D1528309

Slavery, Propaganda, and the American Revolution

SLAVERY, PROPAGANDA, and the AMERICAN REVOLUTION

Patricia Bradley

UNIVERSITY PRESS OF MISSISSIPPI — *Jackson*

01   00   99   98   4   3   2   1
The paper in this book meets the guidelines for permanence and durability
of the Committee on Production Guidelines for Book Longevity of
the Council on Library Resources.

Library of Congress Cagaloging-in-Publication Data

Bradley, Patricia, 1941–
Slavery, propaganda, and the American Revolution / Patricia
Bradley.
p.   cm.
Includes bibliographical references (p.   ) and index.
ISBN 1-57806-052-4 (cloth : alk. paper)
1. United States — History — Revolution, 1775–1783 — Propaganda.
2. United States — History — Revolution, 1775–1783 — Afro-Americans.
3. Press and propaganda — United States — History — 18th century.
4. Antislavery movements — United States — History — 18th century.
5. Slavery — United States — History — 18th century.   I. Title.
E210.B73   1998
973.3'88 — dc21   98-12915
CIP

British Library Cataloging-in-Publication data available

Portions of the following have appeared in "Slavery in Colonial Newspapers:
The Somerset Case," *Journalism History* 12 (Spring 1985): 1–7, and
"The Boston Gazette and Slavery as Revolutionary Propaganda,"
Journalism Quarterly 72 (Autumn 1995): 581–96.

Contents

Acknowledgments

My thanks go in several quarters: to Temple University for a Summer Research Award; to my university colleagues, with special gratitude to the faculty associated with the American Studies Program; to the University Press of Mississippi; to Marie F. Bradley; to my children, Anna C. Bradley and Colin C. Bradley; and to Laurien D. Ward, whose love and support made the book possible and to whom this volume is dedicated.

Abbreviations

A	Almanac
AWM	*American Weekly Mercury* (Philadelphia)
BC	*Boston Chronicle*
BEP	*Boston Evening-Post*
BG	*Boston Gazette*
	Boston Gazette, or Weekly Journal
	Boston Gazette, or Country Country
	Boston Gazette, and Country Journal
	Boston Gazette, or Weekly Advertiser
BNL	*Boston News-Letter*
	Boston Weekly News-Letter
BPB	*Boston Post-Boy and Advertiser*
	Boston Weekly Post-Boy
CC	*Connecticut Courant* (Hartford)
	Connecticut Courant, and Hartford Weekly Intelligencer
CG	*Connecticut Gazette* (New Haven)
CG-NL	*Connecticut Gazette, and the Universal Intelligencer* (New London)
CH	*Christian History*
CJ	*Connecticut Journal, and New-Haven Post Boy*
ConJ	*Continental Journal* (Boston)
EG	*Essex Gazette* (Salem, Mass.)
	New-England Chronicle, or the Essex Gazette
EJ	*Essex Journal, and Merrimack Packet, or the Massachusetts and New-Hampshire General Advertiser* (Newburyport, Mass.)
	Essex Journal, or the New-Hampshire Packet

FJ	*Freeman's Journal* (Philadelphia)
GG	*Georgia Gazette*
GM	*Gentleman's Magazine* (London)
HSP	*Historical Society of Pennsylvania*
IC	*Independent Chronicle* (Boston)
MG	*Maryland Gazette* (Annapolis)
MG&BN	*Massachusetts Gazette and Boston News-Letter*
MG&BPB	*Massachusetts Gazette and the Boston Post-Boy and Advertiser*
MS	*Massachusetts Spy, or Thomas's Boston Journal*
	Massachusetts Spy, or American Oracle of Liberty (Worcester)
NEC	*New England Courant*
NEJ	*New England Journal*
NEWJ	*New-England Weekly Journal*
NJG	*New Jersey Gazette*
NJJ	*New Jersey Journal*
NLG	*New-London Gazette*
NM	*Newport Mercury, or the Weekly Advertiser*
NP	*Norwich Packet, and the Connecticut,Massachusetts, New Hampshire, and Rhode Island Weekly Advertiser*
NYEP	*New-York Evening-Post*
NYG	*New-York Gazette, and the Weekly Mercury*
NYJ	*New-York Journal, or the General Advertiser*
PC	*Pennsylvania Chronicle, and Universal Advertiser*
PEP	*Pennsylvania Evening Post*
PG	*Pennsylvania Gazette*
PJ	*Pennsylvania Journal, or the Weekly Advertiser*
PM	*Pennsylvania Mercury, and the Universal Advertiser*
PP	*Pennsylvania Packet, or the General Advertiser*
ProvG	*Providence Gazette*
RNY	*Rivington's New York Gazetteer*
SCAMG	*South-Carolina and American General Gazette*
SCG	*South-Carolina Gazette*
USC	*United States Chronicle: Political, Commerical, and Historical* (Providence, R.I.)
VG-Dixon	*Virginia Gazette*

VG-Dixon and Hunter	*Virginia Gazette*
VG-Pickney	*Virginia Gazette*
VG-Pickney and Dixon	*Virginia Gazette*
VG-Purdie	*Virginia Gazette*
VG-Purdie and Dixon	*Virginia Gazette*
WNYG	*Weyman's New York Gazette*

Note: Since several *Virginia Gazettes* were published at the same time, they have been differentiated by their publishers.

Introduction

In 1764, the Boston lawyer and firebrand James Otis transcended his local reputation and parochial interests to publish the first major pamphlet of the revolutionary era. In a theme that would come to define the American Revolution, Otis argued against taxing measures on the basis of colonists' natural rights. But in another theme that would not take hold with the same tenacity, Otis was led to ask: "Does it follow that 'tis right to enslave a man because he is black? Will short curl'd hair like wool, instead of christian hair, as 'tis called by those whose hearts are as hard as the nether millstone, help the argument? Can any logical inference in favour of slavery be drawn from a flat nose, a long or a short face?" (Otis 29).

Otis was among the cadre of colonial Americans whose call to freedom did not ignore those who were unfree in the American colonies. A growing antislavery movement existed in secular and religious circles in the decades before the American Revolution and included such resolute patriots as Virginian Arthur Lee, Bostonians John Allen, Nathaniel Appleton, William Gordon, and Philadelphians Benjamin Rush and Thomas Paine. Antislavery sentiment was also heard in private patriot circles. In a long-remembered letter to John Adams, newly arrived in Philadelphia for the First Continental Congress, Abigail Adams wrote: "I wish most sincerely there was not a Slave in the province . . . It always appeared a most iniquitous Scheme to me — fight ourselves for what we are daily robbing and plundering from those who have as good a right to freedom as we have" (*Adams Family* 1:161–62).

Antislavery activity in Massachusetts had been responsible for attempts at antislavery legislation in 1767, 1771, and 1777. Although not successful in Massachusetts, antislavery legislation of some degree was passed in several colonies, including Virginia, Pennsylvania, and Connecticut, before independence, and there was a veritable rush to abolition by the end of the Revolution. Accompanied by a vigorous public debate, eight northern states abolished slavery between 1777 and 1804, Vermont not even waiting for the conclusion of the war (G. Moore, Zilversmit).

But neither the existence of antislavery activity during the revolutionary period nor antislavery legislation at the end of the Revolution should be equated with the position of the patriots or their propaganda. Indeed, those patriots who had voiced antislavery sentiment were not among the leaders of the larger antislavery movement, choosing to subsume their antislavery activities to other forms of participation in the American Revolution. The survival of abolitionist thought into the new republic had more to do with the ability of its nonpatriot adherents to keep the flame alive than with the approval of patriots or the support given to antislavery by the propagandists of the American Revolution.

Antislavery did not become a patriot cause. Instead, revolutionary propagandists chose to transform slavery into a metaphor to represent the level at which the British regarded the American colonists. As a result of this metaphor, I suggest that the legacy of American revolutionary propaganda vis-à-vis slavery was not a commitment to abolition at the earliest opportunity, a traditional defense given for the compromises of the founding fathers (Rossiter 231), but rather helped transfer into the new republic long-standing white attitudes toward black colonists. Despite the early successes of abolition in northern states, it needs to be considered that the patriot use of slavery as a propaganda vehicle encouraged, and even legitimized, white American prejudices toward black Americans and may have served to delay a national solution to the American institution of slavery. Unable to reconcile slavery and the American Revolution, Americans of the new nation fell back upon old attitudes. As Duncan J. MacLeod writes, "The tension between Revolutionary beliefs and the practice of slavery produced a distinctive view of the character of the Negro, to the extent that it seemed to be the very nexus of the problem" (12).

By 1769, just five years after Otis had published his opening salvo, the early tocsin that included abolition in the Whig argument was already being stilled.

By that year, Otis, in face of his increasing mental instability, was losing his position as Boston's leading radical. The passionate argument — "the flame of fire," as John Adams put it (*Life and Works* 10:247) — had become an embarrassment. Three months later he was wondering at his friend's sanity. "He rambles and wanders like a Ship without an Helm" (Adams, *Diary* 1:3523). In face of Otis's dissipating influence, Samuel Adams emerged from the second-in-command post to the leadership of Boston's radical cadre. Accompanying Adams's rise was the disappearance of abolition from the patriot agenda. The issue of slavery would still have its role in the propaganda efforts of the patriot press, but not in ways Otis and other patriot antislavery adherents may have wished.

Sam Adams was the single most important individual in establishing the Revolution's public voice. The ideology of the American Revolution had many authors, but it was Sam Adams who shaped public opinion in the most direct methods — drawing to his influence men of similar beliefs, establishing a chain of command from the gentlemen's circle of leadership to the burgher leaders of the Sons of Liberty, drafting the Massachusetts Circular Letter, establishing the Committees of Correspondence, and, the subject of this work, orchestrating the newspaper press. Indeed, whether one considers the American Revolution as representative of radical change, a continuation of elite dominance, or the introduction of a middle-class meritocracy, one thing is clear: the role of persuasion and argument. Historic changes in government, including the Glorious Revolution that the American Whigs so admired, have been most often put in place by military coups, secret cabals, or the terror of the moment. The American Revolution was not put to a plebiscite, but no other revolution gave a larger role to argument and persuasion. The American revolutionaries *sought* popular support by means high and low. Ideological argument replete with classic allusion coexisted alongside propaganda that ranged from insinuation to intimidation. As Arthur M. Schlesinger Sr. summarized, "From the inception of the controversy the patriots exhibited extraordinary skills in manipulating public opinion, playing upon the emotions of the ignorant as well as the minds of the educated" (*Prelude* 20). This work explores the relationship of the revolutionary press under Sam Adams's direction to the issue of slavery. Did the patriot press play on the "emotions of the ignorant and the minds of the educated" when it came to the issue? How did the *Boston Gazette,* the patriots' premiere organ of propaganda, answer the frequent charge that Americans were calling for freedom while denying it to others?

The absence of a patriot public discussion on slavery was noted in the nineteenth century. "The silence of the popular leaders on this question [slavery] is remarkable. It was ignored as a political issue in general politics, though emancipation was fully advocated in pamphlets and newspapers" (Frothingham, *Rise* 570). While modern historians, including David Brion Davis, argue that the economic necessity of slavery made abolition an improbable cause for a movement that sought to establish a united "American system" (256), it is proposed here that under Sam Adams's direction, the propaganda of the American revolution did not simply ignore the question for fear of offending the South but constructed slavery into a lever promoting revolutionary action. The metaphor of slavery, so popular in the revolutionary decades, cannot be considered simply a reference to political writing of a previous time, but carried with it understandings that were anchored in the reality of American slavery and colonial attitudes toward black colonists. Its influence was furthered by decisions of the revolutionary circle — the selective reporting of the Somerset decision, the refusal to support antislavery in Massachusetts or elsewhere in active ways, the refusal, even, to engage in the antislavery discussion, and the continued portrayal of blacks and slaves along familiar lines. Given the level of sophistication of revolutionary propaganda as a whole, this was not an accidental accumulation but can only be considered as part of the overall campaign.

This work appears in a much different period than its two notable predecessors, Philip Davidson's *Propaganda and the American Revolution* in 1941 and Arthur M. Schlesinger's 1957 study, *Prelude to Independence: The Newspaper War on Britain, 1764–1776.* Both books came from a Progressive tradition, calling on a paradigm established by Charles Beard at the beginning of the century that "organized American history around a restless sea of conflicting material interests" (Rodgers 12). Indeed, an emphasis on the role of propaganda would seem most suited to a tradition that interprets history in terms of conflict and its accompanying anxiety. I suggest, however, that the study of propaganda is not an either-or proposition that ignores ideology in favor of conspiracy and economic determinism. Certainly, it is in the name of ideology that propaganda derives its power for those whom it affects, the men and women who seek larger worlds to explain the social, economic, and political dislocations that lead to the call for the absolute break of revolution. As a shaper of views in vulnerable times, propaganda plays a role in the formation of a nation's ideology. Recording the history of the new nation in the early national period, David Ramsay and Mercy Otis Warren, both ardent Whigs, set the stage for subsequent historians to adopt the Boston Tea Party and the Boston Massacre as spontaneous expressions of American ideology rather than contrived events. We might also consider that the refusal of Americans in the new nation to accept the Constitution without the accompanying assurance of a bill of rights cannot be divorced from the rhetoric of the Revolution that turned on the issues the Bill of Rights subsequently encapsulated. That the Bill of Rights did not provide for the equality of black Americans may also be considered the legacy of a revolutionary rhetoric that refused to address the subject. In 1790, the *Boston Gazette* observed, "The publisher of a newspaper is highly responsible to God and his country, for the sentiments which he propagates among the body of a people" (*BG* 11/15/90). It was an odd note of caution emanating from what had been the patriots' most radical rag, which, in the revolutionary decades, had been most interested in the revolutionary efficacy of its message rather than long-term consequences.

The works of Davidson and Schlesinger appeared when consensus history was dominant, but the fact that Davidson's book was published at the time of the United States' entry into World War II and Schlesinger's book arrived amidst the tensions of the Cold War suggests their acceptance was a prelude to a changing historiography. In breaking new ground, however, neither Davidson nor Schlesinger noted the slavery discussion of the period, even as a backdrop to the revolutionary world. Nor was slavery addressed in a 1980 collection of essays devoted to the revolutionary press (Bailyn and Hench). In contrast, this work calls on an exploding body of work on black life and slavery in the age of revolution (Berlin and Hoffman; D. Davis; Essig; P. Foner; Frey; Genovese; Horton and Horton; Jordan; Mullin; Piersen) that now carries forward the previously lone voices of Aptheker and Quarles. Moreover, as post-Progressive historians took center stage, revolutionary history began to build upon the work of Carl Bridenbaugh's benchmark work, *Cities in Revolt Urban Life in America*, to include new emphasis on the lives of artisans and "lower-sorts." This was not just bottom-up history, focusing attention on groups of people who had been overlooked or underrated (although that was part of the movement), but gave discussion to the tensions of the times in economic, social, philosophical, and religious terms (Bonomi; Greene; Heimert; Heimert and Miller; Hodges and Brown; Kerber; Lemisch; May; Nash; Olton; Rosswurm; Ryerson). The work of this generation of historians is of particular interest for a study of propaganda that must consider that social and economic unease is the traditional seedbed for propaganda of many sorts. I have been able to continue the study of propaganda first articulated by Davidson and Schlesinger because of this new body of scholarship and an approach to history that does not ignore the less definable factors of myth, symbol, and social psychology (Jordan; Wood, "Conspiracy"; Zuckerman).

Foremost among the contextual settings that this work takes into account is the consideration of racial attitudes in colonial Boston. Even though black inhabitants composed a relatively small proportion of Boston's total residents, fewer than a thousand black colonists out of a total population of sixteen thousand, the suspicions of white Bostonians toward black Bostonians were reflected in both the legal system and in everyday practice. In fact, it is probably a mistake to compare Boston's race relations to other cities and colonies as this assumes a judgmental continuum, with the West Indies and South Carolina representing one end while positioning the Northeast, including Boston, as the most enlightened. Such a continuum takes the attention off Boston in terms of the racial attitudes that were to imbue, as I argue, the revolutionary propaganda that emanated from the city and its radical circle. Prompted by its own particular culture and history, Bostonians held perceptions toward blacks and slaves that could intercept with those of other colonies but by no means were simply the lighter end of the racial continuum. As Boston's propagandists marketed their own view of the world and attached it to the revolutionary cause, included in this export were specific views of black colonists.

This work thus begins with an overview of news items that appeared in the Boston press in the years before the Revolution. Attempting to explore attitudes is no easy task, and to assume that portrayals of black colonists in news items automatically represented the overall views of readers is to tread dangerous ground. However, colonial readers traditionally expected a range of views in their newspapers and were able to receive it by the colonial practice of reprinting news stories verbatim from other publications, domestic and British. By providing the sources of the items, colonial printers expected their readers to put information into the context of their origination points. This colonial printing practice served to provide for the dispersal of a variety of political views, and, not incidentally, made it possible for early radical propaganda to appear in newspapers that were not radical themselves. The practice failed, however, when it came to news and information about black colonists. Long before the revolutionary decades, the Boston newspapers reflected a narrow public environment for an understanding of black colonists. In the public arena provided by the Boston newspapers, definitions of black worthiness seldom exceeded the definitions set out by the slave advertising. Indeed, given that newspapers published information of black colonists in terms of crime and conspiracy, it was the slave advertising, usually seeking to sell slaves on the basis of merit, that provided the *positive* public view. But even here, Bostonians seemed unable to give more than grudging approval. "Negroes will do" a Boston slave advertisement noted in a stretch of accommodation (*BG* 12/2/72). If we are to judge by the public world of its colonial press, Boston recognized no black heroes, no black talents, and made no statements of black worth outside of occasional for-sale advertisements.

One explanation for the lack of counterweight is the colony's obsession with conspiracy. As Gordon S. Wood has noted, colonists were products of "the great era of conspiratorial fears and imagined intrigues" ("Conspiracy" 407). There surely could be no better lookouts at the entrance gates of conspiracy than the Massachusetts colonists, the products of a Stuart England who coupled the maintenance of freedom with their ability to heed early warning signs of those who would bring it down. Facade of any sort was regarded suspiciously: plain dress, unostentatious living, and unadorned worship were to be reflections of ambitions of purity; churchgoers were exhorted to forgo temptation in its many disguises; even language was to be plain. Beauty was to be found in order — "the order of things as they are, not as they appear," as Perry Miller put it (Miller and Johnson 1:62). But what could be said about men and women whose very color was one of God's warning signs, whose Africanisms were demonstrative, and whose arrival had been involuntary? Insured perpetual difference by physiognomy, black colonists had little chance to overcome Puritan distrust, no matter how much they met standards of behavioral virtue set down by their Boston overseers. Against this backdrop, the news stories that never failed to report news of black revolt, including those of household servants, were likely to be seen not as logical outcomes of enslavement but rather as evidence of the treasonable hearts that could exist behind the most pleasant of miens.

Samuel Adams was a recipient of such cultural biases, proudly so, as indicated by way he signed his first essay, "The Puritan." Moreover, the revolutionary propagandists found conspiracy a useful theme in building opposition to Great Britain and mitigated against any impulse to overcome these same attitudes on the basis that they impinged upon the understanding of black colonists.

While Adams and his circle called upon ancient Puritan fears in their reification of conspiracy theory, it should also be considered that Adams's call to return to an earlier time of Puritan history, as exemplified by suspicion of things foreign, appeared in the unstable economic decades that preceded the American Revolution, which, for Boston, had been a way of life even when other colonial cities were prospering. After 1763, the economic downturn was accompanied by a stratification of colonial society. Taverns, social clubs, even churches, in Boston and elsewhere, split along class lines. As white colonists were finding fewer opportunities to achieve the "decent competency" of former times, their society was also shutting doors on the basis of predetermined assessments. Artisans, losing traditional positions of authority and leadership, found themselves in danger of being clumped with the "lower sorts." One of Adams's brilliant moves as a propagandist was to harness the sense of liminality occasioned by the drop in artisanal status by bringing into the revolutionary column artisans and small merchants who could exercise the traditional leadership of their class as members of the Sons of Liberty and the Loyall Nine.

Two of these men brought to the cause were John Gill and Benjamin Edes, the printers of the radicals' *Boston Gazette.* Like other members of the revolutionary generation, Adams and Edes shared a personal knowledge of what it was like to drop to second-class status. Under the revolutionary banner, Benjamin Edes, like Adams, was able to replicate the leadership that his father had exercised in the preceding generation. Adams also translated concerns with status into revolutionary propaganda by his unceasing drumbeat that Great Britain did not treat American colonists with the respect and status due them. Inevitably, concern of status, real and imagined, would intersect with the American bondsman as the ultimate example of life without status.

As modern history tells us — Germany's Weimar Republic being the classic example — a society in which substantial numbers of inhabitants experience economic and social decline does not bode well for its least accepted members. In the revolutionary decades, Bostonian black colonists labored yet under an even more conspicuous burden, not only representing the danger of conspiracy but increasingly providing the example of the bottom rung that could seem leeringly close to white colonists in economic or social declension. How far would Americans have to descend to satisfy British prerogatives? To the level of slavery, the propagandists answered in their favorite metaphor. To white colonists, who may have viewed themselves just scrapingly above that status, it was a metaphor less anchored in the political dialogue of the previous century than in the reality of actual slavery that, if not observed in their daily lives, was brought to them weekly by the slave marketplace provided by the colonial newspaper. If we are to look to U.S. history, North and South, we see that when the economic status of whites begins a decline to the economic status of poor blacks, black and white groups do not bond to defeat common enemies but further stratify along lines of color. From Bacon's Rebellion into the modern world, whiteness has taken on increased value in hard times. There was nothing in Boston's colonial culture that was likely to prevent that trajectory.

Finally, Adams and his circle of propagandists operated in a city in which attention to the reality of slavery had been focused by two fronts: Boston's anti-slavery activists and events of the time that involved black colonists. In a city whose religious history was not always useful to the perceptions of black colonists, Boston's religious leaders had nonetheless articulated antislavery concerns from Samuel Sewall's famous call in 1700. Neither Boston's antislavery activists, however, nor those of other colonies found they could dent the increasing patriot control of the colonial press. Turning to printers associated with the British loyalism to make their case, antislavery activists found themselves cornered: to be antislavery was not only to be out of step with patriot ideology but to be considered pro-British. Isolated by the propagandists, the antislavery clerics, the Quaker pamphleteers, and the voices of the black colonists were never able to establish themselves either *on* or *as* a patriot beachhead. Scholars of the slavery discussion have often equated the lack of broad-based discussion to the lack of a significant antislavery movement. "Lacking widespread opposition to slavery, its defense was usually sporadic and local," Larry R. Tise writes in this vein (16). There indeed may not have been widespread opposition to slavery in the American colonies, but an active and intercolonial movement did exist. The limitations of its discussion had most to do with patriot refusal to include it on the patriot agenda.

This early curtain of silence put in high relief the public representation of black colonists in ways that reinforced long-held attitudes. In Boston, as antislavery activists were writing and campaigning for legislative redress mostly behind the scenes, the Boston press continued to forge a public world of black violence, at home and abroad. Notable occurrences in Boston's prerevolutionary era were the execution of two domestic servants in a poisoning plot against a Charlestown resident in 1755 and the execution of a slave in the next decade for the rape of a Worcester woman, an event coinciding with the British occupation of Boston and British rumors of slave insurrection. Occurring at the peak of this racial discord, the "whitening" of Crispus Attucks in Paul Revere's famous print of the Boston Massacre was to express the history of a colonial city whose intersections with race had been longstanding and complicated.

Nonetheless, the history of the city cannot lead to the automatic assumption that Adams and his circle invented issues of racial beliefs for use as American revolutionary propaganda. What can be pointed up is the charged racial atmosphere that existed at a time when radical leaders were composing the propagandistic messages. Adams and his circle did not have to invent racial motivation in their revolutionary propaganda but could instead take advantage of that charged atmosphere to advance revolutionary propaganda along intercolonial lines. This book attempts to illustrate that Adams and his circle utilized assumed racial attitudes in underreporting, selective reporting, and remaining silent on issues related to black colonists.

Adams and his circle were skilled in the techniques of propaganda that seek to influence by the means at its command, including selective information, misinformation, and campaigns and slogans that do not hesitate to call upon the inchoate feelings that may be hardly understood by those who carry them. The status of slaves, the assumption of particular colonial attitudes toward slaves, and instigation of fear that continued British rule would result in a mythic reversal of power in which slaves would occupy, literally and figuratively, the place previously occupied by white Americans advanced the overall themes of American propaganda. Yet readers will find no patriot essays calling for the continued subjugation of black colonists as a theme of the revolutionary press.

As Adams was the inheritor of Puritan attitudes that impinged upon views of black colonists, Adams was also the inheritor of a mature political press tradition from both sides of the water. Like conspiracy, the revolutionary generation viewed revolutionary propaganda as a Jacob's coat of many colors. Adams's skills had been honed on Massachusetts political controversies from the days of the *Independent Advertiser* (Boyer), when to expose a hand was to draw direct fire. Despite the invention of the grand events, the Boston Massacre and the Boston Tea Party, Adams was as skilled in the use of silence, subtlety, and innuendo, all of which would have particular relevance for the propagandistic message when it came to the issue of slavery.

In his early days as a propagandist, Adams had followed the example of the British *Craftsman* as the model for his anti-excise tax campaign of the 1740s (Boyer), but it would be John Wilkes's *North Briton*'s campaign in the 1760s that would teach him most about the use of what we might now call "hot buttons," bringing to the fore deeply buried fears that would have relevance for the Whig campaign as it touched upon the slave issue. In a campaign that would be closely followed by an American audience, the *North Briton* sounded the theme that the king's close advisor Lord Bute could not be trusted because, as a Scotsman, he could be expected to plot for the return of England to Scottish, that is, Catholic, domination. Indeed, the first and primary objection to Lord Bute was "He is a Scot... from the time of that of the Stuarts, of ever odious memory, first mounted the throne, the Scots have over-ran the land" (*NB* 1/22/63). The conniving of Scotsmen knew no bounds, and Bute was charged with a sexual liaison with the Queen Mother to gain influence in the royal household. The scurrility and charges grew bolder until artifice and sarcasm had been replaced by a frontal attack on Bute as a Scotsman and his accompanying "attachment to France," that is, Catholicism, and the dread implications for the overthrow of the Glorious Revolution.

The generation that responded so readily to Wilkes's propaganda was less than a quarter of a century removed from the Battle of Culloden and its promise to end the threat of Catholic domination in the British Isles. The undertow simmering in British popular consciousness since that time, the fear to which Wilkite propaganda so clearly attached itself, was that Catholicism might reappear. To a nation glorying in its British nationalism as the flower of protestantism, the fear of Catholicism in high places was to pose the threat of national extinction. It was no disadvantage to British politicians that the "Stuart bogey," as one historian labeled the fear of a Catholic monarchy (Brewer 172), lacked the hard edges of literal truth. Indeed, its amorphous nature worked to enhance the propaganda of Wilkes and his coeditor, Charles Churchill, who found that the idea of renewed Stuart ascendancy could ignite popular fear whenever its boggy underside was hauled forth.

Adams's essays in his early political campaigns were quick to stir the fear of Catholicism as the example of ongoing conspiracy. After the conclusion of the French and Indian War ended the French threat on colonial soil, attacks on "popery" lessened. What I suggest replaced Catholicism as the simmering undertow of colonial fear was the debasement represented by slavery. The "Stuart bogey" carried less weight, even in anti-Catholic New England, than an American bogey with a black face. While Boston's annual and unruly "Pope's Day Parade" proclaimed Bostonian freedom from Catholic hegemony, it cannot go unnoticed that the devil's imp was in blackface. Indeed, the black colonist could be viewed to have many of the characteristics of the Roman Catholic—the desire for exotic dress, a private language, a secret world of rite, a conspiratorial bent, and a potent sexual nature that could remove white identity from succeeding generations. The fear of "popery" provided ready and fertile ground for Bostonian attitudes toward black colonists.

There were also lessons of implementation to be learned from the Wilkes episode and a man described as "a propagandist whose skills fell little short of genius" (Brewer 166). In 1768, preparing to return from exile to certain imprisonment, Wilkes put in place a campaign that sought popular appeal from all classes and resulted in making him a hero across the British world. In this second stage of the saga, Wilkes's popularity soared as he came to personify increasingly lofty principles. Indeed, the higher the principle, the broader the appeal to "the middling and inferior class of people," as he put it (Brewer 168). Calling for "law and liberty," a new slogan for the time, Wilkes turned himself from a partisan politician into the persecuted Everyman: the honest citizen standing up to the encroachments of arbitrary government. "Law and liberty" did not supplant the famous "Forty Five" that was reinvigorated by Wilkes's imprisonment, causing William Franklin to complain to his father, "The nonsense about No. 45 is almost as much attended to in the Colonies as in England" (Franklin, *Papers* 16:5).

As in England, the American popularity of the slogans, notably "45," served to expand meanings beyond immediate political ends into a fanciful, optimistic message of faith in popular power and was imitated in the American campaign. Similarly, Wilkes's ability to pull to his support men and women who interpreted the slogans as meaningful to their own concerns was to be adapted to American propaganda. By the culmination of the Wilkite controversies, American radicals had developed a pantheon of slogans—"taxation without representation," "join or die," "Boston Tea Party," and the use of the word "slavery" to represent "slavery" to Great Britain. Use of the metaphor of slavery gave first evidence that the issue of real slavery was not to have a part in the revolutionary messages. Upon this base, the metaphor of slavery, patriot propagandists constructed a movement that had as example the level to which white Americans could sink at British hands.

CHAPTER ONE

The Metaphor of Slavery

On an early fall night in 1769, John Adams recorded in his diary a famous account of what had become a weekly ritual: "Supped with Mr. Otis, in company with Mr. Adams, Mr. William David and Mr. John Gill," he wrote. "The evening was spent in preparing for the Next Days newspaper — a curious Employment. Cooking up Paragraphs, Articles, Occurrences, etc. — working the political Engine" (Adams, *Diary* 1:3523).

By 1769 these were men experienced in the shaping of public opinion across the American colonies by means subtle and outrageous. Certainly suspected Tory printers such as John Mein and James Rivington, the target of patriot mobs, could have attested to the role of intimidation. Despite such intimidation, the patriot propagandists succeeded in becoming the dominant voice less because of a campaign of terror than by their understanding of colonial communication in all its layers, contexts, and audiences. Sermons, broadsides, pamphlets, poetry, plays, almanacs, popular song, and, particularly, newspapers plucked at the themes of history, religion, philosophy, and prejudices of the colonial experience. The loyalists, even with their influence, could not match the propagandists' breadth. Thomas Hutchinson, the royal governor of Massachusetts, responded to the attacks of the *Boston Gazette* by patronizing supporting newspapers, then established his own newspaper, the *Censor* (Lathem 10). But by 1771, to rely on a purely political organ was to send a ship to sea with a single sail. By contrast, the patriots caught the wind from many directions. Samuel Adams ingratiated the patriot message into the weave and woof of colonial life.

By the late sixties, Adams, his core of writers that included his closest ally, the young doctor Joseph Warren, and the minister of Boston's Brattle Street Church, Samuel Cooper, along with the printing firm of Edes and Gill had made the *Boston Gazette* into the colonies' premiere organ of propaganda. By the time of the Stamp Act, it not only cooked paragraphs, it invented and embroidered events, established heroes and villains, played on prejudices, and expanded the revolutionary tent by the language of hyperbole. Clearly recognizing the *Gazette* as the "instrument of raising that flame in America which has given so much trouble," Massachusetts governor Frances Bernard sought to have Edes and Gill arrested and the paper closed (Frothingham, *History* 48). The patriot response was brazen. Adams's second, Joseph Warren, charged the royal governor with "jesuitical insinuations" and "slanders" (*BG* 2/29/68). But even in face of new libels, Bernard was unable to raise support, either in the Massachusetts House of Representatives or in the grand jury. By 1770, the *Gazette* had friends in powerful places.

Bernard was eventually recalled to Great Britain. For the next half dozen years nothing restrained the *Gazette,* although complaints were plentiful. Richard Draper, the traditional publisher of the *Massachusetts Gazette and Boston News-Letter,* later an organ for the government, was compelled to take the unusual step of speaking in his own voice: "I can truly affirm . . . that the rudeness, Unfairness and Indelicacy of the writers on the *Boston Gazette,* have brought the Weekly publishers of this Town into great discredit" (*BNL* 3/26/72). A government spokesman fumed that the newspaper simply suppressed what it did not want to hear. "Is this Liberty! Does this agree with the principle of the Patriots, that the Press should be free as air?" Then, coopting the propagandists' own metaphor, the writer concluded, "No, my countrymen, it is the highest degree of slavery" (*BNL* 8/9/72). But Peter Oliver, as a spokesman for the new governor, the native-born Thomas Hutchinson, eschewed high-flown metaphors. "We suffer the repetition in print of pretended grievances until it has become perfectly nauseous" (*BNL* 6/4/72).

Tolerance was clearly stretched, and for good reason. Bernard's warnings to the British home office having been ignored, Adams and his circle transformed the *Gazette* from a local institution into an intercolony voice. By the early 1770s, the *Boston Gazette* had established the "Boston Massacre" and the

"Boston Tea Party" as revolutionary events that represented *all* colonies. By that time, noticeably in operation was the decision that the only slavery that would receive attention in the *Boston Gazette* was the slavery of the American colonists to Great Britain. The frame of the Revolution vis-à-vis slavery was set.

The metaphor of slavery, as other slogans and metaphors of the American Revolution, may be studied by the same scholarly paradigm that undergirds the modern-day study of slogans (Stewart, Smith, and Denton). As in modern slogans, slogans of the Revolution benefited from their initial ambiguity that allowed for individual interpretation. A slogan has been compared to a bridge that allows consumers to take positions anywhere along its span until the target audience agrees on the "new and fixed meaning" (Duncan 8). Connected to vigilance and virtue, the metaphor of slavery could be understood by a New England farmer and his wife far from the centers of political discourse in ways that were embedded in their own history. Slavery as a symbol of degradation at the hands of the British would find no argument at a southern gathering. It is argued here that slavery became a metaphor of such strength because embodied with the political meanings of the word were the day-to-day understandings of the institution and of black colonists in particular. Colonial racial attitudes, I suggest, provided a baseline of common understandings for white Americans by giving example to the metaphor. It is to ignore the history of the colonies' racial relations to separate the metaphor from its racial moorings, and it is to ignore the radicals' sophistication to believe the metaphor could be used unknowingly as a revolutionary banner without call to its multiple layers.

For the initial colonial writers and speakers who took to the metaphor so readily, however, the phrase was anchored in its long-recognized political venue. If colonists did not vigorously oppose the American Act of 1764 authorizing the sending of British military forces to the American colonies, Colonel Eliphalet Dyer of Windham, Connecticut, predicted, "they may for the future, bid Farewell to Freedom and Liberty, burn their Charters, and make the best of Thraldom and Slavery" (*CC* 9/16/65). When the language was taken up by the Boston minister Jonathan Mayhew's attack on the Stamp Act, it took on gendered connotations. Liberty was about to depart and leave in "her" place "that ugly Hag Slavery, the formed child of Satan" (Akers, *Called* 215). Representing the many less-powerful pulpits that took the language to heart, the congregational minister Joseph Emerson called the repeal of the act "a deliverance from slavery; — nothing less than from vile, ignominious slavery" (Baldwin 97). The town fathers of Newburyport, like those of other communities, found the language of slavery most appropriate for its formal resolution to the Massachusetts General Court. "That a People should be taxed at the Will of another, whether one man or many, without their own Consent is Rank Slavery" (Labaree 18). Philadelphia's William Smith told the Continental Congress that "the skins of wild beasts [are] a more honorable covering than all the silken vestments *slavery* can bestow" (*VG*-Pickney 6/15/75).

Political writers, however, found the metaphor of slavery of most use. A *Boston Gazette* writer had used the word literally in the 1754 controversy when he charged the opposition considered the "lower sort of People are but a Degree above Slavery" (*BG* 12/31/54). But a decade later, Otis, even in the pamphlet that drew attention to real American slavery, also used the word as metaphor. The American colonists likely would remain loyal to the king unless the terms were ones of "absolute slavery" (Otis 2). John Dickinson, owner of the largest number of slaves in Philadelphia, used the analogy without self-consciousness in 1768 when he sent to Otis for use in the *Boston Gazette* the lyrics of what would become the "Liberty Song." "In freedom we're born, and in freedom we'll live; Not as *slaves*, but as *freemen* our money we'll give" (Silverman 114). Adams's acolyte, Joseph Warren, reflected the theme: "Awake! Awake! my countrymen." Warren wrote in his first published letter to the press in 1765, "Defeat the designs of those who would enslave us and our posterity. Nothing is wanting but your own resolution" (*BG* 10/7/65). Adams utilized the rhetoric perhaps most of all. As "Candidus," Adams equated the struggle against the Stamp Act as a successful struggle "against that slavery with which they were threatened" (*BG* 9/9/71). As "Candidus" again, he argued that if the British constitution could not protect property, men bound by it "are *slaves* not *free men*" (*BG* 1/20/72). As *Valerius Poplicola*, again on the subject of taxes, he asked, "Is it not High Time for the People of this Country explicitly to declare, whether they will be Freeman or Slaves?" The administration of justice without involvement of the people could not form an idea of slavery "more complete, more miserable, more disgraceful" (*BG* 10/5/72).

To the eminent revolutionary scholar Bernard Bailyn, such widespread use indicated that "slavery" was not a rhetorical device but rather represented a commonly understood political concept. Use of the word should not be viewed as hyperbole or indeed even a connection to the existence of real slavery, Bailyn has argued in his classic work, but as reference to the loss of political rights that colonists believed would result with the lapse of constant vigilance. The use of "slavery" in this political context referenced the loss of political rights as demonstrated by the history of Russians, Danes, Turks, and Poles and the "condition that followed the loss of freedom, when corruption, classically, had destroyed the desire and capacity of these people to retain their independence" (Bailyn, *Ideological* 233–34).

But what is interesting about the colonial use of the phrase as a political metaphor is that by the time of the revolutionary decades, the metaphor was out of favor with British political writers. Although the British had most to do with the introduction of the metaphor as a political concept, British political writers almost never used the language at the time when it was in the very ether of the American colonial world. The slavery metaphor was not used by either the British administration's organ, the *London Gazette,* or by the Whig opposition paper, the *London Chronicle* (Holmberg 100). Nor was it a phrase found in the *North Briton,* despite the newspaper's ongoing implication that Stuart ascendancy was paramount to giving over the nation to the control of Rome. The American propagandists took many lessons from the *North Briton,* but the language of slavery was not one of them. At a time when British political organs, including the *North Briton,* seldom used the analogy, the word "slavery," even without the associated words of "tyranny" and "oppression," was in the lower half of the most used political words from 1765 to 1776 in the *Boston Gazette* (ranking thirty-second out of a list of fifty). It reached highs of usage in 1767, 1772, and 1776, each time almost quadrupling its frequency of use from 1765 (Holmberg 98, 104).

American writers, much less propagandists, were not adverse to taking arguments from a previous time and putting them in the revolutionary context, witness the frequent American republication of the British *Cato's Letters,* the more than a hundred essays by political writers John Trenchard and Thomas Gordon originally appearing in British newspapers in the 1720s. For Americans to reach back for the metaphor of slavery suggests that the language of slavery brought to the political meaning a colonial context beyond hyperbole. In a colonial world that daily saw the existence of the institution, it is difficult to see how the use of the language of slavery could not *but* bring to the political metaphor common beliefs about the people who occupied that status. If the Danes, Poles, and Turks had lost their freedom because of lack of vigilance and the practice of the necessary virtue, the implication for the enslaved Africans of the American colonies was that they bore responsibility for their own enslavement, and on the same basis—an inability to maintain the necessary qualities of vigilance and virtue. These were perceptions that Adams and his cadre of writers knit into the propaganda of the American Revolution for dispersal across the American colonies.

For Bostonians, the wages of ignoring the twin commandments of vigilance and virtue were close at hand. In the 1760s Boston, with a population of about fifteen to sixteen thousand (Bridenbaugh, *Cities* 216), was the third largest city in the American colonies, behind Philadelphia and New York. The black population had been highest in the 1750s, at about fifteen hundred, then began a decline as the revolutionary era approached so that by 1776 Suffolk County contained fewer than seven hundred black inhabitants clustered around Boston, which included a small free black community of perhaps no more than fifty (Levesque 33). Most New England black colonists served as household servants, often living with the families they served, like Sully, the lifelong slave of Sam Adams and his family. However, because of some residential clustering on the North and West ends of the city, African traditions persisted and black leadership was given an opportunity to develop (Piersen, *Black Yankees* 18).

Black colonists in Massachusetts, slave and free, had a legal status that included legal counsel, trial by jury, and the right to testify in court, this last point making it possible for the testimony of three blacks at the trial of the British soldiers after the Boston Massacre. Slaves were not automatically found guilty of crimes of which they had been accused (*NEWJ* 2/24/35) and even in capital offenses extenuating circumstances could be considered for blacks as well as whites (Twombly and Moore 233). Moreover, New Englanders often chose to call their slaves "servants"—a tacit distancing from acceptance of their real status. "Servants" were permitted membership in the white-dominated churches, permitted baptism, freedom of movement, and a degree of education that was unheard of in other colonies. Further, in the world of work, blacks and slaves demonstrated a range of skills, as attested by slave advertising.

Boston was also home to a circle of antislavery activists, black and white, who made consistent attempts in the years before the Revolution to end slavery in the province. Slavery was abolished in Massachusetts before the turn of the century, although in a confused way (Zilversmit 114–15). And, finally, in a world where slaves and slave owners shared close quarters and often worked side by side, affection from both sides may not have been unknown (Piersen, *Black Yankees* 146). Compared to the slavery of the West Indies and other parts of the American colonies, Massachusetts' slavery has been considered a mild institution (Greene, *Colonial New England*).

The underside to Massachusetts's mild institution was the connection of blacks and slaves to conspiracy, immoderate behavior, and violence and an assumption of black limitations premised on those beliefs. Samuel Sewall's famous 1700 attack on slavery in *The Selling of Joseph* came at a time when the colony was passing increasingly stringent laws affecting blacks and slaves—establishing curfews, regulating manumissions, demanding public service from blacks and overseeing their private life (Ames and Goodell 1:535, 578, 606–7). Sewall himself saw no place for the black in white society. "Few can endure to hear of a Negro's being made free; and indeed they can seldom use their Freedom well" (*Diary* 90).

One scholar of American proslavery thought points out that in the elaborate response to Sewall's essay, the slave owner John Saffin articulated some twenty of the twenty-six arguments to be found in proslavery arguments before the Civil War (Tise 18). Notably, all these arguments were put aside for Saffin's concluding poem that was anchored in perceived racial traits:

> *Cowardly and cruel are those Blacks Innate,*
> *Prone to Revenge, Imp of inveterate hate.*
> *He that exasperates them, soon espies*
> *Mischief and Murder in their very eyes.*
> *Libidinous, Deceitful, False and Rude*
> *The Spume Issue of Ingratitude.*
> *The Premises consider'd, all may tell,*
> *Now near good Joseph they are Parallel*
> (Towner 47–48)

The "Imp" of the second line was a reference to the devil's imp that was a part of Boston's annual Pope's Day parade celebrating, like Guy Fawkes Day in England, the discovery of the gunpowder plot in time to prevent the usurpation of Protestant rule. The imp was traditionally represented in blackface well into the late colonial period, as indicated by Pierre Du Simitiere's sketch of the celebration in 1767 (Du Simitiere).

For some white Bostonians, perceptions of blacks and slaves were likely premised on work and personal relationships, religious conscience, and the Enlightenment legacy of a logical turn of mind. Nonetheless, there could be no escape from attitudes that regarded blacks and slaves as appropriate to a secondary position because of an innate nature that was libidinous, immoderate, and prone to crime. In a Puritan world where symbol was considered the godly mode of communication, the color of black was itself a symbol of evil.

Congregational ministers by no means invented that use or even used it any more than any other religious group, yet the use of the color black and its associated word of "darkness" carried particular strength given the congregational emphasis on rhetoric. The witchcraft hysteria produced claims that the devil was seen in the form of a "Blackman" (Twombly and Moore 225). Mather Byles of Boston's Hollis Street Church reminded his congregation of William Bradford's remark: "'Alas, in this wild heart of mine, are the seeds of all these blackest Sins' " (Byles 14). Cotton Mather said atheism was to be hissed out of the world, unable to be supported by "even the darkest recesses of Africa itself" (Pearce 206). According to an execution sermon delivered in 1754, "As this Sin of murder is thus singularly *foul* and *black* in the Estate of God, so it is likewise in the Account of Man" (*Horrid Nature*). For Jonathan Edwards, color was another example of the way God communicated: "Sin and sorrow and death are all in Scripture represented by darkness of the color black" (Edwards 18). As Richard Slotkin points out, Puritans routinely used black and white to represent sin and salvation. "This conventional image of 'whitening' conversion and 'blackening' sin persisted in all its simplicity even after the heyday of Puritanism had passed" (Slotkin 9).

There was little in the public weal to contradict the perceptions that blackness was related to evil or its corollary that black colonists had a penchant for criminality. In the colonial newspapers, certainly, the only news of blacks or slaves came in reports of black violence. Slave advertising represented "runaway" slaves in terms of evil and good slaves in terms of obedience. It is not surprising that revolutionary antislavery writers such as Anthony Benezet emphasized the nature of African justice and equality and that slave petitions were routinely couched in the most inoffensive and pious language. Bostonians always had before them ongoing examples of black conspiracy and black crime in part because of the vigorous colonial press of the city, as many as four or five newspapers as the revolutionary era approached (Lathem 8–10). Meantime, black virtue was seldom acknowledged in the public prints, even in the limited spheres where it was allowed to exist.

The importance of eternal vigilance over external danger was promoted by what must have seemed regular appearances in the Boston press of the much-feared specter of black crime at home and abroad. The efficient system of exchange newspapers brought news of slave insurrections from the islands: the 1745 plot of Jamaican slaves (*BEP* 4/1/45); a slave rebellion in Curacao (*BPB* 8/13/50); another in Jamaica in 1760 (*BEP* 7/14/60; *BNL* 7/17/60). Similarly disturbing news was an ongoing theme from sister colonies. Bostonians could read of the 1712 New York slave revolt resulting in nineteen executions in which suspected perpetrators were burned alive, broken on the wheel, or hanged. The New York correspondent reported that it was "fear'd that most of the Negroes here (who were very numerous) knew of the Late Conspiracy to murder the Christians" (*BNL* 4/21/12). In 1730 Bostonians learned that South Carolinians had put down a suspected insurrection "by the Negroes, who had conspired to Rise and destroy us." The published letter written by a South Carolinian could give Bostonians further reason to suspect black entertainments: "They soon made a great Body at the back of the Town and had a great Dance, and expected the Country Negroes to come & join them" (*BNL* 10/15/30; *BG* 10/19/30). The following month the Bostonians learned of conspiracy in Virginia where four slaves had been executed. Virginia's governor placed the militia on active duty in order to inspect Norfolk's slave quarters on a nightly basis (*BG* 12/7/30). New Jersey supplied news of a slave plot in 1734 (*BNL* 1/24/34). Thirty conspirators were arrested, some hanged, some whipped, and some mutilated. The following year the Boston press carried news of a South Carolina burglary ring conducted by slaves (*BPB* 7/21/35).

South Carolina, indeed, provided an ongoing example of a siege state. In 1739 "several Negroes" collaborated with two white men, a Spanish and Irishman, to kill a white man and injure three others (*BNL* 5/24/39). This was a prelude to what would be remembered as the Stono Rebellion in which rebelling slaves were finally defeated in a pitched battle (P. Wood 308–26). News of it likely came to Boston from several sources, but certainly by way of the ever-vigilant *Boston News-Letter* in an account in November (*BNL* 11/1/39). The next year dread news arrived of yet a "new Negro plot" (*BNL* 7/3/40; *BPB* 7/7/40; *BEP* 7/7/40). Before the year was out, the South Carolina city was devastated by fire blamed on slave arson, later said to be an accident (*BNL* 1/15/41; 4/30/41). In 1741, fire broke out again in South Carolina, and slave arson was again blamed. The *Boston News-Letter* provided an account: "By private letters from Charlestown South-Carolina we are inform'd that the Town is in much Confusion, not only on account of the insolence of the Spanish but also from Apprehensions of Domestick Treachery, the Town having been several times alarm'd by Fire which too visibly appears to be willfully occasion'd by their Blacks" (*BNL* 8/27/41). At least two executions ensued, a man and woman, although it was the male who was burned to death (*BNL* 9/24/41).

There could be no escape from the hysteria occasioned by New York's "Negro plot" in 1741 (T. Davis). Eleven blacks were burned at the stake in the episode, covered in all its grisly detail, rumor, and related incident by the Boston press (*BNL* 4/9; 5/7; 6/4; 6/18; 7/2; 7/16; 7/23; 8/6; 8/27; 9/3; 10/8/41). And, as in the past, news of slave plots in one colony attuned other colonists to suspect their own servants. In the same year as the New York plot, the Boston press carried the account of two New Jersey blacks convicted of setting fire to a barn and burned alive as punishment (*BNL* 5/17; *BEP* 7/6/41). Some years later, Bostonian readers learned of similar executions of two other New Jersey slaves after shooting their mistress (*BEP* 7/9/50).

The memory of the two New York conspiracies was slow to die. In 1755, Bostonians were informed of the New York "Act to Regulate the Militia," less an act of regulation than one of carte blanche permission to murder, permitting militia members who came across a slave one mile or more from home "to shoot or otherwise destroy such Slave or Slaves, without being impeached, censured, or persecuted for same." It was, the *Boston Evening-Post* introduction noted, "the most severe that we have seen before" (*BEP* 3/10/55).

In 1767, a plot of Virginia slaves resulted in the death of several overseers, news of it again reaching Boston (*BG* 1/11/68).

There were in these years persistent and ongoing reports of slave conspiracy and arson from other colonies, reported so thoroughly in the Boston press that present-day historians have heavily relied on their accounts to reconstruct the events.

News from other colonies could only intensify understandings of similar kinds of activities in Boston and other Massachusetts towns during the same years. From 1721 to 1723 a series of suspicious fires believed to have been set by slaves wracked Boston and New Haven. Cotton Mather feared the opening salvo of the "laying of the Town to Ashes" (Mather 2:687). In 1723, after a spring and summer of arson, a Boston slave was tried, found guilty of arson, and put to death. The *Boston News-Letter* provided frequent accounts from April to November (*BNL* 4/4; 5/2; 5/9; 7/4; 8/8; 10/10; 11/14/23), which, thanks to the exchange system that brought news to Boston, also spread news of Boston's troubles to other parts of the colonies.

The fires moved Boston's town council to instigate controls. A list of regulations known as the "Boston Articles" severely restricted slave and free black activity under penalty of sale to the West Indies. A gathering of more than two slaves who were not on the business of their masters ran the risk of the lash for the offenders. A black or slave did not have to be in a group to be regarded uneasily, however. Across the river, Charlestown's city's selectmen ordered Robin, a free Negro, to leave town because he seemed suspicious (Frothingham, *History* 250). In 1728, Boston blacks, mulattos, and Indians were forbidden to carry canes or sticks lest they be used as weapons (Winsor 2:485). But legislation did not stop a Salem slave from attempting to burn his master's house in 1730 (*AWM* 8/27/30). In 1735 arson was put aside in favor of a more deadly method. A Boston family was murdered when the family cook laced chocolate with arsenic, an event that resulted in a further call for restrictive legislation (*BPB* 8/4/35; *NEJ* 9/2/35).

Racial tensions were rising in Boston, a result of both local activities and news from South Carolina and New York. A Boston writer urged local masters to take a firm hand with their servants. "The Great Disorders committed by Negroes, who are permitted by their imprudent Masters, &c. to be out late at Night has determined several sober and substantial Housekeepers to walk about the Town in the sore part of the Night . . . and it is hoped that all lovers of Peace and good Order will join their endeavors for preventing the like Disorders for the future" (*BEP* 7/14/40). In 1741, when fear was in full throat from the news emanating from New York, a Roxbury mob laid their hands on a slave suspected of stealing money, strapped him to a tree where he was "whip'd in order to bring him to confess the Fact after which he was taken down and lying some Time upon the Grass was carried into his Masters House but died soon after" (*BNL* 7/23/41). Yet such lessons seemed to go unheeded. In 1745, Bostonians learned of a slave's ax murder of his master (*BEP* 9/16/45). The Boston response to a 1747 riot against impressment was to insert Boston's black population alongside "foreign seamen, servants . . . and other persons of mean and vile condition," and the instigation of a new slave curfew (*BEP* 11/20/47).

But curfews offered little protection when conspiracy was within Boston's own bosom, or nearly so, across the river in Charlestown, in the house of the prominent John Codman. A male slave, Mark, was accused of securing the arsenic that was administered over time by a female house slave, a result of which was that Codman's "lower Parts turned as black as a Coal." Mark was hanged on Cambridge Road; Phyliss, perhaps strangled first, was burned at the stake ten yards from the Charlestown gallows. The third slave, Phoebe, who had revealed the plan, escaped execution and was sold to the West Indies, a dubious reward for loyalty (*BEP* 7/7/55; Goodell).

The executions and banishment could only linger in the memory of both the city of Boston and the sister village of Charlestown. As described in the

Boston Evening-Post, "After execution, the body of Mark was brought down to Charlestown Common, and hanged in chains on a gibbet erected there for the purpose" (*BEP* 9/22/55). When the executions were described to him, Westborough's minister Ebenezer Parkman recoiled: "A frightfull Spectacle!" But he still saw the event as a generalized warning of what awaited in eternal life, not an episode connected to enslavement. "May all hear and fear! especially to be punish'd Eternally in the Flames of Hell. May my own Soul be suitably affected with the Thought!" (Parkman 295). The event also gave birth to both an execution sermon and a fourteen-stanza popular broadside that united sin, crime, and color in a trinity of its own: "Their crimes appear as black as Hell justly so indeed / And for a greater, I am sure / there's none can this exceed" (*A Few Lines*).

Significantly, long after Mark's body had rotted in its chains, the gibbet remained in place for the next twenty years (Frothingham, *History* 264), not just providing a warning to the pious but reminding servants of their duty and, to Charlestown and Boston's white population, providing the reminder that treachery could simmer just below the surface.

Before the year was out, two Boston papers, including the *Boston Gazette, and Country Journal,* in business since April, reported another murder by a slave in which the slave owner's child was taken from his bed and thrown into the well "where it perished" (*BG* 8/11/55; *BEP* 8/11/55). In 1760 yet another Boston slave was arrested after setting fire to her master's barn and house. It was, she admitted, an act of revenge (*BEP* 1/28/60). In colonial society, fire, needing no cohorts, was the great equalizer. Certainly, nowhere in the public realm was the view represented that slave "treachery" was a predictable response to involuntary servitude.

A short period of quiet came after the turmoil of the Codman affair. Then in 1763, a sixteen-year-old Boston slave was executed for the murder of a white girl. This gave birth to both broadsides and a sermon printed by the *Boston Gazette's* Edes and Gill (Bristol). Five years later, in 1768, when the revolutionary era well commenced, the slave Arthur was executed for the rape of a white woman in nearby Worcester. Occurring during the turmoil of the British occupation of Boston, the execution of Arthur was the subject of a popular broadside and a published execution sermon (Arthur). Here was yet another platform that increased awareness of black crime and used black crime as the warning traditionally accompanying Puritan sermonizing (Slotkin 31). The warnings were several, including notice to all members of a subservient class not to push boundaries; to masters, to expect no better if they did not discipline their servants; and a call to all for white vigilance.

Despite Boston's relatively small black population, there could be no escape from an awareness of black crime, unpredictable as the periodic outbreaks of smallpox that struck the city. Further, the fear of black crime worsened with the suspicion, as in the New York plot, that blacks might align themselves with colony enemies. The fear of black violence conspiring with the white enemies of the Bay colony was a theme that traveled from Catholic plots to a fear that the French would use black slaves along with Indians in the French and Indian War, and culminated in the fear that the British would arm slaves in the American Revolution.

As the metaphor of slavery had as a backdrop examples of black crime and conspiracy, it also represented the political understandings of slavery in the classic terms of vigilance and virtue. As we know, from the time of the arrival of Africans on Virginia shores, white colonial Americans had established a cluster of characteristics for black colonists (Jordan 1–43). In addition, New Englanders had their own set of perceptions forged from their history and illustrated by a tendency to twin concepts, conspiracy *and* crime, that is, crime as a result of conspiracy; virtue *and* vigilance, one not existing without the other. The metaphor of slavery served as a meeting place, a common ground of participation where definitions could be proffered, bartered, and sometimes even exchanged.

Not surprisingly, the foremost progenitor of the metaphor of slavery as well as the foremost expositor of notions of vigilance and virtue was Sam Adams. In public and private spheres, from his first contribution to the *Independent Advertiser* and running through his private correspondence, Adams's views on the necessity of virtue and vigilance were an unchanging theme for forty years. Influenced by the Great Awakening in the 1740s, the importance of virtue was immovably in place by the revolutionary decades. "We may look up to Armies for our Defence, but Virtue is our best Security. It is not possible that any State should long remain free, where Virtue is not supremely honored," he wrote to James Warren (S. Adams 3:325). "We shall succeed if we are virtuous," he assured a member of the Continental Congress. "It is the Disgrace of human Nature that in most Countries the People are so debauched, as to be utterly unable to defend or enjoy their Liberty" (S. Adams 3:403). By

1782, his views were rigid: Men "will be free no longer than while they remain virtuous," adding ominously, "Sydney tells us, there are times when people are not worth saving; meaning when they have lost their virtue" (W. Wells 3:114).

Adams's public writings and those of his fellow *Gazette* propagandists echoed the emphasis on vigilance and virtue and the implication that slavery could only result for those who did not abide by their strictures. A "Candidus" article began, "I Believe that no people ever get groaned under the heavy yoke of slavery, but when they deserv'd it. This may be called a severe censure upon by far the greatest part of the nations in the world who are involv'd in the misery of servitude: But however they may be thought by some to deserve commiseration, the censure is just" (*BG* 10/14/71). In the classic understanding of virtue to which educated American colonists subscribed, virtue was best exercised in the civic realm by responding to the call of leadership. But virtue became democratized fairly early in the colonial experience when good habits became part of the understanding of virtuous behavior. Virtue thus defined made it possible for all colonists to be virtuous, even if they were not called to leadership. It is not surprising that the Bostonian-by-birth, Benjamin Franklin, and his writing partner, Joseph Breintnall, chose to use virtue in this sense in one of "The Busy-Body" essays, for here was virtue that was as practical as it was accessible. As Franklin wrote, a man who had "learnt to govern his Passions, in spite of Temptation, to be just in his Dealings, to be Temperate in his Pleasures, to support himself with Fortitude under his Misfortunes, to behave with Prudence in all Affairs and in every Circumstance of Life" was of "much more real Advantage to him . . . than to be a Master of all the Arts and Sciences in the World beside." In this sense, "Virtue alone is sufficient to make a Man Great, Glorious and Happy" (*AWM* 2/18/29). Franklin's subsequent pursuit of virtue, as we know from his *Autobiography,* was by way of thirteen steps, beginning with temperance and concluding with humility. Despite Franklin's substantial move into public life during this part of his career, he does not include civic duty as one of the elucidated virtues.

As the revolutionary decade approached, the notion of virtue, either as a male prerogative of civic leadership or as appropriate and useful behavior, was further mitigated by the role of women. As a counterpart to Britannia, American radicals put forward a female heroic figure, Columbia, arrayed with shield, spear, and helmet. In actual fact, patriots saw the role for women in revolutionary activity less as heroic than as one constructed on the idea of virtue as housewifely expertise: women could be helpful to the cause by spinning and weaving and in the rejection of tea and luxury items. Thus, in 1772, it was not out of place for the colonies' fiercest and most radical printers to publish the British cookbook, *Frugal Housewife, or Complete Woman Cook*. To fit in with the patriot call as well as to be in line with the new understandings of women's roles, the founder of what would become the Daughters of Liberty, Esther Reed, couched her call for women's participation in nonimportation in the approved domestic idiom: "Who amongst us, will not renounce with the highest pleasure, those vain ornaments?" ([Reed]; M. Norton 178–80). Interestingly, a much more dramatic call from the Daughters of Liberty, beginning, "That woman is born a free and independent Being; that it is her undoubted Right and Constitutional Privilege firmly to reject all Attempts to abridge that liberty" (*BPB* 10/18/73), found no patriot publisher but appeared instead in the Tory *Boston Post-Boy*.

The patriot call for women's involvement along lines of domestic virtue was not a patriot invention as much as a patriot framing of a male colonial preoccupation. It was not to encourage nonimportation or demonstrate patriot virtue for the same *Boston Post-Boy* earlier to have published a recipe for "The Good Wife" (*BPB* 8/20/70). In 1771, another delineator of the good wife insisted on "no Learning; no Learning" (Hutchins). As David Copeland chronicles, the colonial press had long provided a barrage of advice in which virtuous women were defined as women who served the interests of home and husband (Copeland 152).

In a construct that was not so different from the presentation of vice and virtue in a black framing, the emphasis on virtuous women was accompanied by suspicion that women might not be virtuous. Indeed, by Copeland's count, the colonial press was much more likely to present women as "vicious" than otherwise. A vituperative essay in Philadelphia's *American Weekly Mercury* concluded "the Modern Woman" was a woman of idleness (*AWM* 8/13/30). "The best of the sex are no better than Plagues," another Philadelphia polemic concluded (*PG* 3/4/34). Philadelphia was fortunate that such polemics were regularly challenged by the city's femal poet and wit, Elizabeth Magawley. "As in your *Sex* there are several Classes of Men of Sense, Rakes, Fops, Coxcombs, and down-right Fools, so I hope, without straining your Complaisance, you will allow there are some Women of Sense comparatively" (*AWM* 1/5/30; Shields 92). But in the colonies overall there were few female voices to counter charges that women were playing cards instead of looking after their children (*BG* 12/8/35) or that women were murderers of children (*NYG* 4/8/65; *CG* 3/14/75; *NLG* 12/21/70); poisoners and betrayers of husbands (*AWM* 5/15/35; *NYEP* 3/12/50); and adulterers (*VG*-Rind 3/8/70).

Such suspicions were more likely to be displaced than allayed by the revolutionary emphasis on the virtuous woman. At a time when political writers called for the reluctant necessity of severing familial relationships across the sea, the emphasis increased on clearly defined family relationships at home. Despite the calls for domestic tranquility, however, the positions of woman and the home were undergoing change in the colonial period because of factors over which colonists themselves had little control. Demographic changes resulted in a surplus of unmarried women on the eve of the Revolution while economic dislocation increased the hardship of widows (Wilson 896, 400–402). Although women's economic status was acutally in decline, a male colonial sensibility that revolved on conspiracy could easily find support for suspicions that women might be as conspiratorial as other segments of the society. Hannah Snell served in His Majesty's Army under the name James Gray and her sex was not detected even during a whipping because "her arms being drawn up, the protuberance of the breasts was inconsiderable, and they were hid by her standing close to the gate" (*BNL* 12/5/50). Like so much of life in the late colonial era, nothing was sure, even, in this case, gender.

Growing in fervor during a time of increasing uneasiness, the elevation of domesticity into higher and higher levels of virtue might be considered another face on the traditional understandings of women's virtue in terms of sexual inviolability. The call to domestic virtue in tumultuous times gives some indication of the sexual tensions that were abroad in the colonial world, and the insistence on domestic virtue was one way to assert control over women in the name of patriotism. Not surprisingly, the colonial sensibility resonated to the British Whig piety campaigns. The *North Briton*'s efforts to unseat Lord Bute by intimations that he curried influence in the royal bedroom has already been mentioned. In 1772 another piety campaign focused on the king's sister, Princess Caroline, at her marriage to a Danish prince, the references to loss of Danish liberty could not be avoided. In the summer of 1772, in thousands of words appearing in all colonial papers, none less than in the *Boston Gazette,* colonial readers followed the story of Princess Caroline's affair with the Danish court physician, her subsequent betrayal by the Queen Mother, the ensuing trial, and the eventual deaths of the lovers. Colonial readers were presented a multichaptered story of aristocratic malevolence, cunning, and punishment for their sensual summer reading, down to the execution of the physician-lover, bloodily drawn and quartered.

What is noteworthy about the campaigns is that both turned on female sexual impropriety, considered powerful enough to have imperial consequences. Neither women, even Princess Caroline, engendered much sympathy when female virtue was the key to international stability. Closer to home, in Worcester, another sexual dalliance gave evidence to the danger posed by unbridled female sexuality. In 1778, Bathsheba Spooner was executed for complicity in the murder of her husband following an afternoon of sexual adventures with three British soldiers. In the Massachusetts tradition, the condemned soldiers were allowed to explain the circumstances of the crime in an execution broadside. Bathsheba Spooner's public voice found barely a footnote: "Mrs. Spooner said nothing at the Gallows" (Lowance and Bumgardner 95).

Unlike later periods, it was a long-standing Boston practice to report news of rape, murder as a result of domestic violence, and occasional reports of prostitution and sodomy (*BEP* 11/12/50; *BEP* 8/18/35; *BG* 11/19/45; *BEP* 6/16/55; *BEP* 7/2/70). Nor were women immune from the Puritan tradition of public punishment despite later regret for the atrocities of the Salem witch trials. The *Boston Evening-Post* reported that four Portsmouth women had been fined for prostitution and then given ten stripes each on their bare backs (*BEP* 4/22/65). In 1770, another contributor reported, in the same amused tone that Henry Laurens would later assume at the idea of freedom for slaves, that four women in Boston had appeared before a judge on charges of fornication (*BEP* 7/2/70).

Meantime, giving credence to colonial fears, petitions for divorces increased in Massachusetts (Cott, "Divorce"), and premarital pregnancies rose — as high as 30 percent before and after the Revolution (Wilson 404). Franklin's grisly 1765–66 etching of a dismembered Britannia (*Magna Britannia*) may have as much to do with a perceived need to maintain female purity at home as with opposition to the actions of imperial Great Britain abroad.

British satirists were quick to locate female sexuality as a nexus of colonial vulnerability. In a famous print published in the aftermath of the Boston Tea Party, Columbia was stripped of her armor in favor of the centuries-old idea of female vulnerability as sexual availability. Here, the female figure portraying America has been forced to the ground by British political figures, tea poured down her throat while the lascivious Lord Sandwich peers up her robes. The scurrility and offensiveness of the print did not stop Paul Revere copying it for the patriot *Royal American Magazine*. In the patriot setting, the prone Columbia connected sexual virtue to American virtue as a whole but could also suggest that colonists themselves, like Lord Sandwich, sought proof of female virtue even at the cost of female humiliation. The concept of American virtue as threatened sexual invasion would be highlighted during the occupation of Boston with patriot implications that the occupying soldiers were on the brink of ravishing young women. These various ideas of womanly virtue in the late colonial period set the stage for women's later confinement to Republican motherhood, the completion of the desexualization of women begun by domestic virtue and the armor-clad Columbia.

The point I seek to make in this sketch is to propose that in this revolutionary cusp, the interpretations of American female virtue as sexual inviolability would inevitably cross with white perceptions of black sexuality. This intersection has been explored in a southern context in the colonial period (Clinton and Gillespie), but black and white sexuality was also a theme in the Massachusetts colony despite the colony's relatively small black population. Massachusetts was one of two northern colonies (Pennsylvania was the other) to prohibit not only marriage but sexual intercourse between white and black (Ames and Goodell 1:578–59). At the proposal of the 1705 law, Samuel Sewall noted his consternation: "If it be pass'd, I fear twill be an Oppression provoking to God, and that which will promote Murders and other Abominations" (Sewall, *Diary* 179). Because of Sewall's efforts, the final act permitted marriages between slaves amid the restrictions on black-and-white sexual liaisons. As Horton and Horton note, a 1761 act emphasized control over all "dissolute persons" (Ames and Goodell 4:462), including those whites who would consort with blacks (Horton and Horton, *In Hope* 49).

Massachusetts shared in the many-layered fears connected to miscegenation: the fear that whiteness would be subsumed; the belief that black men lusted for white women; and the suspicion, fueled by the white male belief that black men possessed larger penises, that white women might prefer black sexual partners (Jordan 152). Such themes are reflected in an item published by two Boston newspapers, which reported in a jocular tone, a New London, Connecticut, incident in which a white man, perceiving what he regarded as a rape in progress, pulled out a knife and "cut off all his [the attacker's] unruly parts smack and smooth." The account concluded, "We here relate as a caveat for all Negroes meddling for future with any white Woman least they fare with the like Treatment" (*BNL* 3/3/18; *BEP* 3/3/18). Nor could Bostonians, given the ongoing news they received of slave revolts, avoid the attached mythology that implied white women were spared death in order to provide for the later sexual pleasure of the insurrectionists (Jordan 153).

Notions of black sexuality as endangerment to white female virtue surfaced in 1763 with the execution of a sixteen-year-old slave for the murder of a white girl, prompting the merchant and radical leader James Bowdoin to sell one of his slaves to the West Indies, fearful of the white response to a slave engaged "in an amour with some of the white ladies in the Town" (Jordan 144). Four years later slave sexuality was again in Bostonian public consciousness when a Worcester slave, Arthur, was executed for the rape of a white woman on the heels of a much-reported remark by a British officer during the British occupation calling upon slaves to slit their masters' throats.

The sermon that accompanied Arthur's execution has prompted Daniel Williams to call Arthur "the first black rapist in American literature" (200). Execution sermons most often were reserved for crimes of murder; just 6 percent focused on rape (Slotkin 17), suggesting ambivalence about the crime itself. Although Massachusetts authorities were not loath to invoke the death penalty for various capital crimes, the crime of rape rarely received the death sentence (Powers 281). In the revolutionary crux of female virtue and black crime, however, such ambivalence disappeared. Encouraged by the execution of Arthur, rape became a symbolic crime against home, hearth, and society. Execution narratives emphasized perpetrators as increasingly unrepentant, degenerates in a downward spiral who sought to attack the family unit by the "theft" of women's virtue and who were unable to leash carnal appetites. The crime and the personality of the perpetrator were interwoven, as if inevitable, given that perpetrators were outside civilized society. It is noteworthy that the next two accused rapists in Massachusetts after Arthur were Irish Catholic outsiders who shared a status that was little higher than black bondsmen and that translated into a similar narrative fate and hangman's noose. By 1790, the popular narrative that accompanied the execution of the Philadelphia-born mulatto Joseph Mountains rejected even cursory repentance, suggesting the hardening of stereotypes. In 1796, the accused rapist Thomas Powers of Norwich, Connecticut, was similarly characterized as unrepentant in the several publications of the execution sermon that also prominently identified him as "a Negro" (Williams).

Like an unspoken Stuart bogey, the black presence hovered close behind any understanding of American virtue as sexual inviolability. Surely for "Eleutherina," a rare female correspondent in the *Boston Gazette,* the metaphor of slavery included implications of miscegenation. "But our hearts are in anguish for our dear, dear posterity the offspring of our bowels," she wrote in language that was not so far removed from the Quaker antislavery style. "Our children are human flesh, and English blood and English spirit . . . How can we endure the prospect that they shall be converted into beasts, driven, beaten, trampled on, by those who are no better that they" (*BG* 1/26/72).

Adams brought to the propaganda of the American Revolution definitions of virtue that represented both the classic understanding of virtue as the civic duty that maintained political freedom and the personal and social usefulness of virtue represented by appropriate and moral behavior, including sexual behavior. These understandings of virtue appeared not only in the front-page essays Adams and his colleagues supplied to the *Boston Gazette* but in the inside pages where propagandists found American behavioral virtue could be highlighted when contrasted with the lack of it in the British by way of the piety campaigns. But there was no impetus for Adams and his coterie to include black colonists as representatives of colonial virtue. Black colonists had long been denied access to Bostonian notions of virtue. In a broadside published about 1760 in connection with a Boston election-day festivity, black involvement is seen in terms of immoderate behavior while white companions are viewed as "trulls," that is, prostitutes.

> *Long before Phoebus looks upon*
> *The outskirts of the horizon.*
> *The blacks their forces summon.*
> *Tables & Benches, chair, & stools*
> *Rum-bottles, Gingerbread & bowls*
> *Are lug'd into the common.*
> *Thither resorts motley crew.*
> *Of whites & Blacks & Indians too*
> *And trulls of every sort.*
> *There all day long they sit & drink.*
> *Swear, sing, play paupaw, dance and stink*
> *There Baccus holds his court*
> (Piersen, *Black Yankees* 123–24)

Comic stereotypes that turned on immoderate behavior and sexual impropriety were also in place by the late 1760s. In the popular British play, *The Padlock,* which had some forty colonial American performances before 1774, the black character of Mungo performs in dialect and is the go-between that enables the female character to be freed from her chastity belt and to unite, presumably sexually, with her lover (Silverman 1976, 105). There was no missing the implication of the role of the black male, comic or not, in setting the stage for white female promiscuity. The play was well known enough, even in Boston, for "Mungo" to become a commonly understood character type and a name Boston radicals used in their campaigns against Frances Bernard. The *Boston Gazette* published a forty-five-stanza parody in which Bernard, in explaining his leave taking, refers to himself as "Mungo."

> *My noble Master, Sirs! I tell you,*
> *Conceives me such a clever Fellow.*
> *As to command me to repair*
> *To court — and bring my Budget there:*
> *Where I sir Mungo Nettle'em, Bart,*
> *By Lying, Pimping, Fraud and Art*
> (BG 7/3/69)

The British were no kinder, introducing a promiscuous black female comic character in a play during the occupation of Boston as a way of bringing attention to patriot hypocrisy (Silverman 292–94).

A related campaign had relevance for white perception of black modes of dress. British Whigs made it a point to ridicule those who tended toward any kind of high style, including overdone hairstyles, as posing as "macaroni" princes, or lower-level aristocracy. In its patriot incarnation, "macaroni" came to represent all aristocracy, British as much as French, and eventually the word came to serve as shorthand for loyalism, as in the patriot jingle, "Yankee Doodle Dandy." The Yankee "dandy" who stuck a feather in his hat and called it macaroni both ridiculed British aristocracy and substituted Yankee down-to-earth humor in its place. By the early 1770s, references to macaroni were recognized parts of patriot speech. In a discussion of social norms that probably did his antislavery position little good, Benjamin Rush asked, "Where is the difference between an African prince, with his face daubed with Grease, and his Head adorned with a Feather; and a moderen [sic] Macaroni with his artificial Club of Hair daubed with Powder and Pomatum?" (Rush 30).

The campaign for plain dress was useful to the patriots in promoting the nonimportation agreements, but clearly, for Bostonians such as Samuel Adams, elaborate dress was a sign to be heeded. Elaborate dress signaled idolatry and the call to luxury but perhaps most of all, like the Stuart king supporters, told of treasonable hearts below the fine linen. As Piersen tells us, however, attempts at elaborate European dress were early characteristics of slaves brought from Africa, carrying forward an African tradition that emulated European clothing (Piersen, *Black Yankees* 101–2). Such traditions were not to be admired in Boston. Slaves in fine dress, or in imitation thereof, not only blurred class lines (as it would in artisan circles discussed later), but raised suspicions that slaves were not what they seemed. In 1721, James Franklin's anti-Mather *New England Courant* provided an account of an elaborate black wedding in terms of its presumed intention to ridicule the government (*NEC* 25/12/21). One explanation for New England slave advertising that gave so much attention to the dress of slaves is to consider the New England suspicion that dress signaled intent.

Considered conspiratorial, violent, and promiscuous in dress and behavior, black colonists had few calls on understandings of virtue by white Boston standards except for those definitions that were most useful to white society. Fearful of black violence, colonial religious leadership inculcated virtue as an expression of approved behavior. Cotton Mather established a Society of Negroes in 1693 that included among its rules warnings against drunkenness, cursing, lying, stealing, and disobedience to masters. In the wake of suspected slave arson in 1723, Mather further inculcated virtue in a slave context, urging the emulation of the "Dutiful Behaviour of their Superiors" (Mather 2:689). Mather and other congregational ministers offered slave baptism and church membership. Franklin undoubtedly echoed the faith in the social values of religion for those "who have need of the Motives of Religion to restrain them from Vice, to support their Virtue, and retain them in the Practice of it till it becomes habitual" (Franklin, *Papers* 7:294–95).

Taken together, virtue for black colonists was not to quarrel with the status of enslavement, to avoid entertainments, and not to flaunt sexuality or dress. Black colonists could not participate in the classic sense of civic virtue, and, by the time the propagandists chose to use virtuous behavior as a way to question the British right to rule, the construction of virtue along lines of moral purity and moderation had eliminated most black colonists. Indeed, before the propagandists chose to find British virtue wanting when compared with their own, American colonists had imposed the same template on black inhabitants and come to a similar conclusion.

Black piety received rare acknowledgement in colonial America. Responding to a request of black colonists, George Whitefield preached to "a great number of negroes" (Winsor 1:509) in his first New England visit. But even in a religious setting, black gatherings were not encouraged. Indeed, Whitefield was later considered a cause of the 1741 New York plot because he actively sought black conversion (T. Davis 215). Black piety certainly found no home in the revolutionary press. Slave petitions to the Massachusetts legislative bodies, no matter how couched in pious and inoffensive language, were not published in Boston despite access to them by Samuel Adams and James Bowdoin.

There was no better example of congregational virtue than Phillis Wheatley, baptized in Boston's Old South in 1771 and a writer of poetry celebrating her own salvation from "heathenism" as well as polemic verse on patriot matters. But whether pious or patriotic, Wheatley did not receive publication in Boston's Whig press. Her most popular, and perhaps least controversial publication, was her elegy at the death of George Whitefield in 1770. As discussed in a later chapter, in Boston this was published by the definitely non-Whig press of Ezekiel Russell. It should be noted that the Whig press was not breaking precedence in refusing to find a place for her as a representative of either black or literary virtue. Wheatley's predecessor, the Calvinist Jupiter Hammon, found few public venues for his work even when he preached continued subservience. Briton Hammon's 1760 narrative, steeped in Indian captivity tradition rather than Quaker antislavery, found publication only in the loyalist shop of Green and Russell (Hammon). John Marrant's 1785 narrative, also in the captivity mode, was published in London.

One Boston slave petition suggested the exhaustion of trying to maintain piety unrewarded. "Let their Behavior, be what they will, neither they, nor their children to all Generations, shall ever be able to do, or to possess and enjoy any Thing, no, not every Life Itself, but in a Manner as the Beasts that perish" (*Appendix* 10; Aptheker, *And Why Not* 6).

Finally, efforts of black colonists to prove virtuous behavior by service in the revolutionary war similarly failed. Black service to the Revolution, despite its use in New England, was generally ignored until brought to light by the nineteenth-century abolitionist movement (Nell). A researcher notes that the service of more than five hundred free black Haitians in making a patriot retreat possible during the 1779 Siege of Savannah received bare mention outside the Tory press and delayed its recognition by American historians (Rhodes).

What was the reason for the refusal of Adams and the revolutionary circle to allow black colonists to bear the mantle of virtue, even without an attachment to antislavery? One might consider the long history of denying virtue to black colonists, the prejudice to color, the need to bring the South to the cause, and even Adams's own beliefs. But from a propagandistic viewpoint, the denial of virtue to a class of subservient people was to give example to the reality of a descent into "slavery." From Puritan sermonizing to the use of boys in blackface as devil's imps in Boston's Pope Day parades, slavery as metaphor was the logical outcome of an ongoing colonial preoccupation with the use of blackness and darkness to represent betrayal and evil. A language that equated the color black with evil, the widespread acceptance of the institution in the North and South, the themes of virtue and vigilance that had no place for black piety, and the political understanding of the word "slavery" conspired to give the metaphor of slavery sufficient layers of meaning for attachment to a variety of colonial sensibilities. Once transposed into metaphor, slavery could serve to unite white colonists of whatever region under a banner of white exclusivity.

CHAPTER TWO

Slave Advertising

The Colonial Context

For the newspaper propagandists of the American cause, the revolutionary message, whatever the cast of the moment, had, at its literal back, advertisements that sought to buy slaves, sell slaves, or recover slaves who had escaped. There could be no confinement of the word "slavery" to a rhetorical flourish or to political metaphor when colonial readers saw the existence of slavery, if not in day-to-day contact, each week in the newspapers. Slave advertising occurred routinely in newspapers of all colonies, and because "runaway" notices crossed colony borders, colonists far from concentrations of slavery had before them examples of the construction of slavery from all parts of the colonies.

About a fourth of newspaper space was generally devoted to advertising—separate, small paragraphs of information that occasionally included a small woodcut display and a boldface "headline." Set amidst these notices of ship arrivals and departures, land for sale, runaway indentured servants, and lost horses, the slave advertisement was not unusual even in areas served by newspapers where the slave and free black population was low. Here, in the context of legitimation provided by the colonial newspaper, slave owning was presented as an accepted routine of colonial life, and, for the price of the advertisement, the slave owner was free to construct identities and dispense and disperse attitudes that were most useful to the slave-owning community.

In the Northeast, for example, "good" slaves were the competent workers and appropriate members, like indentured servants and apprentices, of a stepladder society. In Virginia and Maryland, slave advertising reflected the integral role slavery played in the definition of the society. "Runaway" advertisements reminded Virginians that their definition of self depended on slaves remaining loyally in the place Virginians had prescribed for them. In South Carolina, the slave advertisement was the town crier, calling out that white dominance could only be maintained by vigilance and loyalty of white to white.

Under the umbrella of the colonial newspaper, these differences were not so much sharp contrasts as varieties off the same stalk. The printer served as the middlemen in the transactions. In the North, the names of William Bradford of Philadelphia, John Peter Zenger of New York, and Benjamin Edes of Boston appear in the advertisements from their regions as much as their counterparts, William Rind of Williamsburg and Peter Timothy of South Carolina appear in the southern press. Tory or patriot affiliation made no difference. The typographical displays of slave advertisements were alike, even to the use of running figures for notices of escaped slaves.

Slave descriptions also came from a narrow band of choices that served to present slave transactions in terms of colonywide commonality. By the eve of the American Revolution, slave advertisements had anchored in place an array of slave characteristics that included renderings of the "bad" slave as untrustworthy, demonic, and violent, depending on his or her resistance to the condition of servitude, and the "good" or virtuous slave as one who accepted servitude. Thus, with the exception of arriving slaves sold in "parcels," slaves were characterized in colonial advertising in ways that indicated slaves were different from the free because they embodied particular characteristics that made them appropriate to the status of slavery. Reading the slave advertisements across the colonies, these characteristics fall into two categories: the suitability of black bondsmen and women to accomplish the work of the colonial society, and the need to maintain white control over a body of people whose perceived inborn characteristics, notably violence, threatened the larger society.

This was a different rationale for slavery than in traditional Mosaic law, which viewed slavery as a state of labor and circumstance but not necessarily related to viewing a group of people in agreed-upon ways. It also differed from the "just war" rationale for slavery provided by John Locke and colonial proslavery essayists, who asserted slavery was appropriate when men and women had been captured in a just war, that is, not a slave-catching expedition, when the alternate to enslavement was immediate death. Like Mosaic law, slavery by way of the Lockean loophole was based on circumstance, not inborn characteristics related to race. The rationale offered by slave advertising had most in common with that offered by the Old Testament in its account of Ham, who, along with his descendants, was condemned to servile status forever. Slave advertising called upon a notion that slavery was an unchanging status regardless of circumstance largely because of shared personal characteristics that made them unfit for freedom. Prominent among these characteristics was the danger black people, freed or enslaved, posed for whites. Thus, no matter how "good" the good slave, the skills, behavior, or demeanor would never be good enough to warrant freedom. The tip of a sunny iceberg did not preclude the existence of danger below, a constant reminder provided by advertisements for escaped slaves.

The practice of slavery differed markedly from region to region in the American colonies, but the slave advertising of colonial newspapers might be considered a place where these varied attitudes found common ground. Because slave advertisements crossed regional boundaries, particularly in the advertising for escaped slaves, which often appeared in mid-Atlantic and northeastern newspapers in areas of suspected havens, regional differences toward slaves found widespread distribution. But rather than appearing as bizarre in a new context, slave advertising emanating from one region provided the opportunity to tap into common perceptions. Once on the common page, southern slave owners and New England slave owners could determine they were equally fearful of slave conspiracy. A description of a slave by his or her "leering underlook," a common expression that indicated untrustworthiness, even revolt, for the southern slave owner, might not lead to the apprehension of the slave in question but clearly reinforced any reader's suspicion, North or South, that slave loyalty could not be taken for granted. Competence was an aside in face of the apparent proof provided by the advertisements for escaped slaves that only the thin line of white vigilance protected society from slave uprising. Warnings of the perils of "harbouring" in the revolutionary decade of the 1770s were as apparent in advertising from the North as from the South.

Taken together, the slave advertisements of the colonial press called upon and reinforced perceptions about racial characteristics. While abolitionists such as Granville Sharp pointed to the advertisements in horror and argued that property and humanity were irreconcilable, slave owners found that perceived and specific characteristics of slaves buttressed the rationale for the institution.

Proof of humanity by way of personality traits, as the abolitionists would have it, thus made no difference in the status of freedom; existence of personality traits was not in question. Instead, the characterization of the slave in what would become commonly understood ways provided a vocabulary that accepted the patriot metaphor.

Scholars have long examined slave advertising for the information it can provide about the institution itself, about slave life, and as examples of slave resistance (Frey, Hodges and Brown, Mullin, P. Wood). Several studies also use slave advertising to examine regional differences (Smith and Wojtowicz, White, Parker). Here, however, the emphasis is on slave advertising as a construct of white control and has most in common with Shane White, who writes, "Consider for example, the accounts of the physical appearance of blacks contained in the runaway advertisements. Such descriptions appear to be dispassionate, illustrating well the 'objectivity' of the advertisements, but we need to understand that the language used in them was loaded with meanings... there was a direct and readily discernible link between appearance on the one hand and character and intellect on the other" (White 119).

Set in the various contexts of legitimation provided by the colonial newspapers in a message composed for the benefit of slaveholders, the slave advertisements provided ostensible evidence that human characteristics not only were insufficient claim for a nonfree status but offered a paradigm that defined *particular* characteristics as those indicative of a subservient class. Proof of humanity by way of personality traits thus made no difference in the status of freedom, but their existence instead proved that blacks and slaves *should* remain subservient, for the benefit of all. For the master seeking a runaway slave, the escape proved the slave was not suited for freedom, for the act of running away made the slave "artful," "conniving," and "disloyal." Escaped slaves, the advertisements suggested, in often demonic renderings, should be turned in for the protection of the greater society. Meantime, sellers of slaves sold them for "no fault," often with acknowledgment of their skills, none of which was considered a prelude to life as a free person.

Political position apparently played no role in the amount of advertising carried by a newspaper. For example, a moderate newspaper such as the *Pennsylvania Gazette* carried many columns of slave advertising—in 1772, for example, twice as many (by my count) as its competitor, the *Pennsylvania Journal*, most likely because of the *Gazette*'s substantial circulation. The *Boston Gazette* carried only slightly more slave advertising than Richard and Margaret Draper's conservative *Massachusetts Gazette and Boston Weekly News-Letter.* Printers had no politics when it came to slave advertising, a business proposition.

Besides advertisements for slaves for sale and advertisements for runaway slaves, advertisements also appeared, in much fewer numbers, for slaves wanted and by jailers advertising for the owners of individuals who had been apprehended on suspicion of being runaway slaves. The for-sale advertisements exceeded, although not overwhelmingly, the advertisements for runaway slaves. The slave-wanted advertisements, by contrast, occurred irregularly and, particularly in the Northeast, tended to be calls for individual slaves with specific skills. Despite the fewer numbers of these slave-wanted advertisements, readers of the *Boston Gazette* would have had difficulty in avoiding the advertisement by a slave dealer that called for "Any persons who have healthy Slaves to dispose of, Male or Female, that have been some years in the Country, of 25 Years or Under, may be informed of a Purchaser by applying to the Printer." That advertisement appeared sixteen times between December 1772 and July of the following year, an unusual number of repetitions. Most advertisements appeared two or three times.

In the Northeast the "good slave" of the for-sale advertisements was articulated most prominently. To the colonial reader of Pennsylvania, Massachusetts, and New York, the slave of the for-sale advertisements was hardworking, healthy, and skilled, and sold for "no fault" or "for want of employ." Occasionally, those phrases would be elaborated upon, as in the advertisement of "A likely Negro WENCH, about 22 years of age, fit either for town or country business. She is sold of no fault, but the want of employment, as her mistress has quit keeping house" (*PG* 4/25/70). Four years later, in almost identical language, another "likely young Negro Wench" was advertised for sale, "The cause of her being sold is her Master's removing out of the Province" (*PG* 11/5/74). Purchasers were sought for children on the same grounds, as in the advertisement of the "strong Healthy Negro Girl 10 Years of Age" who was to be sold "for Want of Employ" (*BG* 4/6/70).

Only occasionally did an advertisement include an indication that the slave in question was not faultless, as in the advertisement of a "likely Negro wench, about 25 years old with a Female Child, about 4 years old." Potential buyers were told that upon inquiry "the real cause of her being sold will be made known" (*PG* 12/7/75). Another Pennsylvanian, advertising a mother and her two sons, indicated "There faults will be candidly told" (*PG* 5/15/76). However, one New York advertiser had no hesitation in expressing candor in the center of the advertising marketplace. The advertised slave had no faults "except a too great fondness for a particular Wench in his old neighborhood" (*NYJ* 10/19/75). Two *Boston Gazette* advertisers were similarly frank: "To Be Sold, a hearty, likely strong Negro Fellow of about 18 years old, he has some good Qualities, he is sober and good-natured, but is a runaway, a Thief and a Liar. If such a Negro will suit any Person to send out of the Province, they may hear of him if they apply soon to Edes and Gill" (*BG* 12/10/70). The week before an advertisement in a similar vein had appeared: "Very handy at all kinds of Household Work, but does not like it, is discontented with his present service and by keeping bad Company in Town, is grown very impudent and Saucy" (*BG* 12/3/70).

But such indications of problems were rare, so rare in fact that, in an unusual insertion, the *Boston Gazette* noted the trend toward faultless slaves with some sarcasm: "WANTED A Negro Man from 18 to 30 Years of Age that will steal, lie and get Drunk. Any person having such a one to dispose of, may hear of a Purchaser by applying to the Printers hereof" (*BG* 7/18/74).

Slaves for sale shared a number of other positive characteristics, particularly that of being "likely," a somewhat all-purpose eighteenth-century word of affirmation that suggested suitability to task, health, and physical attractiveness, as in the description of a slave as "likely to look upon" (*NYJ* 1/12/75). But perhaps the most valuable quality the word had for the advertiser was that it was all-encompassing. Men, women, and children could all be described as "likely," whether they were house servants, artisans, or sold on the auction block straight from the Middle Passage. "Likely" served as a common description for all slaves, a word, significantly, generally not used in the advertisements for indentured servants. Its popularity may be explained by the fact it served as a way of ascribing similarity to men and women who were not always similar. It thus served as a way of working against the individualization of slaves into personalities and put the onus of developing the "likeliness" or the potential of slaves onto the shoulders of the master.

A description of a slave as "likely" was often joined by a description of strength and health, as "A very likely, strong Negro Boy of Good Temper, about 12 years of age," who, naturally, was to be "sold for no fault, but only for want of Employ" (*BG* 9/1/72). It was a selling point if a slave had had smallpox and measles and the resulting immunization that the successfully survived diseases provided in a society that was periodically racked by epidemics.

Once it was ascertained that the slaves were sold for no fault, were "likely," and were strong and healthy, all attributes that commonly were shared among slaves for sale, slaves were only then individualized by their talents. The talents were considerable and crossed a number of occupations. Not only were slaves advertised as being good farmers and cooks, the advertisements indicate they had skills in a variety of trades — as millers, coopers, butchers, hairdressers, tanners, carpenters, wheelwrights, and bakers. Language ability, English as well as others, was considered worthy of mention, as the advertisement that promoted "a likely Negro lad, 17 years old, speaks English and French" (*BG* 4/4/74).

Good temper was occasionally mentioned, but the emphasis was on usefulness and the attributes of skill, strength, and health that would contribute to that usefulness. A slave-wanted advertisement called for a boy "of a good disposition, and willing to learn the necessary qualifications for a waiting man" (*PJ* 9/13/70).

Even in the context of the for-sale advertisements, there are glimpses of slave independence and the recognition by advertisers of their wants and desires: "The cause of her being sold is her Master's removing out of the Province, and she not willing to go, as her Parents live near Philadelphia" (*PG* 5/11/74). Another: "The cause of his being sold is that he is not inclined to farming" (*PG* 6/29/74). A third: "They are sold for no fault, only not agreeing with the freeman of the business they are at present employed in" (*PG* 4/10/70).

Obedience may have been assumed, but owners of slaves for sale did not consider it either sufficiently factual or important to use meek behavior as a selling point. Indeed, the use of the phrase "down look," presumably a depressed, hangdog attitude, was seldom used to describe slaves in the Northeast, but frequently used to describe runaway indentured servants. However, the lack of description of slaves as subservient cannot be interpreted to mean that the slave had some control over his or her destiny. Despite the concern of an occasional kind master, the majority of the slave advertisements indicated that slaves existed for the benefit of the owner regardless of the personal consequences for the slave. Small children were sold with or without their mothers. In one Pennsylvanian advertisement, a husband and wife were advertised for sale as a pair, not a common occurrence, but the family unit did not automatically include their child. "They have a fine promising male child, 2 years old, that has had the smallpox, likewise to be sold with them if the Purchaser chooses" (*PG* 12/7/75). A New York advertiser offered a similar option to potential buyers. "A likely Negro Wench, not quite twenty years of age, with or without her child, a Boy, about 2 years of age, as may suit the purchaser" (*NYJ* 8/2/79). A five-year-old child was advertised separately from her mother with a sanctimonious note: "The owner intends to break up house-keeping, otherwise he would not choose to part with them" (*PJ* 5/11/74).

Boston advertisements, however, provide the most compelling evidence that points to the vulnerability and isolation of the black child. In Boston, black babies were regularly "given away free." Between 1770 and 1774, the *Boston Gazette* and the *Boston News-Letter* together carried twenty-five such advertisements for free babies, as in this typical one: "To Be Given Away. A very, likely Negro Female Child, of as fine a breed as any in America. Enquire of the Printer" (*BNL* 1/30/73). In other colonies, advertisements for free babies were rare, suggesting that the owners found other solutions for unwanted or orphaned black children.

By the age of seven or eight, children were useful enough to be sold. Children of the eighteenth century, of course, did not inhabit a special place of dependency and need later defined as childhood. Work began early for both black and white children. But perhaps one benefit of the harsh rules of the eighteenth century that only recognized a short period of physical rather than emotional dependency of childhood may have been the lack of characterization of blacks as childlike, a characterization that was to hound future generations.

If runaway slaves had not been advertised in the northeastern newspapers, the image of the eighteenth-century colonial slave portrayed by the northeastern papers would be one of competent servant. But the existence of advertisements for runaway slaves belied that image. Not all of these advertisements for escaped slaves were from northeastern owners. The location of Philadelphia made its newspapers recipients for advertisements from southern colonies, particularly Maryland.

The major negative characteristic of slaves in the runaway advertisements was connected to their disappearance. By the act of escaping, the slaves could be characterized as "arch," "sly," "cunning," "lying," and "crafty." The act of escape was seen as betrayal, even abandonment. The advertisements bristle with antagonism. Personality traits of the escaped slaves were described as if they were warning signs to others not to be similarly fooled. A Boston runaway by the name of Samson, although "sprightly and active," spoke with a "learing under-look" (*BG* 8/19/76). Nor did skillfulness and hard work guarantee a loyal slave. Jem was described by his Philadelphia owner as "a cunning ingenious fellow" despite a remarkable number of admirable traits — a "good workman in a forge" who could do "any kind of smith or carpenters work necessary about a forge, and can also do any kind of farming business" (*PJ* 8/5/72).

Indeed, there seemed no protection from artful behavior, a theme in the escaped-slave advertising that appeared in the Northeast. Even religious demeanor was no guarantee of a dutiful slave. Moses Grimes, for example, was "very religious, preaches to his colour, walks before burials, and marries." He was still "very artful" — so artful, in fact, that "if spoke familiarly to, pretends to simplicity and laughs" (*PG* 12/25/72). Another slave, who had escaped with his wife, was described as a preacher and also "smooth tongued, and very artful" (*RNY* 1/6/75). In these advertisements, pleasantness was not viewed as a natural characteristic of slave personality, as it was in later rhetoric, but as an indication of cunning.

The examples also illustrate that artfulness was frequently connected to the slave's conversational interaction with the master, reflecting the master's lurking suspicion that slaves did not always mean what they said. The advertisement for the Philadelphia slave, Buck, could work as a reminder to other whites that a slave's pleasant demeanor was no guarantee that disloyalty was not far under the surface. He was "artful and deceptive in conversation, firm and daring in his efforts to perpetrate villainy, though of mild temper and plausible in his speech" (*PG* 12/4/75). The same phrases, "deceptive in conversation" and "plausible in speech" were used the following year for a slave named Harry (*PG* 12/26/76).

The appearance of these and similar phrases in the runaway advertisements indicate that slave owners established for themselves a rhetoric that protected them from the acknowledgment that the men and women who ran from their custody might have reason to seek their independence. In some cases, the rhetoric served as a public expression of grief as much as a call for the return of property, as in this advertisement by a Virginia master that appeared in a Pennsylvania paper:

> I tell the public he is the same boy who for so many years waited on me on my travels through this and neighboring provinces (and his pertness, or rather impudence, was well-known to almost all my acquaintance) there is the less occasion for a particular description of him. I think it not amiss to say he is a very likely young fellow, about 20 years old, about 5 feet 9 inches high, stout and strong made, has a remarkable swing in his walk, but is much more so by a knack he has of gaining the good graces of almost everybody who will listen to his bewitching and deceitful tongue, which seldom or ever speaks the truth. (*PG* 4/27/74)

The runaway advertisements, like the advertisements for runaway apprentices, can be characterized by their predictability. As in the for-sale advertisements, the runaway advertisements of the Northeast usually conformed to a pattern. Some newspapers, particularly the *Pennsylvania Journal,* perhaps the most typographically advanced colonial newspaper in terms of advertising layout, used an African running figure or other illustration with the advertisements. The block of copy most usually began with the word "RUNAWAY" capitalized, followed by the location of the place the slave left, the name and a description of the slave, a detailed description of the clothing worn and taken, a description of skills, and occasionally a description of personality traits, as already discussed. The advertisement closed with a reminder of the amount of the reward and the name of the owner or an "Enquire of the Printer." A final postscript often warned "all masters of vessels" not take up the slave or anyone to "harbour" the slave on pain of legal penalty. As in the for-sale advertisements, the physical description of the slave was dominant in words that affirm as much as describe: "A very stout well-made fellow" (*PG* 2/3/73); "well-featured," "a likely, well-made fellow" (*BG* 11/8/71); "strait-limb'd" (*BG* 3/25/76); "very strong made" (*BNL* 6/15/75); "spare and active" (*BNL* 9/28/75); "stout well-set Fellow" (*BNL* 7/8/73). These general statements were followed by precise physical descriptions — height "five feet seven or eight inches" — with particular attention paid to physical marks of identity, some of which were striking. A Boston slave, Prince, although "well-set," had "had his Jaw Bone broken, it is an obstruction to him in Eating, has had his right leg broke, and is a little crooked, has lost two or three Toes of his Foot." If those disabilities were not sufficient to make him a marked man, his former master noted his red waistcoat and yellow breeches (*BNL* 6/7/70).

Not regularly, but on occasion, an advertiser noted that the slave was wearing an iron collar, certainly a reminder to northeastern readers of the status of slaves. An eighteen-year-old Philadelphia girl was identified by the iron collar she was wearing at the time of her escape (*PG* 2/6/70). And another slave escaped with a collar and a chain on his leg, although his owner warned that he nonetheless "pretends to be free," a favorite phrase. It was noted he took a hammer and chisel with him (*PG* 5/10/70). The slave Cuff escaped with "an iron collar around his neck" but was also identified by his stutter (*PG* 10/25/75).

Where such obvious identification marks were not available, owners did not fail to use minutia. The physical description of a Maryland slave advertised for in Pennsylvania included mention of a small bald spot and "one of his little fingers stiff" (*PG* 2/8/70). Another youth "has been lately cured of a sore on one of his great toes, and one on his shin bone a little above the instep" (*PG* 10/12/74).

The closeness of the master's observation of the men and women in his or her custody was again illustrated in the descriptions of the slave clothing. Although owners acknowledged that the runaway slave would likely change his or her clothes, that did not stop them from listing every stitch down to the shade of the buttons that the slave was wearing at the time of escape. Another close description was given to clothing the slave took along: "Had on when he went away, a brown Homespun Coat, lined with the striped woolen, old leather breeches, a Pair of New long striped Linen Trousers, and took with him a new homespun brown lappel coat and Breeches lined with the same colour, and brass Buttons, the collar lined with red quality, black Calico . . . and a homespun Great Coat with metal Buttons and divers pair of Stockings, striped Woolen shirt and a white linnen ditto" (*BNL* 3/18/71).

The master of Philadelphia runaway Dick noted that the "pair of pretty good leather breeches" he ran away in were without any seam between the legs (*PG* 6/7/70). The owner of the slave Pompey concluded his already detailed clothing description with the information the slave's shoes, although decorated "with copper or pinch-back buckles," still "appeared too long for him" (*PJ* 11/20/76). The amount of clothing that was available for the escaping slave Be to take on her flight to freedom, and her master's knowledge of the wardrobe, invites speculation as to her special status. In addition to the considerable amount of clothing she was wearing, she also carried along "an half worn scarlet coat, new purple and yellow checked stuff jacket and petticoat, white linen ditto, blue and white stample linen ditto, cambrick apron, red and white calico short gown, and black bombazein quilted petticoat" (*PJ* 11/20/76).

The minute physical and clothing descriptions certainly indicate one level of intimacy between the slave and his master. But the intimacy appeared limited to these spheres of observation. Owners of the runaway slaves advertised in the Northeast appeared, at least from the advertisements, to have little personal knowledge of the men and women who served them. Unlike slave owners in the southern colonies, northeastern slave owners tended not to offer speculation on where the runaway slaves may have fled to, suggesting these owners had little interest or even much concept of the familial and emotional ties of the slave. When such acknowledgments existed, the tone sometimes suggested surprise that the tie to the master was not always paramount, as when one owner complained that when he gave his female slave a pass to visit her child in Philadelphia, "she never returned" (*PG* 2/20/72). Another female slave left "three young children, a good master and mistress, and is going towards New-York, after a married white man who is a soldier in the Continental service there" (*PG* 8/7/76).

Another black-white relationship was noted in an advertisement in which the emphasis was on the kind of white women that would flee with a slave. "Said Mulattoe took with him a white woman, which he says is his wife, she is very remarkable, as all the fingers are cut off her right hand, and is a thick-set, chunky, impudent looking, red haired hussey, pretty much given to strong drink" (*PG* 11/1/70).

Most advertisements that speculated on whereabouts did not have this intensity. Advertisements simply noted that it "is supposed she will go towards New-York, where she has Relatives" (*PG* 8/8/71). The Philadelphia slave Mingo was "supposed to be gone off with a White Woman, named Fanny" (*PG* 6/28/70). In a footnote, an owner added that his slave Jack, since he was born in Maryland, "is on his way to his old master, to see his mother and father" (*PG* 10/21/72). There were occasional mentions of family units fleeing to freedom. "A young female child about eight months old" was taken in the flight of a man and woman, "which may be a good mark to know them both" (*PG* 11/1/70). Similarly, another couple by the names of John Sharper and Nan took with them the three-year-old Ishmael (*PJ* 5/7/72).

These examples come from the Philadelphia papers, which carried the largest amount of slave advertising of the northeastern papers. In Boston, with less advertising from southern colonies, family connections or speculation to the whereabouts of runaways were almost totally ignored. The *Boston Gazette* carried only one such advertisement from 1770 through 1776, that for a slave named Dillar, who "had carried off with her a Child of about 5 Years of Age" (*BG* 2/6/75).

Runaway advertisements suggest that slaves did not escape without some planning. The frequent mention of the clothes they took with them, even their "artfulness," suggests the leave-taking was not impulsive. Those factors would indicate that slaves probably had some rather specific plans on where they were going. But many northeastern slave owners, particularly in Massachusetts, although observant enough to note the fit of a shoe and shape of a buckle, appeared to be ignorant of the lives and concerns of slaves outside their connection with the white world.

Escaped-slave advertisements composed a small portion of northeastern advertising in general, and a small portion of advertisements when compared to the advertisements for runaway servants and apprentices. At first glance the slave runaway advertisements seem almost indistinguishable from the advertisements for runaway servants. Indeed, there were many similarities between the two, including close physical descriptions and the offering of rewards.

There were differences also. Slaves were never advertised with a surname, and servants, including free blacks, were given both names. The use of the single name, in fact, was the immediate indication that the individual in question was a slave. Additionally, there were certain rhetorical nuances. The use of "likely" for slaves and not for servants; the use of "down look" for servants more than slaves (although in Virginia, the use of "down look" was also used in slave descriptions); and the occasional use of "wool" to describe the hair of a slave. Unlike descriptions of white women servants, black women were described as "wenches" (although "woman" was also used); black youths were frequently "boys" and "girls," whereas white male youths were described as "lads." But most important, the advertisements made unequivocally clear that the sale of slaves was the sale of the individual but that the indentured servant was not for sale; it was his or her *time* that was for sale. These differences, or lack of them, bring up the notion proposed by Oscar Handlin and Mary F. Handlin in connection with the origins of the slave system in the South. They argue that slavery grew out of a tradition that accepted various levels of non-freedom, beginning with medieval villenage, rather than perceived inherent differences of the black race. If we apply that model to the Northeast, advertisements indicate that colonists did not simply view slaves as on the bottom rung of servitude out of happenstance or history. They were acknowledged as different from indentured servants and were given characteristics, including violence and cunning, that were less applied to indentured servants. Nonetheless, the existence of other servant classes could suggest that slavery might be more easily accepted by northeastern colonists as yet another level that existed for the overall good of a functioning society. Emphasizing the function of the slave in the white world, advertisements can be viewed as illustrations of the proslavery arguments of the period that claimed enslavement was part of the natural order of the world because it promoted the happiness of the whole rather than individual benefit.

In December of 1774, an advertisement in the *Maryland Gazette* sounded the feared note of slave uprising. The advertisement was for the runaway Will, a slave whose escape had not been artful or deceitful, whose getaway had been engineered not by a smooth tongue, who had run without wife or child or even additional clothes, who had no plan of escape and ran to no secret harbor. Will took the action that colonists feared the most—he rose up and attacked the white man in whose charge he had been placed: "Having resisted his overseer, by throwing him down, throating him and striking him sundry times with his fist, it is therefore to be hoped that as he has been guilty of so flagiteous [sic] a crime that all masters of negroes and servants will encourage the taking of him . . . it cannot be doubted but all overseers will be vigilant on this occasion" (*MG* 12/15/74). In face of slave unpredictability, here, indeed, was a call for white vigilance.

The advertisements of the southern press suggest vigilance was not limited to such dramatic calls. It existed on many levels, and its front line of defense was depersonalization. Slaves advertised for sale in the Virginia press, and to a lesser extent the Maryland press (that exhibited characteristics of both southern and northern regions), lost the characterizations of skillful workers of the northeastern advertisements. Slaves became members of "parcels," men, women, and children known only by their common enslavement. In Virginia the context of the slave advertisements shifts from that of people to that of property. The advertisements no longer appeared amid those for runaway indentured servants but were found among the advertisements of what appears to be an extraordinary number of lost, strayed, or stolen horses.

In the early 1770s, the number of advertisements of slaves for sale and those for runaways were fairly similar. But in the Virginia press the advertisements represented many hundreds of slaves for sale, rather than the few dozen of the northeastern press. William Rind's *Virginia Gazette* for 1770 contained more runaway advertisements than sale advertisements. Yet the number of slaves represented by the runaway advertisements amounted to perhaps thirty-four; the slaves represented by the advertisements for sale numbered more than fifteen hundred (by my count).

Many of those for-sale advertisements were for slaves to be sold by professional dealers from parcels as large as 240; others from groups of 20, 30, or 80 slaves, all to be sold at auction, not at private sale. So organized, slaves were described in limited ways—"choice," "valuable," and the ubiquitous "likely," those terms usually a part of the headlines along with the place of birth: "Just arrived from Africa" or "Virginia-born." Health was prominently mentioned. But only when the parcel was the result of the death of an owner, or sold by "a gentleman who declined to go into planting" did the advertisement generally include the mention of the skills represented in the group: "Nine choice Negroes," including a "good carpenter, good shoemaker" (*VG*-Rind 3/1/70). A group of 80 "Virginia-born" slaves included "likely young wenches, sundry carpenters, a good blacksmith and a master skipper" (*VG*-Pickney 4/13/70). But even these descriptions, which tended to characterize the parcels rather than individualize the men and women who comprised the parcels, were scarce. Even when small parcels of slaves were sold, in groups as few as two, the opportunity to individualize was ignored. The advertisement of the slave Minny was rare. "He is supposed to be as good a skipper as any in the colony; is well acquainted with the bay, and all Virginia and Maryland" (*VG* 10/12/75). And by Virginia standards the for-sale advertisement of a house servant was effusive. The young man was "exceedingly likely," "a very good house servant," understood "taking care of horses," and was even "a tolerable good cook." The seller offered to take the young man back if the purchaser was not entirely satisfied within a month (*VG*-Purdie 4/14/75).

For the most part, however, Virginia owners were faint in their praise for the slaves they wished to sell. A parcel of slaves might include "sundry carpenters" and "a good blacksmith" (*VG*-Pickney 4/14/70), but such descriptions were insufficient to make much difference in the representation of slaves. The definition of slaves as individuals was left to the purview of the runaway advertisements.

As in the northeastern advertisements, the physical description of the slave dominated the runaway advertisements. But the Virginia advertisements lacked the minute detail of the northeastern advertisements. Virginians were satisfied to describe the slave simply as "middle-sized" or "well-made," rather than convey size in exact feet and inches. Virginians did share with the slave owners of the Northeast a particular concern with color. Virginians, as other colonists, could be specific about shade: "yellowish complexion" was a frequent term of description. "Pass for a white man," "very black," "remarkably black," and "dark Mulatto" were important distinctions. As in the Northeast, speech was seen as a means of identification — stuttering, speed, plainness, and even "talkiness" was noted, but noted, of course, when there was something unusual and usually negative about the speech.

Apparel was given little emphasis, sometimes dismissed as clothes "that are commonly given to Field Negroes" (*VG*-Purdie and Dixon 5/23/71). Ben escaped "wearing such clothes as Negroes occasionally wear in summer" (*VG*-

Purdie 11/3/75). Even in cases where the escaped slave was known to have taken clothes with him, owners had difficulty being specific or, unlike the northeastern owners, found the enumeration of clothing unimportant, as in the advertisement for Essex: "He is a great rogue, and had a great variety of clothes on him, 21, middle-sized, very straight, talks fast, has large eyes, thick lips and had several times had a swelling under his throat, which has frequently broke, the scars of which are plainly to be seen" (*VG*-Rind 5/31/70). Caesar carried off "several suits of clothes, but do not remember any except those he went off in" (*VG*-Pickney and Dixon 7/27/70).

The mention of scars and physical difficulties were frequent, and the advertisements made a point of noting that the markings or disabilities were the result of accidents rather than mistreatment. The runaway Will was partly identified by the scar under one eye received from an ax blow (*VG*-Rind 11/8/70). Ben was identified by a mark "occasioned by burn when young" (*VG*-Purdie 11/10/75). Some masters appeared sensitive to the subject of mistreatment. The Virginia owner of the slave Sam made it clear his slave could not have escaped because he was treated badly: "His thefts were certainly the cause of his flight, to avoid the Gallows, for he was never punished whilst with me, nor ever complained, neither had he had Cause to be dissatisfied at his Treatment" (*VG*-Purdie 3/7/71). But the owner of another slave, also named Sam, offered 25 pounds for the slave's head. "He has broke open my Store, and stole many things. . . . I will give Ten Pounds Reward for his Head, if separated from his Body. He has been much whipped for the Crime he committed, and expects to be hanged if taken; therefore he must be well-secured" (*VG*-Pickney and Dixon 2/2/71).

The same edition carried an advertisement that certainly served to remind Virginians that slavery was supported by the colonial government and that an owner had the right to call for the death of an escaped slave. "As he is outlawed I will give TEN POUNDS for his head, or for a property Certificate to entitle me to be allowed for him by the county."

But neither the tone of the advertisement for Sam nor the angry, punishing words of the last two advertisements was typical. Those advertisements reminded Virginians in a particularly strong way that slaves, after all, were not loyal, and that in the end, discipline was the only support. The message was more typically carried in the characterization of the runaway slave as deceitful or artful. Charles was an "artful cunning fellow," a sawyer and shoemaker who "reads well and is a great Preacher from which I imagine he will pass for a freeman" (*VG*-Purdie and Dixon 4/25/71). Jack had a "deceitful smile"

(*VG*-Rind 2/15/70), as did Joshua, who also was of a "cunning and of a roguish disposition" (*VG*-Purdie and Dixon 2/15/70). Another Jack was described as "slim, clean made, talkative, artful, and very fancey fellow" (*VG*-Purdie and Dixon 12/5/71). Artfulness was frequently connected to some aspects of speech. Venus, for example, advertised along with the second Jack, was characterized as "very smooth tongued" (*VG*-Purdie and Dixon 12/5/71). Caesar was identified as "cunning, smooth-tongued, sensible fellow, has a remarkable good countenance and talks much, especially when in liquor to which he is pretty much addicted" (*VG*-Purdie and Dixon 7/26/70). The mention of alcohol addiction occurred periodically in advertisements throughout the colonies.

As in the northeastern advertisements, the Virginia advertisements that refer to runaway slaves as deceitful and artful composed less than 10 percent of the total advertisements, despite the power of the description when it occurred. Indeed, Virginia masters did not characterize their slaves as deceitful or artful in any significantly greater numbers than advertisers of the Northeast.

Nonetheless, the appearance of the description "artful" and its corollaries in the runaway advertisements suggests Virginians were not as impersonal about their slaves as the for-sale advertisements would seem to indicate. Other aspects of the advertisements evidence that Virginians were far from impersonal in their relationships with their slaves. And, unlike their northern counterparts, Virginians demonstrated a far-ranging awareness of the personal history of their slaves and a realization of the multiplicity and strength of familial and emotional connections that caused slaves to abscond, as the Virginians phrased it, from "their duty."

"I gave him leave to go see his wife, who lives at Mr. Cornelius Loften's in this country, and he is supposed to be lurking around in the neighborhood. It is supposed that he had had dealings with a woman of infamous character in this neighborhood . . . and that she advised him to run away" (*VG*-Purdie and Dixon 9/6/70). On a similar theme, it was noted that Sall Cooper, one of the few slaves who was given a surname in the runaway advertisements, "has been for some time past much in the Company of a white Man who has lately gone to Norfolk, she is probably lurking in that place" (*VG*-Purdie 11/21/71).

Such advertisements provide glimpses into the lives of slaves; occasionally, an advertisement provides a complete drama. A ten-pound reward was offered for the capture of Sam: "About three years ago he purchased his freedom of his old master, Mr. Francis Slaughter, and continued in that state until this spring, when it was discovered he was attempting to inveigle away a number of negroes to the way of Indian country (where he had been most of the last summer) upon which the neighbors insisted on his being reduced to slavery once again; and I purchased him. I imagine he will endeavor to pass as a freeman; he having served in the expedition against the Indians last fall" (*VG-Purdie* 6/23/75). Sam's knowledge of the "Indian country" may have helped his escape. His ability to survive is suggested by what he took with him—a gun, an ax, and a pot.

Interestingly, the Virginia slave owner did not routinely regard his runaway slave as deceptive. Deception was a consistent but nonetheless minor theme, suggesting that the response of their slaves to Lord Dunmore's call for them to join the British, as explored in the final chapter, may have been of surprise to their patriot owners and helps explain the sense of betrayal that characterized Virginians' response to that episode.

Slave advertisements of the South Carolina press offered slaves in "parcels" and individually, the individual advertisements picturing the slave as skilled and useful, as did those in the Northeast. Yet the advertisements for runaway slaves portray a society that viewed itself under siege, protecting itself by the methods of a police state in response to the astounding increase in the number of slaves between 1730 to 1767 (Parker, P. Wood). As in other colonies, description of slaves to be sold included some characterization by their skills. Some parcels of slaves were advertised as including such trades as "a cooper, porter, cook, seamstress" (*SCG* 3/18/70). Other parcels were simply described as "choice plantation slaves" to be sold "by a gentleman about to decline planting" (*SCG* 2/15/70), a fairly common reason given for the sale of groups of slaves. Individual slaves were similarly characterized by their skill—a woman as "an extraordinary good Washer and Ironer" (*SCG* 6/7/70), a young man as understanding "extraordinary well taking care of horses" (*SCG* 1/1/70). The South Carolina advertisers seldom mentioned that their slaves were "sold for no fault," and there were only occasional explanations for the sale, just two in 1770, including this glimpse into a master-slave relationship: "The only reason his being offered to sale is, that his present employment is to attend a store, which does not seem to suit his inclinations, his present owners are willing part him, as they want one chiefly to attend the store. Enquire of the Printer" (*SCG* 1/25/70). Five years later a young woman and three-year-old child were to be sold because "she does not like to live in the country" (*SCG* 1/30/75).

But in the harsh slave world of South Carolina, concerns for the inclinations or the desires of the slaves stand out as oddities. The brutality and the costs of an institutionalized slave system were apparent in the slave advertisements.

As in other colonial advertisements, the South Carolina advertisements began with descriptions of the slave's physique and the clothing worn, in the stock euphemism for escape, "when he went away." Physical characteristics dominated, but there was not the precise notation of size and weight or the attention to the details of clothing found in the northeastern press. What most differentiated the South Carolina advertisements from all other colonial newspapers was the particular emphasis on collusion, particularly white collusion, in the escape of a slave.

Routinely, the northeastern press added a paragraph to most runaway advertisements that warned "all masters of vessels" not to take the runaway aboard. Virginians often speculated that escaped slaves were probably "lurking" in various neighborhoods. Authorities in all colonies tended to arrest unfamiliar black men and women as runaway slaves. But in South Carolina, the threat to the system was not so much the escaping slaves but the whites and blacks who made the escapes possible. The code word in the advertisements was "harbour." Thus, the advertisements tended to provide detailed accounts of the purchase history of the slave, as a way of indicating where the slave may have fled. "It is likely he may be gone to, or harboured by some evil minded person, at some of the above places," the owner of a slave named Tom wrote, "I hereby offer a reward of 50 pounds to whoever will prove his being so harboured, to be paid on conviction of the offense" (*SCG* 4/5/70). Significantly, most rewards for "harbouring" included money for information leading to the conviction of the harbourer, particularly if white, as in the advertisement for Neo: "And as I have Reason to believe that he is harboured by some villainous white Person, or free Negroes, or has been shipped off to the Barbadoes, or elsewhere, I will pay 100 pounds currency, for sufficient proof to convict a white person of any offence and Twenty pounds currency for Proof of his being harboured by a free Negro, or Five Pounds by a Slave" (*SCG* 5/10/70). The concern for conviction of "harbourers" remained unchanged, regardless of the number of escaped slaves. In 1770, 50 percent of the runaway advertisements in the *South-Carolina Gazette* warn of "harbouring." In 1775, the percentage was almost the same despite a dramatic decrease in the number of runaway advertisements from five years before (my count).

Although the South Carolina press serves as the most rigid example of the cultural messages of slave advertising, the escaped-slave advertising in all colonies functioned as a way of binding slave owners together, a trade association of sorts, predicated on the assumption that white people would assist in regaining a slave. The confident, even confidential tone, as of one person sharing information with another of similar temperament, translated into the assumption that the advertisements would reach a readership of similar assumptions and expectations. And the advertisements' appearance in the approved setting of the colonial newspaper further sanctioned the message that all white people—assumed to be the nature of the readership—had an obligation to participate in the maintenance of the status quo across colony boundaries.

The distribution of such messages by way of the colonial newspaper provided an appropriate frame for patriot propaganda that was distant from the antislavery discussion. While clearly the existence of slave advertising did not translate into readers' automatic acceptance of the institution, its appearance does indicate that American colonists could not avoid knowledge of slavery and were provided an immediate benchmark that gave meaning to the rhetoric of slavery. Outside of metaphor, however, the slave advertising provided a set of characteristics for slaves and, by implication, for all black colonists that emphasized prejudices already in regional cultures and could only help support the rationale that the institution provided appropriate supervision for this group of Americans. The understanding of black colonists along these narrow constructs was sufficiently deep-seated to negate the examples of the competent black worker that the advertising acknowledged and was experienced on a daily basis by many white Americans who shared with them the worlds of home and work.

What can account for a willingness of the northeastern slave owner to share work but nothing else? For Bostonian Americans, close to the "foundry" of propaganda, one explanation is the certitude provided by long-held positions. A generation of white colonists, coming of age in the changing world of revolutionary America, welcomed propaganda that looked back to sureties of the past.

CHAPTER THREE

Flames for the Cause

By 1768, as Otis became further incapacitated by mental illness, Samuel Adams emerged as the radical leader. One indication that Adams was now at the helm was the appearance of his front-page articles in the *Boston Gazette*. In pieces that tilled the Wilkite legacy of stirring popular ferment by appealing to long-standing and deep-seated fears, Adams dug deeply into New England's fertile anti-Catholicism. As the "Puritan," Adams argued that "popery" posed a more serious threat to Massachusetts than British tyranny, and the members of the General Court who did not support the Boston Whigs were clearly papists. If Protestants did not replace such representatives, Massachusetts tottered at the edge of rule by the Holy See (S. Adams 1:203, 210, 212). Metaphor might have moved into hyperbole, but for New England readers, who viewed the specter of Catholicism as *rule* by outside authority, it was nonetheless a carefully chosen weapon.

Unlike the frontal assaults in Adams's use of anti-Catholicism, the *Boston Gazette* published no fiery articles calling for continued black subjugation. Instead, by a variety of techniques, including silence, innuendo, and selectivity, all as much a part of the propaganda arsenal as Adams's front-page essays, blacks and slaves were portrayed as appropriately placed in their subservient role. Indeed, nothing in the *Boston Gazette* contradicted the attitudes and prejudices found in the slave advertising or news items that appeared in the Boston papers and elsewhere. As the revolutionary decade approached, those prejudices and attitudes were not so much tolerated as they would be put to use in revolutionary propaganda. As Adams was to discover in the Boston Massacre, the status of black colonists could not be ignored in any discussion of power or place. By the time of the Massacre and the manipulation of the race of one of its fallen heroes, Crispus Attucks, Adams and his coterie of writers were long experienced with the use of the press to promote a political agenda. The *Boston Gazette* had been the radical organ since 1755, when Adams put his support behind the paper as the two print shop apprentices, Benjamin Edes and John Gill, started out on their own.

Adams's recruitment of Edes and Gill deserves mention, as the young men were never the hired hands of previous political campaigns. Like other members of the patriot press, they were active partners in the promotion of the radical agenda. Indeed, the recruitment of Edes and Gill set out a template for the construction of the patriot press, drawing to the cause men like Edes and Gill, whose traditional place in the world was undergoing change. Such men were appropriate choices to carry the theme that the British treated the American colonies with the same contempt that white colonists reserved for black colonists.

The New York printer James Parker, writing to his business partner, Benjamin Franklin, wearily commented at one point, "Printers are obliged to work like Negroes, and in general are esteemed but little better, on many Accounts" (Franklin, *Papers* 4:310). Of all the stops on the continuum of the metaphor of slavery perhaps none was more meaningful to white Americans of a certain class than the fear of descent into unacceptable status, a status so clearly illustrated in the slave advertising and kept in front of colonial readers by the rhetoric of slavery that typically warned of dire consequences: "If Great Britain, instead of treating us as their fellow-subjects, shall aim at making us their vassals and slaves" (*BG* 7/24/71). In exploring this thesis, F. Nwabueze Okoye writes: "The outrage of the colonists stemmed from their conviction that only black people in America were deserving of servile status." Okoye contends that underlying the patriot zeal, beyond the use of metaphor, was the fear that colonists were to be treated by Great Britain the way white Americans treated black bondsmen and women. "The great fear of the colonies," he writes, "was equality of status with enslaved blacks" (Okoye 7).

James Horton and Lois Horton take a different view, noting that in the stratified society of the late colonial period poor whites forged bonds with black colonists that resulted in "interracial cooperation among the lower ranks of American society" (Horton and Horton, *In Hope* 281). Such cooperation, if it existed, puts a greater onus on the patriot propaganda, suggesting that the propagandists set about to destroy whatever cooperation existed by enlarging upon the threads of discontent that existed.

The fear of a decline in status, however, was not without basis for the generation that took up the patriot banner. White Americans of the revolutionary generation had indeed experienced various aspects of leveling in their coming of age. The first was welcomed. In the Great Awakening great numbers of colonial Americans, including Sam Adams, eschewed the leadership of local ministers in order to participate in an evangelical, one-to-one experience with God. The second, however, was the economic decline of the 1760s, which translated into a social stratification and a loss of social and economic mobility for artisans and workers alike. As the revolutionary era developed, these changes in colonial society, including Boston, were exacerbated. "The rich became richer, and aristocratic gentry everywhere became more conspicuous and self-conscious; and the numbers of poor in some cities increased," as Gordon S. Wood describes it. The resulting tensions were not out of incipient class warfare, he writes, but rather because the new class lines were out of sync with what had been the "pervasive equality of American society (Wood, *Radicalism* 170).

The increasing stratification for white Americans could be indicated in the most personal of ways. In Charlestown, across the village from Boston, the selectman found it necessary to make it illegal to dress beyond one's rank (Frothingham, *History* 256). Boston's Isaiah Thomas, printer of the fiery *Massachusetts Spy,* resisted the definitions that prompted such laws by dressing "considerably above his social position and had manners which made him accepted to those who, in that caste-ridden age, regarded themselves as superior to any craftsman" (Shipton 133). Benjamin Mecom, the unhappy nephew of Benjamin Franklin, quite literally refused to wear the leather apron, choosing to operate his press in "a powdered bob wig, ruffles and gloves, gentleman-like appendages which the printers of that day did not assume," as Thomas described his contemporary, despite his own proclivities for gentlemanlike appendages (Thomas 141–42). Other printers were said to call Mecom "Queer Notions" after a department in his magazine (Winsor 2:409). But there was no humor when, in 1771, a Harvard student dismissed Richard Draper, a member of one of Boston's old and respected printing families, as "a Meer mechanic . . . below the notices of a Freshman" (*BNL* 8/15/71). Draper became a loyalist, his own way perhaps of remaining true to a former time.

Sudden artisinal concern with dress, however, was not out of step with a late-colonial society that was consumed with new aspects of manners, evidence, according to one researcher, that middle-class culture was emerging earlier than once recognized (Hemphill). Advice books about middle-class conduct, the promotion of female domesticity, the growth of belles lettres, the rejection of hurly-burly taverns in favor of more protected environments all indicate a search for identity by the establishment of new boundaries. But clearly the closing down of what had been fairly permeable layers of society and the accompanying anxieties and self-doubt were useful accoutrements to members of a society promoting radical change. In Anne Norton's theory of the construction of political identity, men and women displaced from their previous places in society become "liminars," occupying a status between existing orders, whether political, economic, ethnic, or class. Out of this state of confusion, in a moment of "unparalleled political importance" comes a new definition of abstract principles—altogether a potent political force (A. Norton 53). What might be added is that men and women in this state, seeking to reaffirm a former status, are not the population likely to open doors to those below them. Of all the rationales put forward for slavery and for the second-class status of free blacks, the most compelling for such colonial liminars was likely unstated—the proof offered by the existence of slavery that white colonists had not yet reached the very bottom. Put into the context of the social upheavals of the period, the metaphor of slavery was not so much a call for vigilance in the face of popish plots as one for the vigilance it took not to slip further down a slippery slope.

Growing up in Charlestown in an environment affected by the sweep of New Light ministry (Budington), Edes and Gill came from families who had experienced the prosperity and status encouraged by an earlier equality. Edes was the second son of a well-known Charlestown man, Peter Edes, a hatter whose interests had expanded into real estate (Wyman 1:319–22). In a not unusual role for an artisan of the earlier period, Edes was one of the founders of the city's oldest fire societies whose members were described as "the owners of many of the prominent estates in the town" (Hunnewell 65). By midcentury the value of Peter Edes's property was among that of the upper half of the townspeople (Pruitt 182–83).

Similarly, Gill came from a comfortable stratum established by his English grandfather, Michael, owner of a Charlestown wharf and a militia colonel. Michael's wife, the former Relief Dowse, was painted by John Singleton Copley in her widowhood in 1759, an indication of the ongoing prestige of the family despite the fact that Gill's father, John, did not match his own father's success (Wyman 409; Parker and Wheeler 82). One of John Gill's younger brothers, however, did replicate his grandfather's success, rising from a Boston brazier to one of the city's wealthiest merchants. By 1781, Moses Gill was one of the colony's chief justices and after the Revolution served as lieutenant governor, then acting governor (Hart 2:581), his wealth and prestige carried into the new nation thanks to his adoption of one of John Gill's numerous children, a son named Moses. Meantime, Gill, despite his revolutionary record, died in reduced circumstances, as did his former partner (Probate Records 84, 102).

The Edes and Gill families may not have had grand ambitions for their sons when they apprenticed them to Samuel Kneeland, printer of Boston's many religious works, including the New Light *Christian History,* but Kneeland was the example of the successful and religious artisan whose hard work and demonstrated virtue allowed him to become "independent in his circumstances" (Thomas 104). The Massachusetts Stamp Tax in 1755, culminating declining circumstances, provided the impetus for the transfer of the *Boston Gazette* to the ownership of the two young apprentices about to embark on their own careers.

It seems apparent that the radical group chose Edes and Gill more carefully than had been the case in the selection of the printers of the radical's previous organ, the *Independent Advertiser,* whose printer, Daniel Fowle, complained bitterly and publicly at his treatment by the radical circle (Fowle). From the *Gazette*'s debut, burdened by the colony's stamp tax, solvency was not taken for granted. The partnership would eventually produce the largest annual amount of printing in the city (Yodelis, "Who Paid"). Some of that was because of public printing, probably a result of Adams's influence in the General Assembly. But early on the shop profited from religious printing, including the growing connection between religious printing and the revolutionary cause. In the 1760s, Jonathan Mayhew's attacks on the Society for the Propagation of the Gospel in Foreign Parts was not only making Mayhew more acceptable to the Boston clergy, the 176-page diatribe and related publications were a boom for the young business. Both Edes and Gill were members of Mayhew's West Church, as was Paul Revere and other ambitious artisans, but it was likely Mayhew, an Adams intimate and no novice in propaganda, who connected the young printers to the Adams circle in its search for a new vehicle and helped provide its economic base.

Given the financial difficulties of the time, Edes and Gill would likely have had little long-term success without the radical connection. Yet even with the radical connection, the marriages of Edes and Gill suggest the sliding status of the artisan (as it also suggests personal preference). Unlike the successful Moses Gill, who made two prestigious marriages in his climb, Edes and Gill made practical matches, and, in the end, neither man was able to parlay the prosperity of the printing house into permanent success. After the Revolution both died in much reduced circumstances.

For Edes, however, the most politically active of the partners, the financial stability offered by the radicals was probably less important than the opportunity to be among the community's political leaders, as his father had been in Charlestown. Two years after the launching of the *Gazette,* Edes was town constable and subsequently was regularly elected to city positions as surveyor of boards, clerk of the market, and collector of taxes, the latter position one that Adams had held almost ten years earlier and which Edes resigned, as had Adams. He was closely involved in Boston's inner political circles, notably the North End Caucus, and in the 1760s he and other artisans were recruited for Boston's artillery company (Robert 2:101, 124, 220). By 1765, Edes was first sergeant in the artillery company and in a position to organize resistance to the Stamp Act. He would serve as emissary when Adams sought to bring together Boston's rival North and South End gangs, turning their frustrations away from attacks on each other into patriot fervor (Cullen).

Adams's recruitment of Edes and Gill as the foremost printers of the patriot cause exemplified how Adams served to put the tensions of the artisan class to use in the construction of the patriot press, as in other areas, and provides an avenue for understanding why the patriot press largely followed Adams' agenda by remaining silent on the issue of slavery. Although the emphasis here has been on the *Boston Gazette,* it should be noted that the early patriot press was composed of a cadre of independently owned newspapers. Despite the conservatism of the colonial printing craft as a whole — not men and women who sought conflict (Botein) — Adams was able to draw together a committed group of patriot printers by recruiting men who could be characterized as, Norton puts it, "betwixt and between." The core members of the patriot press — Edes and Gill, John Holt, John Dunlap, Isaiah Thomas, and William Goddard — were men who did not have the same intergenerational and family ties to the craft as the Boston Drapers and other members of the moderate press, and, except for William Bradford, a later member from Philadelphia, seemed to have become printers because of previous failure or force of circumstance (Miner; Palsits; Shipton; Teeter, "John Dunlap"; Walker). Like Adams, no example of worldly success, they were men whose unsteady personal histories, marked by erosion of rank and diminishing opportunities, were not likely to seek the empowerment of a class of people below them.

The Boston Massacre was the culmination of years of radical activism. Adams's invectives against the colony's governor, Thomas Hutchinson, during the Stamp Act crisis had encouraged a Boston mob to destroy the Hutchinson family home — burning its remarkable library, smashing the expensive glass windows that symbolized wealth and station, and shredding its fine interior. When the British colonial office, fearing a repetition of Wilkes-type mobs in the American colonies, ordered the occupation of the city, Adams was presented the opportunity to take local political action to the intercolonial stage. There could be no better representation of British prerogative than the occupation of a colonial city by a standing army, surely an example all American colonies should heed.

Backed by the proved loyalty of Edes and Gill and the new adherents to the patriot cause resulting from Stamp Act agitation, Adams's understanding of the tools at hand was best illustrated in 1768 and 1769 with a series of items that became known as the "Journal of the Times" or "Journal of Occurrences," prepared for use across colonies by Adams and his circle.

Certainly, one danger of a propaganda organ is that it will preach to the converted. To avoid the encumbrances of its too well-known politics, Adams and the Whig circle turned to John Holt's *New-York Journal,* a newspaper that had benefited from the Sons of Liberty. From their base in Boston, the propagandists also issued the same set of paragraphs it had prepared for the *New-York Journal* (altered slightly to avoid names) for the *Boston Evening-Post,* now published by brothers Thomas Fleet Jr. and John Fleet. The choice of the *Evening-Post* over the *Gazette* was significant because the *Post* was a newspaper recognized for fair-mindedness (Thomas 143). The paper went out of business in 1775, according to all accounts then and now, when impartiality became impossible, although it might also be considered that it went out of business when an impartial newspaper was no longer needed by the radicals. In 1769, however, the impartial *Evening-Post* was an excellent venue for spread of the propagandists' view across the colonies and even into British publications by way of the exchange system, and probably received the widest distribution of any colonial writing up to the time outside of John Dickinson's "Letters from a Farmer in Pennsylvania" (Dickerson viii). The sophistication of the plan also indicated that Otis was no longer a player as a leader of the Boston Whigs. Otis's personality, growing rasher by the day, made it unlikely he could instigate a plan that took restraint.

Under a standing head, the weekly paragraphs eschewed lengthy discussions of American rights in favor of a personal, intimate style that emphasized the role of the British occupation in the lives of ordinary Bostonians. These paragraphs included some accurate news of troop movements, occasional sentences that were clear calls to British readers, news of support from other colonies, examples of Bostonian forbearance despite extraordinary provocation, and warnings that the Daughters of Liberty were capable of replacing British goods by spinning wool and manufacturing needed items at home. But most important were the accounts of the impact of the occupation on everyday lives. Townspeople, on their own business, in a "civil society," found themselves arbitrarily stopped and challenged by British soldiers. Some of these early accounts were hardly narratives of atrocities. One group of townspeople was "stopped and detained so long in the street, in a very cold season, that one of the married ladies, through the cold and surprise, is now much indisposed" (Dickerson 30). However, accounts of physical abuse increased; the specter of rape emerged: "A girl at New-Boston, was lately knock'd down and abused by solders for not consenting to their beastly proposal" (Dickerson 99). By June of 1768 the Journal-reported insults were so numerous that it was unclear "how much a local and prudent people can bear" before they proceeded to "extremities" (Dickerson 107).

Whether minor occurrences or not, the public theme that united all these paragraphs was the subjection of all Bostonians to the leveling aspects of British power. Indisposed ladies may not seem to be the heady stuff of revolutionary propaganda, but for Adams's sophisticated pen there was value in spreading the word of a degradation that spared no one. The theme that the British viewed all colonists alike allowed the propagandists to emphasize an American commonality that crossed colony boundaries and class lines. But the theme also inferred a lack of British sensibility to colonial boundaries of difference. Among all boundaries, of course, race was the most significant. The ultimate betrayal was the notion that the British were not above instigating rebellion among black servants. The themes were explored on large and small stages in the Journal of Occurrences, beginning with the Journal accounts of the use of the whip.

Even into the nineteenth century, it was standard practice for British authorities to use the whip to keep its soldiery in line. Although the Journal writers were eager to convey a sense of the debauchery of the British soldiers, the Journal nonetheless reported instances of whipping with sympathy, noticing on more than one occasion that the whippings were severe enough to cause death (Dickerson 9, 89). This was clearly a powerful image in the South, where the use of the whip was confined to slaves. But by any colony standard, the use of the whip on white British subjects, soldiers or not, was not only severe punishment for bouts of drunkenness but also a humiliating one. To emphasize the humiliation, the *Gazette* made clear the use of a "black drummer" as the whipper in one early account of a flogging (Dickerson 6). This was not a casual piece of information for any colonial reader with its implications that a black whipper meting punishment on a white man was a world of power in reverse.

From its insinuations that whipping was an example of how the British authority could treat its own and, by inference, of British misuse of American colonists, the Journal moved into the most powerful aspect of its propaganda vis-à-vis the black population. These were the reports of British officer seeking to turn black servants against their masters. In November of 1768 (in a article that only appeared in the *New-York Journal*), the British captain James Wilson was heard to tell a group of slaves that "the Negroes shall be free, and the Liberty Boys slaves" if blacks would only "cut their masters' throats." A few days later, "a person of credit" was overheard giving the opinion "'if the Negroes could be made freeman, they should be sufficient to subdue these damn'd rascals.'" Boston selectman responded quickly to these reports of interference with Boston's slave population by instigating a slave curfew; Boston's judiciary lodged a charge against Wilson for his careless words (Dickerson 16).

These Journal accounts appeared at a time of high tension in Boston's race relations as Massachusetts's legislators faced a major thrust aimed at ending slavery, not just the slave trade, in the colony. In March of 1767, a bill that called for an end to the slave trade and the ownership of slaves received two readings in the Massachusetts House of Representatives. On the third reading, the bill was compromised in favor of a new bill laying an import duty on slaves, which was quickly followed by second and third readings. On its third reading, the original abolition bill was now watered even further with the addendum that the act, if passed, would be only be in effect for one year. This was the bill that was sent finally to the Council, approved, and returned to the

House where, as a nineteenth-century historian notes, it was simply lost (G. Moore 127–28).

Shortly after the controversy over the slave trade bill, Bostonians faced one of the deepest fears held by colonial Americans, the attack of a slave on a white woman. In September of 1768, a slave belonging to a Worcester man was sentenced to death for the rape of a white woman. The crime was sensational and, not surprisingly, news of it was reflected in the Boston press (*BEP* 10/3; 10/17/68; *BPB* 10/3; 10/24/68; *BNL* 10/3/68), including a broadside printed by Boston's struggling Kneeland and Adams. In the broadside, according to the ministerial pen recording his last words, Arthur provided an account of his fall into degeneracy. The attack, the reader learns, was no lone, impulsive action but part of a pattern of behavior of drunkenness, thieving, jail breaks, "indecencies" and "black Designs" towards white women. On one occasion, Arthur reported he was one of a group of blacks introduced to a "white Woman of that Place. And our Behaviour was such, as we have much Reason to be ashamed of." It was on his escape from jail as a result of one of these escapades, fleeing to his Indian haven, that "the Devil put it into my Head to pay a Visit to the Widow Deborah Metcalfe, whom I in a most inhumane manner ravished: The particulars of which are so notorious that it is needless for me here to relate them."

Outside of the devil's promptings, the account explains Arthur's action on the basis of the bad company of Indians and other blacks as the final encouragement to Arthur's predilections. What the account leaves in place is the notion of the irrational, "bad seed" black criminality that was often found in slave advertising. Arthur reportedly admitted his master had educated and treated him "very kindly." Facing death, Arthur concludes, "I freely acknowledge I have been better treated by Mankind in general than I deserved."

News of the attack and Arthur's confession and execution coincide almost exactly with Captain Wilson's comments. Arthur, indeed, was put to death just a week after Wilson's comments became known. These were incendiary intersections — a call to slaves to slit the throats of their masters even in the face of what Bostonians may have regarded as proof of essential slave criminality. Further, occurring during the occupation of the city by a standing army, a crime of rape brought with it all the attendant images of despoiled virtue and powerlessness. Whipping was one example of how British authority treated its own and, by inference, the American colonies. But news of the rape of a white woman by a black slave, accompanied by inflammatory comments of a

British officer, could only infer the British had so little understanding of American colonists that they could indiscriminately cross any boundary, including race.

Boston continued to simmer with resentment and frustration. For the radicals, the frustration was increased anew by Scottish printer, John Mein, whom the Whigs found unmanageable. Irascible and hot-tempered, Mein was not to be so easily squashed when a *Gazette* writer, thought to be James Otis, called him a Jacobin. Mein demanded to know the author; Edes refused and provided a public explanation in an effort to discredit Mein. Mein arrived at the *Gazette* office, could not find Edes, and took on the unsuspecting John Gill. The ensuing fisticuffs led to a lawsuit and trial in which Mein was fined (Alden, "John Mein").

But Mein was determined to have the last word. In February and March of 1769, as Boston continued to boil with racial discord, Mein helped connect antislavery to Tory sympathy when he published two antislavery essays (*BC* 2/27; 3/2/69). By August, Mein's Toryism reached new heights with a series of attacks on the nonimportation agreement, culminating in the publication of the names of merchants who had broken faith. At this juncture, the end of October, Mein was quite literally run out of Boston by a mob gathered for the purpose, saving his life perhaps by brandishing a pistol (Schlesinger, "Propaganda"). The importance of Mein as a Tory sympathizer not incidentally connected to antislavery is suggested by the journal of the young Boston printer John Boyle, who had heretofore ignored the occupation and any of the events as related by the Journal. "This Mein had been concerned with one Mr. Fleming, another Scotchman, in printing an infamous News-paper, in which he made it his business to scandalize some of the most worthy characters in Town. Those who signalized themselves as Advocates of Liberty were sure of being aspersed" (Boyle 201).

Mein's departure was followed by the death of the youth in the confrontation over the nonimportation agreements, the public funeral, and the numerous exchanges between city toughs and soldiers leading to the event on a snowy King Street of March 5, 1770. At this juncture — the execution of Arthur, the comments of Captain Wilson, the antislavery proposals, and Mein's refusal to abide by the radicals' standards of behavior all in recent memory — the Boston Massacre brought to the forefront of the revolutionary movement the role of black colonists. Was Crispus Attucks to be a hero, one of the innocents cut down in King Street? Or a rowdy who helped provoke the attack? Could there be an innocent with a tawny skin? Should he be remembered at all? And at what cost?

In an act of transformation, Adams's invention of the "Boston Massacre" moved American opposition to the British occupation from an image of Boston street rowdies into a grander realm, an episode that could only reverberate with Old Testament connotations of the slaughter of innocents. Adams left behind the homely, day-by-day telling that had characterized the Journal and lifted circumstances that were hardly heroic on either side into a lofty, quasi-religious plane, producing, as Schlesinger described it, folk heroes out of "street loafers and hoodlums" (Schlesinger, *Prelude* 21). Now, with this larger-than-life event, the *Boston Gazette* came back to center stage.

The Stamp Act had provided the radicals with important lessons in the elevation of political opposition into the issues of rule. Integral to the lessons was the expression of opposition in symbolic rather than specific terms. In actual fact, the Stamp Act proposed specific consequences and its implementation would have carried severe economic consequences (Westlager). The Whig propagandists, however, seeking a broad audience, chose to emphasize the act as an example of the interference of colonial rights rather than its economic consequences to the narrower band of the colonial elite. Under Otis's and Adams's leadership, a host of metaphoric devices, including various uses of death motifs and the symbolic public burnings of stamped paper, provided the aura of public virtue and worked to cross lines of rank, wealth, geography, and parochial interest. In the Stamp Act opposition, Boston radicals also demonstrated that the best propaganda was a combination of the related word and representative deed. In highly wrought language, the *Gazette* compared Stamp Act agent Andrew Oliver, New England born and bred, to a plantation slave driver who sought to curry favor with his white masters by driving fellow slaves (*BG* 8/19/65). The point was made dramatically when Oliver underwent a mock lynching when Edes and his Sons of Liberty compatriots from the artillery company strung his effigy from the "Liberty Tree" next to a real boot as a connection to the suspect Scottish betrayer, Lord Bute (Gordon 1:175). Like the decomposing body of a real lynching—as in the body of the executed slave exhibited from the gibbet on Charlestown Common—the effigy provided a striking example of what could happen to those who betrayed their own.

The use of Boston's Liberty Tree—one of many designated as symbols of immortality and regeneration—as a focal point for public involvement was a small beginning in Adams's use of mythology that intersected with Puritan history. As Dirk Hoerder notes, violence itself was a symbol, intended to purify not to punish and to provide warning to others (Hoerder 81). Boston crowds had long used violence as warnings, sometimes to higher classes for exceeding norms, but crowd violence seldom resulted in death. "Mobbish Boston" was no invention of the revolutionary generation. Crowd action had been a common occurrence in Massachusetts; Hoerder counts fifty prerevolutionary episodes (40).

Because crowds were seen to have purpose, they were not adverse to direction. Adams, Otis's lieutenant during the Stamp Act crisis, was behind efforts in directing the Loyall Nine to organize the crowds who met stamp collectors at the various colonial wharves in an imitation of a spontaneous gathering (Maier, *From Resistance*). In related actions, stamped paper was burned, mock gallows were erected, and effigies were hanged — all symbols undergirded by warnings of violent ends, like an Edwardsian sermon, for those who did not comply.

Revolutionary propaganda was also largely conducted along lines of inversion, an appropriate metaphor for the world turning upside down. The death of five individuals in suspect circumstances was hardly the stuff of a "massacre" any more than overturning sufficient tea into the Boston Harbor so that ships could not move was a "tea party." The use of thanksgiving days and fasting days were adapted to propagandistic purposes in the various memorial days that surrounded the opposition to the Stamp Act. The public nature of Calvinist punishment found transformation into the street theater of the representational lynching of Lord Bute on the "Liberty Tree," the public burnings of confiscated tea around the colonies, and the tarring and feathering of suspected Tories. As Peter Shaw writes, "The rituals of revolution have been accurately described as reversed ceremonies of legitimacy. But the ceremonies of legitimacy were themselves ambiguous" (221). Like the revolutionary slogans, ambiguity was useful, permitting individual constructions within a revolutionary ether. Tarring and feathering, for example, was a ritual of multiple meanings, one of which was connected to white understandings of blackness. As Peter Oliver described the practice, "First, strip a Person naked, then heat the Tar until it is thin, & Pour it upon the naked Flesh, or rub it over with a Tar Brush . . . [a]fter which, sprinkle decently upon the Tar, whilst it is yet warm as many Feather as will stick to it" (Oliver 94). Given the understandings of black as evil, the coat of white feathers, often supplied by female supporters from bed pillows, suggested ephemerality. The real stickiness was the layer of black tar to the skin, indicating that, for traitors, whiteness was the facade.

Adams's ability to invent the significant event arguably made the Adams propaganda the most powerful lever in drawing popular support to the American Revolution. Joseph Greenleaf's attacks on Hutchinson, for example, were more libelous than those of Adams, but Greenleaf remains a minor figure in the propaganda war because his arsenal did not go beyond an attacking pen. By contrast, Adams attached his pen to an event that was aimed at demonstrating proof of a larger issue, a familiar way of thinking for Bostonians who believed God communicated by external means. The Journal of the Times offered its proof by piling one instance upon another; the Boston Massacre offered a shorter route. As Adams and his organizers were able to move the Stamp Act beyond an unpopular revenue-raising issue into a discussion of parliamentary law and natural rights, Adams's arsenal turned the events of the Boston Massacre into proof that the Mother Country cared so little for her American colonies that her own soldiers would shoot without cause.

For Adams's most resounding propagandistic success, the first step was to call the event a "massacre," an enlargement of the event beyond the facts of the situation, and, some may argue, even a reversal. So naming the event was not an Adams original, however. During the Wilkes episode the previous year — the object of intense patriot attention — taunted soldiers fired upon demonstrators outside Wilkes's London prison. Several individuals were killed, including a young man. In the resulting days of rioting, the shooting became known as "The Massacre of St. George's Field," and the youth was given a public funeral. The trial of the soldier blamed for the young man's death also received notice in the Boston press (*BNL* 10/27/68).

The patriots had already put the Wilkite propaganda to use. When a Boston boy was shot during a radical-inspired protest against a merchant importing English goods less than two weeks before the Massacre, the attending physician, Dr. Joseph Warren, declared the act murder (*BG* 2/26/70) and the patriots assembled a great crowd at the Liberty Tree to escort the body to burial. The patriot response to the subsequent event of March 5 was clearly aimed at escalating crowd attitudes, but the attachment of the panegyric "Boston Massacre" suggested the ultimate aim was its use as a unifying symbol, perhaps to serve the patriot cause as much as the Stamp Act. The Massacre, however, was no Stamp Act; it did not affect all colonies, its implications for parliamentary rule were unclear, and it was a localized event of suspect circumstances. It should be noted, however, that outside Boston the initial response to the Massacre lacked the incendiary spark of the Stamp Act. In at least six colonies, newspapers reflected no particular pattern of outrage or interest as a result of the Massacre (Smith), not only suggesting that British troops on American soil carried different meanings in different colonies but also indicating that Massachusetts's culture of public rite was not so readily adopted by other colonies. The lack of immediate response to the Massacre put particular pressure that the eventual trial of the British soldiers make a place for the Massacre in colonial consciousness.

As the events of the Massacre unfolded, Adams was faced with how to define Crispus Attucks, a free black of Indian and African ancestry, a seaman, distressed by the economic downturn, who was not surprisingly a member of the angry crowd and the first of the fallen heroes. Here was an opportunity not only to continue the theme of the virtuous nature of colonial Americans but to include people of color in that perception.

The Whig account of the Massacre first came at the hands of James Bowdoin, whose propagandistic efforts had heretofore been in connection with his membership on the Massachusetts Executive Council. In that capacity, Bowdoin had consistently given council papers a propagandistic slant and made them available for newspaper publication (Walett). In his pamphlet account of the Massacre, Attucks's name was listed prominently as a victim: "Crispus Attucks, a molatto, killed on the spot, two balls entering his breast." Also clearly noted was Captain Wilson's involvement in "exciting the negroes of the town to take away their masters lives and property and repair to the army for protection, which was fully proved against him" (Bowdoin 11).

But months later, at the conclusion of the trials of Captain Thomas Preston and the British soldiers, Adams was not so anxious to identify Attucks by race. He was simply "Mr. Attucks," another innocent who was "leaning upon his stick when he fell, which certainly was not a threatening posture" (*BG* 12/31/70). The use of "Mr." can be interpreted to mean that, as a dead hero, Attucks had earned the right to be addressed with a note of respect, or its use can suggest that Adams expected readers, particularly outside of Boston, to assume the courtesy title indicated Attucks was white. In Boston, certainly, Attucks's race was no mystery. As a six-foot-two free black, Attucks was an easily recognizable figure in the city, although probably more known by his free name, Michael Johnson. Nonetheless, Nathaniel Emmons, the Congregational New Divinity minister from Franklin, had no problem recalling him by his old slave name. Emmons was a lifelong opponent to slavery, but Attucks elicited no sympathy. "I stood with Parson Byles on the corner of what are now School and Washington streets and watched the funeral procession of Crispus Attucks, that half Indian, half negro, and altogether rowdy, who should have been strangled long before he was born" (Eaton 146). The use of a courtesy title was not likely to change Emmons's perception and suggests the Adams account was aimed at the intercolonial audience that the *Gazette* had been developing by way of Journal of the Times.

The confusion over Attucks's race was further complicated by Revere's famous illustration in which Attucks is portrayed as white. One interpretation of the engraving is provided by Barbara Lacey, who writes that a whitened Attucks indicated his death "is viewed as equal to that of the others who died." That earned equality is similarly represented on the broadside "where Attucks' coffin stands side by side with those of the three other slain patriots" (Lacey 163). In that interpretation, Attucks's sacrifice is comparable to the whitening that Slotkin addresses in the conversion experience of blacks; Attucks's death in the patriot cause permits his elevation to a higher status, which is represented by the absence of his dark skin, as if exterior and interior were finally to mesh. Coming long after the publication of the engraving, the use of the courtesy title could also be explained by the same rationale.

The argument that Attucks was represented as someone who had been elevated into honorary whitehood can be further supported by an examination of the skin colors in the Revere engraving in which three of the British soldiers have been given darkened complexions. We know that Revere, in order to rush the print to the public, commandeered the work of Henry Pelham, and Pelham's print, published after Revere's, indicates the same darkened hues, indicating the original darkening was likely at Pelham's hand. However the portrayals came about, the frequent copies of the print in the revolutionary period include the darkened British soldiers. The darkened visages are particularly noticeable in the engraving made by the British craftsman, William Bingle, for the cover of James Bowdoin's pamphlet (Brigham, *Revere's Engravings*: Plate 19), which had been sped to England on a ship the patriots had quickly engaged so theirs would be first news of the Massacre. Since Bowdoin is clear that Attucks was a "molatto," the darkened faces of the British soldiers may have served as a parallel to Attucks's whitening, suggesting that it was the British who were the real "savages" in the situation.

The darkened complexions disappear early in the national period. By that time, most white Americans were probably unaware of Attucks's racial background, which was reintroduced when antislavery activists backed the publication of William C. Nell's *The Colored Patriots of the American Revolution.* In the frontispiece to this work, Attucks's race is clear; indeed, he has lost any obvious Indian heritage in this portrayal, now the fallen hero at the center of a cluster of concerned patriots (Nell).

Attucks was no hero in John Adams's account as chief defense counsel at the trials of both Captain Preston and the subsequent group trial of the British soldiers. Called as a defense witness, the slave Andrew insisted Attucks had provoked the melee. At both trials, Andrew's master, Oliver Wendell, affirmed that Andrew was trustworthy. Nor did Andrew's testimony stand alone; he was one of three black witnesses and several white witnesses who helped the defense present the event as a disorderly mob seeking trouble.

Adams was not to leave it at that, however. Instead, he provided a summing up in terms of racial and ethnic stereotypes. To make his point that the American colonies were ruled by law and order, Adams argued that the shootings had been instigated by outsiders, "a motly rabble of saucy boys, Negroes and mulattoes, Irish teagues and outlandish jack tars." Jurors only needed to look at two of those who were killed to see what kind of mob it was: the Irishman Patrick Carr and the mulatto Crispus Attucks. In an early linking of immigrant Irish and American blacks into what would become the "black Irish" concept of the nineteenth century, Adams characterized both men as outside agitators, the kind of men that the colonies, and Boston in particular, had been forced to tolerate: "And it is in this manner, this town has been often treated; a Carr from Ireland, and an Attucks from Framingham, happening to be here, shall sally out upon their thoughtless enterprises, at the head of such a rabble of negroes, etc., as they can collect together. [Attucks] whose very looks was enough to terrify any person, [who] had hardiness enough to fall in upon them, and with one hand took hold of a bayonet, and with the other knocked the man down. [It was Attucks] to whose mad behavior, in all probability, the dreadful carnage of that night is chiefly to be ascribed" (Kidder 257–58).

Given the Tory nature of the juries, the defense would have won however Attucks and Car were portrayed. Not-guilty verdicts were rendered in both trials for all but two of the soldiers, who were found guilty of the lesser charge of manslaughter (Zobel 241–94). But in his closing argument, in a few lines,

Adams managed to limn several colonial perceptions of black colonists — physical strength, proclivity to violence, and the danger inherent when blacks joined with colony unacceptables. Colonists outside of the jury box might logically infer that the loyalist jury (only two members of the jury were from Boston) took the testimony of the black witnesses more seriously than the white ones and provided another indication of British carelessness toward its colonies.

The trials were far from a loss for the radicals, who had overwhelmingly demonstrated their respect for the process of law even in the face of a packed jury. Nonetheless, writing in the *Gazette,* Adams sought to fix blame and, like his cousin John, found it in racial stereotypes. "Andrew a Negro — a Fellow of a lively imagination indeed!" Adams wrote, and suggested that the lively imagination led to his invention of stories, including this one. Stirring the pot of New Englanders' fear of slave conspiracy, Adams further suggested that the master did not know his servant as well as he thought and emphasized the theme that blacks were not to be trusted by returning to the Captain Wilson incident: "It is well-known that the Negroes of this town have been familiar with the soldiers; and that some of them have been tampered with to cut their master's throats; I hope Andrew is not one of these" (*BG* 1/7/71). The comment, according to Hiller Zobel, a historian of the Massacre, demonstrated "the radicals' true position on racial matters" (284).

Not surprisingly, the version put forward by the Adamses lingered. The first issue of Isaiah Thomas's radical-inspired *Massachusetts Spy* carried the following:

> *As Negroes and L--rs in judgement agree!*
> *No wonder that vice with her airs is so free!*
> *Device and low cunning do commonly stand!*
> *Related in friendship and join hand in hand*
> *Experience doth teach us that poor black and white!*
> *When blended together, as one, will unite!*
>
> (*MS* 3/7/71)

The Massacre itself would be celebrated in ritualistic ways for the next thirteen years (Ritter), only to be replaced by July Fourth as Independence Day.

Adams's ability to use the blunderbuss event did not negate his continued use of the techniques pioneered by the Journal of the Times. In fact, the use of both strategies indicates how the *Gazette* was able to marry the overstatements of what we usually recognize as propaganda with the older tradition of the impartial colonial newspaper. In the *Gazette,* both large and small events carried implications beyond the facts of the event. This technique was not surprising given Edes and Gill's experience with the didacticism of congregational sermonizing, in which all events, big and small, were indicative of God's plan. Congregational ministers often preached in homely metaphor, but, as their congregations knew, the devil, quite literally, lurked in the detail.

As congregational ministers assumed a universality of existing beliefs, the *Gazette*—as Adams's remarks about Andrew indicate—was not shy in calling on the body of attitudes toward black colonists assumed to be held by most white colonists. The *Gazette* did not have to argue the appropriateness for the secondary place for the colonies' black population but rather legitimized the colonial attitudes that already supported that ranking. This could often be done by a writing style that called upon the readers' involvement to complete the thought, thus avoiding the necessity of debate. A well-placed phrase, ostensibly impartial, could nonetheless play on the perceived prejudices of the reader. In the Somerset decision, explored next, the *Gazette* gave just thirty-nine words for the decision considered to be the foundation of the British abolition movement.

Less momentously, an example of a minimalist approach occurred again in 1775, certainly a period of heightened propaganda. The item seemed innocuous enough: "Cambridge, August 28, 1775—We are informed that the Negroes in Boston were lately summoned to at Faneuil Hall, for the purpose of choosing out of their body a certain number to be employed cleaning the streets; in which meeting Joshua Loring, Esq. presided as Moderate. The well known Caesar Merriam opposed the measure, for which he was committed to prison, and continued the street were all cleaned" (*BG* 8/26/75).

Examined in the context of the *Gazette* as an instrument of propaganda, the flat tone of the half dozen lines establishes standards for the reader. It is the *ordinariness* of the tone that tells the reader that it is appropriate for Caesar Merriman to be put in prison for failing to clean the streets. Were the same half dozen lines to appear in a Quaker publication, for example, the interpretation might be different—the ordinariness of the tone might provide shock value for readers who held opposite attitudes. But the *Gazette* never established any context for its news of blacks and slaves that recognized the possibility of change in the position of blacks and slaves in colonial society, even at a time in which those attitudes existed in Massachusetts and elsewhere.

In Massachusetts the campaign for the abolition of slavery, was not reflected in the *Boston Gazette*. In one instance, the *Gazette* published a letter whose writer called for the colony to forbid the importation of slaves (*BG* 6/15/72), a patriot stance encouraged by the Somerset decision and not necessarily attended by any promise of freedom to the slaves already in the colonies. The paper was silent on the occasion of the several slave petitions that sought representation to the Assembly, even though Adams was presiding officer. By 1771, however, Massachusetts's antislavery activists had again managed to bring an antislavery bill to the Assembly. In his account of the bill's progress to John Adams, James Warren, a member of Boston's radical circle, wrote, "If passed into an Act it should have a bad effect on the Union of the Colonies." He also noted, "A Letter to Congress on that subject was proposed and reported, but I endeavord [sic] to divert that, supposing [sic] it would embarrass and perhaps be attended with worst consequences that passing the Act" (*Warren-Adams Letters* 1:356).

Altogether, the *Boston Gazette* encapsulated a range of techniques to extend its message. Among these were the use of the colonial exchange newspapers to relay its message out, although no contrary messages traveled inward; Adams's hyperbolic essays and his invention and extension of significant events; the use of rhetorical language and slogans; and the utilization of the power of the printer, who extended patriot themes through the choices of selection and silence. Moreover, the printers of the *Gazette* used typeface and placement of stories to convey importance. At a time when most insertions were set in type and placed in the frame as they came to hand, the *Boston Gazette* reserved the front page for Adams's essays. The first announcement of the Boston Massacre was accompanied by crude replications of coffins, each bearing the initials of one of the dead. The annual memorialization further expanded typographical display.

The point here is to emphasize that nothing in the *Boston Gazette,* this premiere organ of patriot propaganda that influenced the entire patriot message, was left to chance. Whether front page or backstairs, in homegrown essays or in selections from other publications, the contents of the *Gazette* advanced an agenda that sought separation from Great Britain. Information about blacks and slaves that appeared in the *Gazette,* and, also important, information that did not, was directed by this overall purpose. Set within the framework of the rhetoric of slavery, the role of blacks and slaves as established by the *Boston Gazette* gave illustration to the reality of loss of power. In its choices, the *Gazette* called upon the colonial and Puritan fear of conspiracy and the conflation of blackness and crime, both situated within the context that did not challenge the institution of slavery. Moreover, the difficulty of blacks and slaves in gaining acceptance in the New England world of demonstrated virtue, and the continued representation of slaves in negative ways served to maintain the rationale that enslavement was a product of the enslaved.

In 1772, however, the British abolition movement challenged these various rationales in a famous case that was to underpin the subsequent abolition movement in Great Britain. That it did not have the same affect in the American colonies may be in part explained by how the *Boston Gazette* chose to present the event.

CHAPTER FOUR

The Somerset Case

One day in the early summer of 1772, South Carolina planter Henry Laurens was at his London desk amidst business correspondence. He had arrived the previous autumn to enroll his sons in a British school and, in an unofficial capacity, look after the interests of South Carolina, including the colony's substantial donation to the defense of John Wilkes (Wallace 162–76). But Laurens's ongoing business interest during that London year was the disposal of an "African cargo," that is, his financial interest in the slaves on a ship headed for Charles Town in South Carolina. He also had some immediate business in connection with a ship in a London dock. "I have a Negro on board of the *Fisher,* a very orderly quiet Lad named Andrew Dross. If the Brigantine is sold be so kind as to dispose of him in such a manner, either under Capt. Chisman's Care, or otherwise as you think best for my interest" (Laurens 8:370).

Laurens was under some pressure to find a quick way to dispose of the young man. The letter was written two weeks before the final decision was expected in the Somerset case, a suit for freedom brought on behalf of an American slave now in England. The case was expected to have reverberations that would address the legality of slaveholding in England, and perhaps even in the British colonies (D. Davis 507). Laurens may also have been concerned about the slave, Robert Scipio, who accompanied his family on the trip. Scipio's name came up when Laurens broke off from a long letter to Gervais about the arriving slaves to mention the trial in an uncharacteristically jocular tone. "They say Supper is ready, otherwise I was going to tell a long and comical story of a Trial between a Mr. Stuart and his Black man James Somerset, at King's Bench, for Liberty. My man Robert Scipio Laurens says the Negroes that want to be free here, are Fools. He behav'd a little amiss one day, and I told him I would not be plagued by him. If he did not choose to stay with me to go about his Business. He said he would serve no body else, and was behaved excellently well ever since" (Laurens 8:353).

Trust in Scipio's devotion notwithstanding, Laurens and his small entourage were out of the country on June 22 when Lord Mansfield, the chief justice of Great Britain's highest common law court, ruled in favor of the American slave, James Somerset. By August 20, back in London, Laurens's tone had changed. He was not pleased with the defense attorney. "In my humble opinion he was not an Advocate for his Client, nor was there a word said to the purpose on either side" (Laurens 8:435).

Gervais never did hear the promised "long and comical story"; perhaps at this point Laurens found it less comical. Indeed, the case may have been a personal turning point for the South Carolinian, who three years later was to condemn slaveholding in a famous letter to his son John and be an influence in his son's subsequent antislavery stance (Hargrove 198–99).

The trial that gave James Somerset his freedom was the first major success for the British abolition movement. It was a victory that was to establish the base of the British abolition movement that over the next fifty years brought unrelenting and finally successful pressure on Great Britain to end its connection to the slave trade in all parts of the world (Klingberg).

James Somerset was African-born and had been purchased in Virginia by a Boston man, Charles Stuart. In 1769, when Stuart traveled to England, Somerset accompanied him as a personal servant, but once in London, he escaped. Stuart ordered him seized and held on board a ship bound for the West Indies, where he was to be sold. The recapture of the slave came to the attention of the Quaker Granville Sharp, who had been searching for a case that would demonstrate what he believed was the illegality of slaveholding in Great Britain. Not only was Sharp interested in purifying English consciences by disallowing slaveholding, the case whetted his long-range ambition for the prohibition of slavery throughout the British colonies. Sharp and his supporters prepared a case that was intended to have far-ranging consequences.

The case was heard in May and June of 1772 before Lord Mansfield in the Court of the King's Bench (Bauer). Five lawyers had been assembled by Sharp and his abolitionist friends. Counsel for the defendant was underwritten by a group of West Indian planters, who, like the abolitionists, believed the decision would have consequences beyond the freedom of a single slave (Wiecek).

After five days of testimony in a courtroom packed with planters, abolitionists, and Somerset supporters — black and white — Mansfield ruled Somerset must be "discharged," set free, although not on the basis that slavery was illegal in England, as the abolitionists had argued. Mansfield's judgment was made on the narrow ledge that Great Britain had no precedent allowing for the forced recapture of an escaped slave outside the country of his or her enslavement. One British press account quoted Mansfield's final, specific statement: "So high an act of dominion was never in use here; no master was every allowed to take a slave by force to be sold abroad, because he had deserted from his service, or for any other reason whatsoever. We cannot say the cause set forth by this return is allowed or approved by the laws of this kingdom, therefore the man must be discharged" (*GM* 7/72).

Despite such precise press accounts, it was popularly believed in Great Britain that the decision had ended slavery in England (Shyllon 25). Lord Mansfield was to go down in popular history as the Great Emancipator, despite his subsequent proslavery decisions. Because of the popular understanding, however, the case came to be a liberalizing influence in Great Britain. In contrast, the eventual influence of the case in the United States tended to be negative. Modern American historians have interpreted the decision as playing a major role in the encouragement of fugitive slave legislation in the United States (Finkelman 38–41). British and American scholars agree that confusion has existed in the interpretation of the case from the time of the trial to the present day.

One American historian blames the colonial press for American confusion. Jerome Nadelhaft claims the *Boston Gazette* "explicitly misinformed" (194) its readers in the version he believes came to dominate the American understanding of the decision. The *Gazette* reprinted a short paragraph taken from the London *Gentleman's Quarterly*: "A correspondent observes, that as Blacks are free now in this country, Gentlemen will not be so fond of bringing them here as they used to be, it being computed there are now about 14,000 blacks in this country" (*BG* 9/21/72).

In contrast, Nadelhaft cites as accurate another short insertion by the patriot *Virginia Gazette*. "Yesterday, the Court of King's Bench gave judgement in the Case of Somerset the Negro, finding that Mr. Stuart, his Master, had not Power to compel him on Board a Ship or send him back to the Plantations, but that the owner might bring an Action of Trover against anyone who shall take the Black into his Service. A great number of Blacks were in West-minster Hall to hear the Determination of the cause and went away greatly pleased" (*VG*-Purdie and Dixon 8/17/72).

Nadelhaft does not speculate on the reason for the *Gazette*'s misinformation, but when the paper is viewed as a propaganda organ, it becomes clear that the *Gazette* had more to gain from the short paragraph of misinformation than from complete coverage. Complete coverage was available from several British sources, newspapers and magazines, used by other colonial newspapers. A study of the coverage of the Somerset decision indicates that the patriot press gave less accurate and shorter coverage to the decision, despite the availability of in-formation, than newspapers that were loyalist in inclination or who had not committed to the patriot cause. The major exception to this pattern was the southern press, whose readers likely had less interest in propagandistic uses of the material than information that might affect their livelihood. The selected use of the Somerset decision by the core elements of the patriot press offers further evidence that the patriot press manipulated the issue of slavery in the Ameri-can colonies to advance the separation of the colonies from Great Britain.

The most dramatic difference between the coverage of the *Boston Gazette* and the coverage given to the decision by other newspapers was most apparent in Boston. The *Massachusetts Gazette and Boston News-Letter* devoted 2,700 words to the story, including a special supplement, giving readers not only trial coverage but also various short paragraphs of opinion as well—alto-gether a substantial sampling of what had been published in the British press and certainly meeting the needs of readers who sought a layered understand-ing of the decision. This pattern of contrast between the *Gazette,* the fiery propaganda organ, and the *News-Letter,* the archetype of the traditional news-paper, held true generally, if not absolutely, throughout the colonies. Newspa-pers that were, or would become, loyalist, and newspapers that were in 1772 already patriot aligned, or would become aligned to the patriot cause, were less accurate on every measure. Patriot-oriented newspapers published fewer words, had fewer insertions, and relied on paragraphs of opinion rather that trial-based coverage. The poorest coverage of all was provided by the most pa-triot organ of all, the *Boston Gazette.* The second poorest coverage was provided by Isaiah Thomas's *Massachusetts Spy,* a newspaper that rivaled the *Gazette* for its fiery radicalism. Other newspapers that gave the subject little cover-age—William Goddard's *Chronicle,* William Bradford's *Pennsylvania Journal,* and John Dunlap's *Pennsylvania Packet*—were all newspapers whose editors played important roles as patriot propagandists before and during the Revolution. The single exception to this pattern is Hugh Gaine's *Mercury,* which had the same amount of information as the *Boston Gazette.* The appearance of the *Mercury* among the patriot propagandists can be best explained in terms of Gaine's idiosyncratic career that tended to follow what he viewed as the most advantageous winds of the moment. Meantime, the newspapers that gave the Somerset decision the fairest and most complete coverage is a mixed group. The two newspapers who gave the decision the most number of words in the most number of insertions are the *Boston News-Letter* (2,711 words in four insertions) and the *Boston Post-Boy* (3,705 words in four insertions) and are traditionally associated with the Tory camp (Bradley 6).

The variety of stories that were available to the colonial printers is illustrated by the *Post-Boy* coverage. The first item was published July 27 and presented the opening arguments from the May 14 court appearance. Another item following this insertion addressed the possible effects of the decision — one of the few articles that appeared in the colonial press to do so: "A correspondent says, this cause pregnant with consequences, extremely detrimental to those gentlemen whose estates chiefly consist in slaves; It would be a means of ruining our African trade; if it should be determined in favor of the negroes, we are apprehensive their black gentry will visit us in too great an abundance, inter-marry with our women and thus we shall become a nation of mulattoes. Some method must be taken to limit or entirely prohibit the importation of negroes."

On August 3, the newspaper published an antislavery letter from a subscriber who had been prompted to write because of the trial. The slave trade was "an infamous bartering of Human Flesh and Blood." On August 31, the newspaper gave the trial conclusion in a version that included Lord Mansfield's final remarks. And on October 5 the *Post-Boy* reprinted a piece from England's *Gentleman's Magazine* that called for recompense of planters whose slaves were to be set free by "the general law of England."

Like the *News-Letter,* it is difficult to determine a stance in the coverage by the *Post-Boy.* Readers could find support for whatever their position or make a choice on the basis of information presented. The writer of an article published in January 1773 and taken from London's *Public Advertiser* reluctantly concluded that slavery was acceptable, but it was a decision that the writer made uneasily on the basis of his belief that slavery by Europeans was less severe than the slavery imposed by Africans on each other.

The *Providence Gazette,* considered a patriot newspaper, also gave Somerset full coverage. Three of the insertions were long summaries of the trial (*PG* 2/17; 7/25; 9/5/72). The newspaper also carried the essay included in the *Post-Boy,* "A correspondent says this cause seems pregnant with consequences" (*PG* 8/1/72), as well as the article suggesting compensation for planters (*PG* 10/10/72). On balance, there may have been more proslavery than antislavery sentiment in the *Providence Gazette,* but the inclusion of the trial testimony places the proslavery discussion within a context that encouraged examination of both sides of the issue, something that shorter coverage did not provide.

The *Essex Gazette* of Salem, Massachusetts, is also considered a patriot newspaper. It opened the year with a front-page attack on Lord Mansfield written by the British essayist "Junius" (*EG* 1/7/72) followed by an imaginary conversation between a ruler and subject on the topic of American independence. "If the present absurd system of policy is passed, I believe a very few years will terminate her authority here" (*EG* 3/3/72). The *Essex Gazette* expressed the patriot point of view but without the hyperbole of the *Boston Gazette* or *Massachusetts Spy.* Its patriot interests, however, did not preclude wideranging coverage of Somerset. It used the "pregnant with consequences" commentary published in the *Post-Boy,* but the *Essex Gazette* also published a letter that predicted the consequences would not be ruinous.

> But it is false that our Colonies would be ruined by the abolition of Slavery. It might occasion a stagnation of business for a short time but it would produce many happy effects. It is slavery which is permitted in America that has hindered it from becoming so soon populated as it would otherwise have been. Set the Negroes free and in a few generations this vast and fertile continent would be crowded with inhabitants. Learning arts, and every thing would flourish in America, and instead of being inhabited by wild Beasts and Savages. It would be peopled by Philosophers and men. (*EG* 8/25/72)

On the Somerset issue, at least, both of these patriot newspapers had more in common with the conservative and Tory *Post-Boy* than with the radical leader, the *Boston Gazette.*

The *New Hampshire Gazette,* which also provided a fair range of material, finally aligned itself with the patriots but was cautious in 1772. However, although the *Providence Gazette* and the *Essex Gazette,* providers of more news on the issue than the *Boston Gazette,* did not participate in the prewar propaganda to the extent of other newspapers, their Whig influences were apparent in 1772. John Carter was described by Thomas as the patriot's "staunch supporter" (Thomas 323). Samuel Hall, printer of the *Essex Gazette,* although nephew and apprentice to Daniel Fowle, who was no friend to the Adams circle since his unhappy days with the *Independent Advertiser,* was characterized as the patriot's "firm friend" (Thomas 178).

Two southern newspapers also are found among newspapers that gave the most complete coverage of the Somerset decision. The *South-Carolina Gazette* used only one insertion, but it was a lengthy one, running 1,400 words. The account was concerned with the fourth day of the trial, that included the argument made by Stuart's counsel that Somerset was bound by the terms of simple contract but included an equal amount of space to Somerset's counsel, who argued that municipal law should take precedence over foreign laws. The majority of the article was concerned with Lord Mansfield's remarks. "The decision, as a matter of law must be governed strictly therefore. It cannot accommodate itself to present conveniences; it must be governed by its own intrinsic tendencies" (*SCG* 8/13/72). The *Gazette* did not use the conclusion of the trial, but even the one insertion presented the trial in terms of its complications, formality, and importance, characteristics that could not be approached by use of the shorter, anecdotal items. Similarly, another lengthy account carried by the Tory *South-Carolina and American General Gazette* included Lord Mansfield's involved summary that clearly showed his reluctance to rule, as the correspondent noted, "Lord Mansfield seems to dread from judgement in favor of the Negro" (*SCAMG* 8/3/72).

In contrast to the South Carolina accounts, the Virginia newspapers carried news of the decision by way of British accounts, particularly those taken from the *Middlesex Journal,* which viewed the trial and the subsequent decision as an example of British liberality (Nadelhaft 193). Alexander Purdie's *Virginia Gazette* told the story in five insertions (*VG*-Purdie and Dixon 5/7; 6/4; 7/23; 8/20; 8/27/72), including antislavery comments reprinted from the British source: "If Negroes are to be Slaves on Account of Colour, the next Step will be to enslave every Mulatto in the Kingdom, then all the Portuguese, next the French, then the brown complexioned English, and so on till there be one man left, which will be the man of the palest complexion in the kingdom" (*VG*-Purdie and Dixon 8/20/72). William Rind's *Virginia Gazette,* the favored Whig newspaper, reprinted a two-thousand-word essay taken from Great Britain's *Gentleman's Magazine,* "Considerations on the Negro Cause" (*VG*-Rind 11/12/72), which included Lord Mansfield's comment, "So high an act of dominion was ever in use here," that provided for Somerset's freedom on the basis of lack of positive law legal but made it less clear that the decision did not outlaw slavery in England. Whether by accident or design, Virginians reading the accounts of the trial by way of the conduit of liberal British thought might be led to beliefs not so very different as those promulgated by the *Boston Gazette* in its short insertion.

Newspapers that gave the Somerset coverage a few hundred words rather than a few dozen or a few thousand, the extremes between the *Boston Gazette* and the Tory newspapers and the southern newspapers, were newspapers that were not early leaders of the Revolutionary cause. Solomon Southwick of the *Newport Mercury,* which provided 870 words on the decision over three insertions (*NM* 8/3; 9/7; 9/14/72), was a strong patriot once the war had commenced (Thomas 254), although he did not participate in the prerevolutionary propagandizing to nearly the same extent as the core patriot printers. By 1772 there was ample evidence, including the coverage given to the Somerset trial, that Southwick was in the patriot camp. The *Mercury,* indeed, published the misinformation that was to appear in the *Boston Gazette* two weeks later, "as blacks are now free in this country" (*NM* 9/7/72), even though the longer essay containing that paragraph had been published in other colonies.

The few words the *Boston Gazette* gave to the Somerset decision appeared in a newspaper routinely written in hyperbole and focused on the British menace. But it was not until September 21, 1772 — after a summer of following the scandal and trial of the Queen of Denmark — that the *Gazette* chose to mention the Somerset case, opening and closing its coverage with the paragraph already quoted and carrying a June 21 dateline from London. It was not likely that the *Gazette* devoted a tardy paragraph to the story because the decision was considered unimportant or already known. The brevity of the item and its late appearance, coming at a time when readers may have already heard of the case from other colonists or from the *News-Letter,* was one of the *Boston Gazette*'s techniques for manipulating reader response.

The phrase "As Blacks are free now in this country," for example, was not only inaccurate, its uncompromising tone indicated there was no possibility of any other interpretation. Moreover, the wording may have suggested to the *Gazette* reader that the British had not given the American colonists a second thought on an issue that was obviously of importance to them. The phrase provided no opportunity for readers to examine the basis for the decision or consider its possible consequences. But, as in other items about blacks and slaves, this lack of information on an issue of obvious interest may have served to increase the impact of the story. Given no information on the obvious questions, readers could only turn to other sources, including other newspapers, of course, but also word-of-mouth, rumor, and personal biases, which may have been the preferred communication network for readers seeking support for entrenched attitudes.

The paragraph, in fact, did more than misinform readers about the Somerset decision. Its very brevity and tone reinforced the *Gazette* rhetoric that Great Britain paid little attention to colonists' concerns on any front, even one as pertinent as slavery. The brevity and tone of the article did not indicate the range of arguments, the formality of the court setting, Lord Mansfield's reluctance to rule on the issue, or, indeed, the narrowness of the decision. Instead, *Gazette* readers saw the subject treated by British authority in what must have appeared a cavalier manner. While the writer noted that the decision might affect the "14,000 blacks in this country," a colonial reader could not be blamed for wondering why the British writer had not addressed the effect of the decision on the many more thousands of slaves in the British colonies.

The anecdotal approach was also primarily used by John Holt, the printer/ editor of the *New-York Journal*. Holt's three references to the trial contain one trial-based story, a minor one, however, having to do with a postponement. However, Holt's readers did learn that the case was not to be dismissed lightly "as this was thought by the court a very important decision, it was postponed 'till towards the end of the term" (*NYJ* 4/30/72). The second reference, which implicated the decision, reinforced the theme of importance and acknowledged that the decision would have impact on the British colonies. "The late decision with regard to Somerset the Negro, a correspondent assures us, will occasion a greater ferment in American (particularly in the islands) than the Stamp Act itself; for slaves constituting the great value of (West Indian) property (especially) and appeals from America in all cases of a civil process to the mother country, every pettifogger will have his neighbor entirely at his mercy, and by applying to the King's Bench at Westminster leave the subject at Jamaica or Barbadoes wholly without a hand to cultivate his plantation" (*NYJ* 8/27/72).

The third and final reference directly reported the trial decision, but without any summary of the trial testimony. Holt chose a colorful, eyewitness account of the final day.

> The great Negro cause was determined a few days ago, and the consequence was that the Negro obtained his freedom. The poor fellow was present in the court at the decision, as were likewise a great many blacks, all of them, as soon as Lord Mansfield had delivered the opinion of the court, came forward, and bowed first

to the Judges, then to the bar, with the symptoms of the most extravagant joy. Who can help admiring the genius of that government which thus dispenses freedom all around it? No station or character is above the law, nor is any beneath its protection. The Monarch and the Beggar are alike subject to it. "Pauperum Taberna Require Torres" are equally guarded by it. (*NYJ* 9/3/72)

The piece was obviously written by a sympathetic observer, and the present-day reader may read the account in the spirit in which it was written. But like other reports from the British liberal press, its reception in the colonies may have provoked a less sympathetic reaction. Indeed, Holt may have chosen the piece because it pointed up the British view of slavery that was in direct opposition to the view held by many of his readers. In July, during the period of the Somerset coverage, the *Journal* carried a lengthy account of an attack of a slave upon his master and the slave's subsequent execution (*NYJ* 7/2/72). Since the attacking slave was owned by a local master, the dangers of manumission loomed menacingly close to readers in a colony where slave insurrection composed a large part of collective memory. Holt's readers may not have been likely to admire "the genius of a government" that placed the white slave owner on the same legal footing as his black slave and, rather than increasing colonial sympathy to the slave, the final Somerset reportage more likely indicated to Holt's readers how removed in understanding the Mother Country was from her American colonies.

Similarly, William Goddard in the *Pennsylvania Chronicle* used anecdotal coverage that his readers may have found disturbing. "On Monday near 200 Blacks, with their ladies, had an entertainment at a public house in Westminster" to celebrate the decision, readers learn (*PC* 8/22/72). For colonial readers, the concept of blacks with their "ladies," not the "wenches" of the colonial press advertisements, drinking at a public house like white people (and even affording five shillings at the door!) clearly had the ingredients of raising the possibility, spectral to some, of equality. Goddard used no story that was strictly based on the trial in favor of the short paragraph used by the *Boston Gazette* (*PC* 8/12/72). Like the *New-York Journal*, the *Chronicle*'s Somerset story occurred in the context of danger posed by blacks. Shortly after news of the Somerset celebration an account was published of a West Indian slave who attacked a white man and was subsequently executed — "staked to iron crows and burnt" (*PC* 9/5/72).

In contrast, the coverage given to Somerset by Isaiah Thomas's *Massachusetts Spy*, certainly a fiery patriot organ, has a somewhat different cast than that of the *Gazette, Chronicle,* or *Journal*. In February the *Spy* reprinted an antislavery letter from the *Pennsylvania Gazette* calling for the education of slaves in order to provide an uplift to their moral life (*MS* 2/27/72), promoting the notion, of course, that slaves were in need of moral uplift. By the close of the year, two *Spy* subscribers were involved in a spirited and lengthy debate on the morality of slavery in a series of essays of the kind that were usually found in newspapers associated with a moderate stance (*MS* 10/1; 10/17/72). A week after the publication of the letter from the *Friend to the Oppressed*, Thomas reprinted a story from Rhode Island in which a slave, apparently drunk, had beaten his "wench," set several fires to his master's property, and finally fallen into a vat of rum and drowned, told in an amused tone (*MS* 3/5/72). During the Somerset period, Thomas included stories about a "very valuable negro" who had been killed trying to retrieve a portion of meat hanging down a well for cooling (*MS* 8/31/72). The same edition contained a short item about a slave uprising in Surinam in which two white men were killed. This handful of items in one newspaper managed to encapsulate several colonial attitudes toward slaves — slaves in need of moral uplift, slaves as inept and foolish, and slaves as dangerous. The *Spy* also contained three references to the trial. The first, at the end of August, even later than the *Boston Gazette,* is short, but, un-like the item in the *Boston Gazette,* it is accurate: "Yesterday the Court of King's Bench gave judgment in the case of Somerset the Negro finding that Mr. Stewart his master had no power to compel him a ship or to send him back to the plantations" (*MS* 8/27/72).

The second reference is an extract from the same account that had been used by the *New-York Journal.* "The great Negro cause was determined a few days ago and the consequence was, the Negro obtained his freedom. The poor fellow was present in the court as were like [indecipherable] a great many blacks, all of whom, as soon as Lord Mansfield had delivered the opinion of the court, came forward, and bowed first to the judges, and then to the bar with symptoms of the most extravagant joy" (*MS* 9/3/72).

Thomas chose to exclude the paean to Great Britain's fairness of government that had been included in John Holt's version of the story in the *New-York Journal.* And one of the few evidences that colonial readers had learned, and were digesting, the decision, came in the *Spy.* The September front page "open letter" to Lord Mansfield used the trial as a peg: "The late cloud of incense gone up to your name for your righteous determination in the Negro cause, we acknowledge is a wonderful display of your regard to the oath of your office, and incites me to go a little farther in the way of your duty." Mansfield's "duty," according to the essayist, was to give his attention more properly to colonial "enslavement." "With what colour of right can you emancipate a man taken in war, and sold to me by his captor for a valuable consideration, and yet hold millions in chains for whom you never paid a farthing?" (*MS* 9/17/72).

Not all patriot printers, or even eventual patriot printers, followed in lockstep to the *Boston Gazette*. But given the colonial context and the use of British writers who were not addressing American concerns, almost any selection might carry meanings for the colonial American that were not intended by the British writer. John Dunlap, later to be the official printer of the United States Constitution but the young printer of the *Pennsylvania Packet* in 1772, told the Somerset story in just two insertions. Neither of them was trial-based and neither was accurate because of its anecdotal nature. Both insertions, however, were written in a satirical manner that lent themselves to whatever position held by the reader. The first was a longer version of an item used by Purdie's *Virginia Gazette* in which the writer suggested that if slavery was to be a matter of color alone, all would be enslaved except the man of the "palest complexion" (*PP* 8/3/72). The second item continued the theme of complexion. In a Swiftean tone, the writer surmised that the Somerset case would result in a law that would determine slavery by the darkness of skin, but such an order would be complicated by a companion order requiring slave ships to collect their cargoes from the port of London, not Africa (*PP* 8/17/72).

The apparent antislavery points in the selections were muddied by heavy-handed efforts to be amusing, possibly useful in providing a middle ground for Dunlap. But neither item served as a doorway to the further discussion of slavery in Dunlap's newspaper. In the following years, as Dunlap became more closely aligned with the patriot cause, he published nothing more on the subject. His Whig career flourished into the new nation (Teeter, "John Dunlap").

The *Pennsylvania Journal's* William Bradford chose just one item to tell the Somerset story. However, it was a trial-based discussion with an accurate summary of Lord Mansfield's final comments. Somerset must be discharged, according to the account, because English law contained no particular law that permitted enslavement. Slavery, Mansfield was recorded as telling the court, was not an institution that could be allowed to exist on the basis of general principles but instead had to be supported by specific or "positive law." Mansfield did not condemn slavery. "The power of a master over his servant is different in all countries, more or less limited or extensive; the exercise of it therefore must always be regulated by the laws of the place where exercised" (*PJ*

9/2/72). In this account Mansfield gave to the American colonies the same rights as a foreign nation. The account clearly makes the point that his decision was of concern only in Great Britain and did not, as Granville Sharp argued, apply to British colonies because colonial law could not exist contrary to the British law from which it derived its authority.

Although the Somerset coverage was less of a polemic in the *Pennsylvania Journal* than in the *Boston Gazette,* the *Journal's* message suggested that the American colonies functioned under separate rules than those of the mother country. But Bradford, at this point, was primarily a follower of the conservative Whig John Dickinson and, like Dickinson, his move to the patriot camp was cautious. Bradford was also connected to Pennsylvania slave trading activities through his ownership of a marine insurance company and was keenly aware of the merchant reaction to efforts to curb the Pennsylvania slave trade (HSP 6). Bradford was neither a supporter of abolition nor an early patriot, but a critic of Parliament's power over the American colonies as exemplified by Great Britain's interference in the slave trade. And, as a newspaper that served merchant interests, it is not surprising to see the Somerset coverage embedded in news of the West Indies. Three weeks after the Somerset insertion, in a front-page article, Bradford published a list of restrictions for blacks in the Danish Royal Islands, including a curfew, restrictions on the sale of goods made to whites, and a warning to planters not to care too much "for the preservation for their Negroes" by supplying them lodging or food if fishing was available (*PJ* 10/2/72).

The *Journal's* competitor was the *Pennsylvania Gazette,* the newspaper associated with Benjamin Franklin, but in this decade under the ownership and management of his former partner, David Hall. Franklin was in London at this point, still lobbying for Pennsylvania to become a royal rather than a proprietary colony. Hall, freed from Franklin's dominance, had more in common with Bradford and the *Journal* than the patriot press. Hall published two Somerset items, including a thorough and even-handed summary of the trial arguments. The items also served to portray Mansfield as an Englishman keeping England inviolate from the evils of slavery. "He concluded with hoping that Mr. Stuart and every other man who arrogated such an unjust, in human, and dangerous dominion over a man when in this country would be told that the laws of England would not endure it, nor suffer the free air of this realm to be contaminated with the breath of a slave" (*PG* 8/12/72). The conclusion of the trial was carried in an "extract from a letter" also carried by the *New-York Journal* (*PG* 8/26/72).

Like its competition, the *Pennsylvania Journal*, Somerset appeared in a context that mitigated against celebratory readings of the decision: advertisements for slaves for sale and slaves wanted (*PG* 9/23; 10/21/72), news of a severe and devastating uprising in Surinam that had not been quelled (*PG* 10/7/72), and news of a hurricane in St. Croix, which had resulted in martial law that, like those in the Danish Royal Islands, placed severe restrictions on black inhabitants (*PG* 10/7/72).

The *Pennsylvania Gazette*'s items point up that any news of Somerset was surrounded by evidence of colonial slavery, and, alongside that, seeming evidence that the notion of freed slaves was incomprehensible in the colonial setting. Moreover, the use of the British press in a desultory way to report the decision had little chance of avoiding a British self-congratulatory air that could not have been well received by American colonists, whatever their politics. The British press was generally in favor of the freedom for Somerset, seeing his freedom as a symbol for what was considered the free air of England. For some British writers the decision appeared to restore confidence in British liberalism at a time when the British public was learning of the atrocities of the famous British tea company, the East India Company, against the native peoples. "The name of an Englishman till of late was admired, as comprehending all that was humane and generous, over the whole world; but now it has become more odious in Asia that even that of the Spaniard was formerly in Mexico and Peru" (*CC* 1/5/73). Indeed, one rationale for the Boston Tea Party was that it was against the corrupt East Indian Tea Company that was being protected by Parliament.

However, the existence of slavery in the British colonies obviously did not fit with this British self-congratulatory moralism that ignored British responsibility for the establishment of slavery in its colonies or its recalcitrance in ending the slave trade. By focusing on the decision as an affirmation of Great Britain's free air, the British news reports served to point up the differences between the countries. Any coverage less than the full trial-based stories emphasized British nationalism and the exclusion of the American colonies. The fuller newspaper accounts, like that in the Drapers' *Massachusetts Gazette and Boston News-Letter* or John Green and Joseph Russell's *Massachusetts Gazette and Boston Post-Boy*, were not only more informative, but, simply by sheer weight of words, tended to mute British self-congratulation and unwittingly served their Tory alignment by quieting colonial irritation.

From a patriot point of view, the truncated coverage served the cause in several ways, emphasizing the irritant factor of the British coverage, making available large spaces of silence to be filled by rumor, helping the spread of misinformation, and by giving such short shrift to the subject, indicating that the British were not so concerned about how the decision would affect the American colonies. Given all the material that was available to the colonial printer from British sources and from other colonial newspapers, the coverage of the issue by the core patriot press can only lead to the conclusion that information on the issue was manipulated.

By 1772, Adams was building an intercolonial movement that avoided direct confrontation on the issue of slavery. Yet to ignore the issue of slavery was also to ignore the American antislavery movement. Outside of the *Gazette*, antislavery essayists were increasingly drawing attention to the incompatibility of calls for American liberty and the existence of American slavery. While there were those patriots who sought to bring antislavery under the patriot banner, the Adams modus operandi prevailed. The *Gazette* continued to use silence in face of continuing public and legislative calls for abolition. From the point of view of a propagandist, silence was a canny choice. A strategist might observe that sometimes simply holding your cards is the best way to play a hand.

CHAPTER FIVE

The Voices of Antislavery

For Granville Sharp, the man who had done the most to bring the subject of slavery to a British court, the Somerset decision meant that slavery was forbidden not only in Great Britain but in the American colonies as well. The tireless writer was quick to his pen, and with equal speed the colonial Quaker printers published his comments in the colonies. "Why is it that the poor sooty African meets with so different a measure of justice in England and America, as to be *adjudged free* in the one, and in the other held in the most abject slavery?" (Sharp vi). Few chose to address the question directly. Certainly not Benjamin Franklin who, writing to London's *Public Advertiser,* pointed to British hypocrisy. "*Pharsical Britain!* to pride thyself in setting free a single Slave that happen to land on thy coasts, while thy Merchants in all thy ports are encouraged by thy laws to continue to commerce where so many *hundreds of thousands* are dragged into slavery can scare be said to end with their lives, since it is entailed on their posterity" (Franklin *Letters* 190).

The *Boston Gazette* had even less to say. The *Gazette* concluded its attention to the Somerset decision and to the slavery debate altogether with its short extract on the decision. Much of the colonial press, patriot and otherwise, followed suit.

But there can be no doubt that antislavery activity in the American colonies heated up after 1772. Activists in Massachusetts, Delaware, Connecticut, Vermont, Rhode Island, Pennsylvania, and Virginia were reinvigorated in their efforts to end the slave trade. Connecticut succeeded in banning the trade in 1774, and other colonies achieved partial successes before the Declaration of Independence. Both Continental Congresses, in 1774 and 1776, adopted resolutions against the slave trade. There was, indeed, a growing antislavery movement in the first half of the 1770s. Its public discourse was supported by pamphlets and newspaper essays as its leaders sought to influence public policy.

The leader of the indigenous American antislavery movement, Samuel Hopkins, achieved his greatest success with the publication of the *Dialogue on Slavery* dedicated to the First Continental Congress. The subsequent resolution by the Congress could only have heartened antislavery activists who saw the action as the first step to abolition in the new nation.

One of the puzzles of the American Revolution is how that early promise could turn into the compromises of the Constitutional Convention. One explanation is to examine the characteristics of the antislavery discourse in terms of the propaganda thrusts of the American Revolution. Clearly, the propaganda of the American Revolution avoided the voices of antislavery. Much of that had to do with the needs of revolutionary propaganda as viewed by Adams. What also played a role was how the antislavery movement chose to argue its case.

Despite their energy and commitment, the antislavery activists failed to make the issue integral to national identity. In terms of its communication, the failure occurred because antislavery remained in religious hands, and *particular* religious hands that—until the collaboration of Moses Brown and Samuel Hopkins—chose not to address political strategy. Unlike Adams, the proponents of antislavery did not adapt their religious discourse into political rhetoric. Because of the commitment to religious conscience as underpinnings of antislavery, antislavery adherents failed to make the kind of connections with the patriot propagandists that could have assisted in framing abolition as a propaganda issue.

Although antislavery activity was invigorated after the Somerset decision, Adams continued on a course that avoided a position on any aspect of antislavery except one on the slave trade, put at British feet. Not only did antislavery voices not appear in the pages of the *Gazette,* no discussion at all, either pro or con, found its way to the national stage provided by the *Boston Gazette.* Such agenda-setting from the patriots' premiere organ could hardly encourage patriots who held antislavery views to pursue a public antislavery stand.

Instead, presumably by design, antislavery activity was left in the hands of those traditionally most associated with the development of antislavery views. The patriot silence put into high relief an antislavery discussion that was often connected to British loyalism and a religious emphasis that ignored secular concerns — the role of the freed slave in society for example — in favor of arguments of self-purification, moral suasion, and affective feeling. Antislavery in the hands of the less committed patriots, British loyalists, and the religious sects that played less, if any, political role in revolutionary politics helped insure it would never move to the patriot center stage. Meanwhile, black colonists had few opportunities to be heard on the public stage.

As we know, the most consistent lance carriers for antislavery in the revolutionary period were members of religious denominations — Quaker; the evangelical sides of the Presbyterians, Methodists, and Baptists; and a branch of Calvinism that was not even embraced by all of New England, New Divinity. Advocates from these denominations preached, wrote, and campaigned for antislavery political action, but in the end failed to provide antislavery with enough of a broad, American public persona to go beyond local venues. Congregational adherents of antislavery, for example, most often framed their cause in terms of God's wrath. As late as 1777, when the antislavery minister and regimental chaplain David Avery preached a sermon of thanksgiving, the war was blamed on God's punishment for existing "sins and abominations." Among these, "our enslaving NEGROES is not the smallest of our crying sins. Doth not this sin cry to heaven for retaliation?" (Avery 1). Such rhetoric flew in the face of revolutionary propaganda that stressed American innocence opposed to British venality and was hardly a speech to engender a fighting spirit to the Connecticut troops it addressed, most of whom who had little connection with the institution. Antislavery adherents failed to erect a banner that, like the patriot propaganda, was sufficiently encompassing, optimistic, or forward-looking to include antislavery as a revolutionary issue, or even engaging enough to lead to a spirited defense of American slavery. The emphasis remained on Congregational didacticism and Quaker sensibility, both welltrod avenues. Whether didactic or persuasive, both forms contrasted with the propaganda as practiced by the patriots and hindered the movement as a national force.

Additionally, the antislavery movement in the final years before Independence was not only in religious hands but often in religious hands that were themselves estranged from the colonial power structure, both political and religious. Quakers, the most well-known of the antislavery advocates, were considered British loyalists (McKeel), thus distancing their position on slavery from the patriot cause. The itinerant evangelical Baptist, Methodist, and Presbyterian preachers were regarded suspiciously by southern slaveholders and traditional churchmen even before they voiced an antislavery message. And the New Divinity sect, representing the branch of Calvinism that was most active in antislavery, was the least powerful of the larger sects when it came to influence on patriot radicals.

In colonial America, as in England, the antislavery movement was dominated by Quakers, and for most of its antislavery history, American Quakers were part of a world Quaker antislavery movement that received its leadership from the English branch. There was, indeed, an indigenous Quaker antislavery movement in the American colonies even before world Quakerism officially embraced the cause. In 1733, Nantucket's Elihu Coleman published an antislavery pamphlet despite a general Quaker ban on antislavery publications (Coleman 1851). In 1753, just two years after Quakers had ended the ban, the Philadelphia Quarterly Meeting declared slavery a sin, a year before the London Yearly Meeting issued its strong denunciation of the slave trade. In 1758 the Philadelphia Yearly Meeting set in motion a campaign against slavery itself (Soderland 17, 30). This coincided with a decision made by the London Yearly Meeting that strongly advised Friends throughout the world against any involvement in the slave trades. American Quakers were quick to support the London advice, and Philadelphia Quakers in particular sought the cooperation of British Quakers in the support of the Pennsylvania Assembly's passage of a slave import duty. Despite the leadership of American Quakers in the antislavery movement, one upshot of this Anglo-American cooperation was that the American opposition to slavery came to be considered a branch of English Quaker antislavery. The connection was further enhanced by the similarity of the antislavery argument on either side of the Atlantic. By the 1770s, little difference existed in Quaker pamphlets whether written by Englishman Granville Sharp or American Anthony Benezet.

The conflation of British and American antislavery was encouraged by Benezet, who, in 1774, sent the American Quaker, William Dillwyn off to England to make connections with British antislavery leaders. The decision removed Dillwyn, who had written one antislavery pamphlet addressing American concerns in 1774 (Dillwyn), from the American antislavery movement and likely further weakened the indigenous movement by drawing it closer to the British model. Dillwyn settled permanently in Great Britain, where he be-came involved in the British antislavery movement.

Benezet quickly came to the attention of Sharp and British Quaker leaders as a result of his first major pamphlet in 1762 (Benezet, *Short*), which set in motion the Atlantic cooperation and the publication of Sharp's work in the colonies. Unfortunate for the American antislavery movement, however, was the fact that the English Quaker antislavery movement carried with it a clearly anti-American edge, and, as the Revolution approached, an antipatriot tinge. Sharp, in a work reprinted in Benezet's pamphlet, could only seem careless of American sensibilities: "The boasted liberty of our American colonies, there-fore, has so little right to that sacred name, that it seems to differ from the ar-bitrary power of despotic monarchs, only in one circumstance, viz., that is its a many-headed monster of tyranny" (Benezet, *Short* 13). Entrapped by a Quaker rhetoric that emphasized the guilt of slave owning in general and the guilt of *American* slave owners in particular, the antislavery writings appearing in colo-nial pamphlets and newspapers were hardly in tune with a patriot movement based on innocence and rebirth. Indeed, British antislavery activists seemed intent not only on appropriating the rhetoric of American purity but on deny-ing any American claim to it at all, as the Somerset decision seemed to come down to the keeping of "British air" free from the contaminants of American slavery.

The man who coined that phrase and directed the case along the lines of British purity was the Somerset attorney, Francis Hargrave, who, in a pam-phlet republished in the colonies, argued that the ruling protected England from the introduction of slavery from "our colonies and from foreign coun-tries" (Hargrave 48). In stressing the role of the purity of Great Britain, Har-grave drew on a long tradition of British exploration that permitted all man-ner of behavior after passage "beyond the line." Adventurers were expected to leave pagan indulgences behind them when they returned to the pristine home country. The American colonies, for all of their own self-perceptions, were not exempt from this way of thinking, and the Somerset decision suggested the American colonies posed as much of an infectious threat to the English air as the West Indies.

America as a guilty party was accepted by American evangelicals and, in-deed, promoted by the emphasis on affective feeling that characterized most antislavery writing, particularly that of the Quakers (Jennings). The Golden Rule, used by so much of Quaker argument, led to a tradition of an outpouring of feeling for the unfortunate, and sentimental tradition became part of the rhetoric of antislavery up until the Civil War. As part of this tradition, Quaker writers established the African as the noble savage, an innocent in the original setting of his native land. Here, in an Eden-like Garden, the African family existed as God intended. The European was the despoiler of the Garden, breaking apart families, subjecting the African to unspeakable cruelties, and turning the African into a victim and a martyr.

But victims necessitate guilty parties and further framed the debate in sin and guilt. For the British antislavery writers, Americans, after the Somerset case, were assigned that mantle. For the British, the Somerset decision appeared to expurgate much of British guilt, and in a mood of self-congratulation after Somerset, the British were happy to move blame to American shoulders. While the view that America was a guilty nation was not so easily transplanted into patriot ideology, its reverberations were not so alien to the consciences of American evangelicals.

The Quaker discussion of antislavery was already under way by the time of the First Great Awakening in the 1740s, the event that had the most to do with the development of colonial antislavery among other Protestant sects. The new evangelicals who sought the eradication of slavery as a rejection of worldliness included Presbyterians Samuel Davis, David Rice, and Jacob Green, British-born Methodist Francis Asbury, follower of John Wesley, and Thomas Rankin and Freeborn Garretson. The New England Baptists who relocated in Virginia were found among the southern antislavery evangelicals, often working in the South as itinerant preachers and becoming the target of suspicion because of their emphasis on black Christianization (Essig). Most of these traveling evangelicals were not writers of pamphlets — a loss indeed when one considers the exception to this rule, the Baptist minister, John Allen, who brought his evangelical message to Boston in the 1770s in fiery pamphlets that conjoined antislavery and patriot ideology (Allen 17). Next to the Quakers, those who were quick to the pen were the New Divinity clerics, so uncompromising in their religious views that they were regarded suspiciously by their brother Congregationalists.

Cotton Mather was the first prominent Congregationalist to address the issue of blacks in colonial society when he established his Society of Negroes, meeting Sunday nights for religious instruction as part of Mather's campaign for the Christianization of Africans. His pamphlet on the subject sought no change in the legal status, but it is memorable for its presentation of slaves as "poor creatures," who needed a paraphrase of the Lord's Prayer and a shorter catechism "brought down to their capacity" (Mather, *Negro Christianized*).

As disturbing as this approach is to a modern sensibility, its ostensible emphasis (if not design) was on the perceived benefits of religion to those in bondage. This was in contrast to Samuel Sewall's famous *The Selling of Joseph* that had called for the discontinuance of the slave trade on the basis of its sinfulness against white conscience. The emphasis on white sinfulness continued even when secularity was taking on an enlarged role not only in society but, as indicated by the congregations of Jonathan Mayhew and Samuel Cooper, even in church settings. For colonial Americans who were increasingly secular, concern about individual or even national sinfulness was mitigated by secular concerns that had to do with the role of the African, freed or not, in the larger society.

In its own way, the Mather pamphlet had struck out on a road that was less concerned with the sinfulness of the slave keeper than the benefit of religion to those in bondage. Mather's successors shifted the emphasis to white sin. It needs to be considered than in doing so, African colonists largely lost the opportunity to participate in the shared world of New England religiosity and a focus in which bondsmen and women held a modicum of power in their ability to demonstrate virtue. By contrast, the emphasis on white sin bound bondspeople to white decision and had consequences for the colonial antislavery movement. In a patriot ideology of innocence, taking on the mantle of sinfulness was limited in its appeal. Further, the emphasis on white virtue had little room for black voices, since, in essence, white colonists were not so concerned with saving black souls as their own. The emphasis of antislavery as white sinfulness also stilled other voices, the voices of the enslaved and, from a practical standpoint, white writers who addressed secular concerns. Finally, the sect most connected to antislavery as sinfulness also represented a sect that was far removed from the levers of practical power.

Led by Samuel Hopkins, the New England antislavery movement in the years before the Revolution was most in the hands of the New Divinity ministers (Lovejoy), a legacy of the Great Awakening. The Great Awakening had significance for the subsequent antislavery movement as well as for the Revolution. Alan Heimert argues the Awakening divided American protestantism into two streams of thought, the rational and the evangelical, and it was from the evangelical stream that the American Revolution most owed its genesis. The propaganda of the American Revolution certainly owed a debt to the evangelical stream. Indeed, it was the form apart from the content that one scholar believes was "Evangelicism's enduring legacy." This was a new mode of order, Harry S. Stout writes in revisiting the Heimert thesis, "that would refine the norms of social order" (Stout 525). Chief among the characteristics of the new form was its emphasis on communication to large numbers of people who would find transformation despite a generally anonymous setting.

Unlike the tightly woven and often intergenerational congregations of the New England church, those who gathered to hear the traveling New Light preachers were likely only connected to each other by their knowledge and admiration of the man on the stump. Isolated outside the powerful skein of a New England church congregation, individuals who came to hear an itinerant preacher had no power over him, no responsibility to community, and no opportunity for individual interaction. At the same time, the worshiper had the opportunity to experience the freedom that comes with the removal of associations. Momentarily stripped of the definition given to him or her by society at large, perhaps thankfully so, and set in a context of powerlessness, the evangelical follower was presented with the evangelical tour de force of simple messages strongly spoken. Encapsulated by a simple frame that was unmitigated by community standards or critical discussion and pressured by the knowledge that the opportunity, like the preacher, was transitory, the evangelical convert had the likelihood of accepting the evangelical message in its full force, often responding with the often-noted explosion of wailing and shrieking. "It was a very frequent Thing to see an House full of Out-cries, Faintings, Convulsions and such-like both with Distress, and also with Admiration and Joy," Jonathan Edwards reported to Boston's New Light periodical *Christian History* (*CH* 1/15/43), published, it should be noted, by Samuel Kneeland during Edes and Gill's apprenticeship.

The preacher on the stump was transitory, but what was long lasting was the permission given worshipers to understand God's intention through his or her own interpretation instead of biblical or ministerial mediation. Edwards argued that God communicated to the world through natural and contemporary events that composed a divinely organized system of symbols, or, as Edwards put it, the "certain sort of Language, as it were, in which God is wont to speak to us" (Knight 532). This typology traveled from Edwards to the very non-Edwardsian church of Jonathan Mayhew, who interpreted the Boston earthquake of 1755 in terms of God's coming retribution (Mayhew 1755:136). Thomas Prince, New Light minister of Boston's Old South Church, reported that a thunderstorm breaking out during a church service in 1742 produced near-panic when congregants believed they were hearing God's voice of displeasure. The congregation was panicked again when the rumblings of an earthquake "excited the shrieks of many, put many on flying out, and the Generality in Motion" (*CH* 2/18/43). In 1750, Bostonians struggled with the question of whether the installation of lightning rods would blunt God's call for sinners to repent (Cohen).

The reading of God as open to anyone who could read the physical world renewed the Puritan emphasis on outside appearances and, in terms of this discussion, its implications that God would not have assigned a skin color that connoted evil without reason. It also breathed new life into the Puritan habit of understanding conspiracy by means of signs and symbols — a mode of interpretation carried into revolutionary propaganda by Puritanism's most ardent son, Samuel Adams. Not only were his *Boston Gazette* essays characterized by the sure and simple language of the evangelical preachers but his dots, dashes, and exclamation points seemed an effort to replicate the emotion of the stump.

Congregational ministers originally welcomed George Whitefield and his fellow evangelicals in the preaching swath across New England. Whitefield's emotional sermons seemed destined to revitalize the Congregational church. As it turned out, the success of the evangelicals eventually failed to strengthen traditional churches. Moreover, the ministerial elite, trained at Harvard and Yale for the most respected profession the colonies could offer, reacted negatively to the leveling aspects of these new preachers, who needed no years of education, family background, or permanent congregations to take on their powerful roles. And the emphasis on individual emotion was a disturbing portent for a leadership class that revered social order. The resulting split led to the well-known division of the New Lights and the Old Lights.

There was not so much new about the New Lights. The New Lights eschewed the Half-way Covenant as too permissive because it had found a middle ground between Calvinism's most conservative theology, which maintained God's only promise was to save a portion of mankind but made no promises about who would compose that portion, and the more liberal view that held men and women had some power over their salvation. Still, even Congregational ministers did not move in lockstep, and New Light theology offered a spectrum of beliefs. The "Consistent Calvinism" or New Divinity branch of the New Lights returned to a strand of Calvinism that stressed God's absolute sovereignty in the view that a supreme God hardly needed to make bargains. Samuel Hopkins's refutation of Mayhew's "rational religion," the despised Arminianism, became the defining event in shaping New Divinity as a thread separate from the New Light drift to the liberal left of "conditional Calvinism" (Conforti; Breitenbach). Adherents to the New Divinity movement not only reaffirmed the traditional covenant theology but narrowed its theology to more conservative ground. Men and women were dependent wholly on God's will to the point that a worshiper needed to be so submissive that he or she ought to be willing to be dammed for eternity for God's glory. It was from this most conservative and doctrinaire religious wing that Calvinistic antislavery emerged.

In terms of the political achievement of antislavery goals, this alignment of antislavery with the New Divinity branch of Calvinism posed some practical problems. First was that in attacking less conservative conditional Calvinism, New Divinity men were attacking some of Boston's most powerful churches and home to the Boston radicals while New Divinity's most prominent adherents were in the hamlets of frontier Connecticut and the pastorates of rural Massachusetts. It is safe to say there were no members of the patriot power elite in the impoverished congregations of Jonathan Edwards's Northampton parish, Samuel Hopkins's first parish in Great Barrington, Massachusetts, or among the worshipers who gathered to hear Levi Hart in Preston, Connecticut.

For the New Divinity men, there was no shame in serving the small and remote — indeed, it was a tenet of the faith that humble circumstances were essential to the virtuous life. But the consequence of New Divinity's expression in the small and remote pastorates was to weaken its antislavery component at the center of power in Boston. Indeed, the New Divinity pastors in Boston and nearby had difficulty maintaining their positions of influence, much less promoting a political agenda. John Bacon accepted New Divinity theology only after he was installed in Boston's Old South Church. His subsequent rejection of the Half-way Covenant led to his dismissal in 1772 (Hill 2:158–59). Andrew Eliot was pastor of New North Church with its large but lower-class congregation that was not universally behind his tenure. Eliot's antislavery position was not as public as that of Samuel Hopkins, but he was prominent in opposing the Anglicans' Society for the Propagation of the Gospel in Foreign Parts by offering conversion to people of color through the Congregational organization. He early refused the gift of a slave presented by his congregation. But he was later called "Pope" and "Andrew Sly" by the unhappy church members who sought his removal (Sprague 1:420). William Gordon of nearby Roxbury's Third Parish was a vigorous New Divinity man, antislavery activist, essay writer, patriot, and chaplain to both legislative houses in Massachusetts. However, British-born Gordon fell out of favor with American revolutionary leaders and was dismissed from his chaplaincies. He also offended members of his church and was finally dismissed from his congregation, whereupon he returned to England to write a respected history of the Revolution (Winsor 2:350). Given Gordon's antislavery activities, John Adams's complaint about him may suggest the role antislavery played in his patriot disfavor. Adams wrote of him in 1775: "I fear his indiscreet Prate will do harm in this city. He is an eternal Talker. Very Zealous to the Cause, and a well-meaning Man, but incautious, and not sufficiently tender to the character of our Province, upon which at this Time much depends" (Adams, *Diary* 2:174).

Adams also noted that Gordon was fond of thinking of himself as a "Man of Influence," suggesting this was hardly Adams's view. In fact, the dismissals of Gordon and Bacon represent another characteristic of New Divinity men that lessened their influence in patriot circles. Products of rural life and modest circumstance, they were men who generally lacked the powerful friends and family that advanced careers of the Old Lights. Hopkins, the leading member of the group, was the son of a miller, as was Nathaneal Emmons (Park 53). David Avery, the son of a small farmer, was originally expected to be a carpenter (Dexter 3:305–10). Without powerful friends, their political influence was further lessened by their own career visions, seeking pulpits that would provide opportunities for reflection and study rather than political or social status. Indeed, the New Divinity men, embracing the antislavery cause as another repudiation of the worldly life, welcomed the oppositional position vis-à-vis the power structure provided by an antislavery stance. Persecution for an antislavery stance was as much evidence of personal virtue as other suffering. These characteristics lessened the likelihood of New Divinity antislavery becoming an influence on a majority agenda.

Additionally, the time period of the development of New Divinity tended to play against the impact of the antislavery discussion. Tucked away in the Joseph Bellamy parsonage, New Divinity's future leaders such as Hopkins, Edwards the younger, Ebenezer Baldwin, and Hart spent the 1760s codifying a way of thought that would lead to antislavery. But it was not until Hopkins moved to Newport, Rhode Island in 1769, that his philosophy of "disinterested benevolence" was transferred to the slavery issue. Similarly, Emmons, after completing his studies in 1769, did not receive the call to the Wrentham, Massachusetts, pastorate until 1773 (Park 53). But by the 1770s the Boston radicals had set out the revolutionary agenda on their own terms.

What was peculiar about the rejection of New Divinity from the patriot ideology was that New Divinity's belief in the sanction and surety of a Puritan past reflected Sam Adams's views. Adams himself was a son of the Great Awakening, coming of age during the height of its influence when he was completing his master's degree at Harvard, although not meeting his father's ministerial ambitions for him. It was also the time of the public humiliation occasioned by the loss of his father's fortune at the hands, as Adams would always believe, of the colony's later governor, Thomas Hutchinson. As his biographers agree, the influence of the Awakening, occurring at a crux of the Adams family's crisis, seemed to establish in Adams a personality of blame, suspicion, and an exaggerated sense of morality, as described by his portrait in *Sibley's Harvard Graduates*: "He had no close friends, and even those of his associates who greatly admired him regarded him with some apprehension and distrust . . . he disliked and feared everyone who achieved prominence in business and public life. Let any man succeed, and Adams would begin to deprecate his talents and services" (*Sibley's* 10:425). So described, Adams's personality comes close to what is put forward by Michael Zuckerman in his examination of an exaggerated sense of morality in the early American "fabrication of identity." "They are driven to define others as adversaries," Zuckerman writes, "as if to vindicate their own uncertain worth by assaults on those around them." Calling on the work of social psychologists, he further notes; "They embrace identities defined primarily by their aversion to iniquity, as if to salvage a satisfactory sense of self in circumstances in which that sense is imperiled" (Zuckerman 193). In Adams's case, these were not the traits of a generosity of spirit that would serve to encourage a change in black status. But had another confluence of circumstances occurred, Adams may have adopted New Divinity and with it, the antislavery stance.

Meantime, the consistent Calvinists who came to the fore in the generation after the Great Awakening found no ready audiences, even in the impoverished, remote posts that had difficulty finding pastors. One third of New Divinity were dismissed by their congregations at least once (Conforti, *Samuel Hopkins* 92–93), suggesting dissatisfaction not only with their conservatism but perhaps with their lack of other ministerial attributes. Some of the congregations' discontent may have been related to a public speaking style that was not up to the standards of their New Light predecessors, the senior Edwards or Joseph Bellamy, and could not compete on the rhetorical stage with someone like Jonathan Mayhew, whose liberal views did not include rejection of the fiery style of the older Puritan tradition. The ministers certainly raised none of the excitement of the original New Light preachers. Eschewing emotionalism for metaphysical discussion not "readily appreciated by the common mind," younger congregants fled from Hopkins's ministry in Newport. "The effect of his preaching was that nearly all the young people of the town went to other churches," a memorialist recalled, which left "a larger proportion of aged people in his congregation that I remember ever to have seen in any other" (Sprague 433). Ezra Stiles predicted Hopkins would "preach away all his congregation" (Conforti, *Samuel Hopkins* 101), and Hopkins was not being modest when he despaired that his congregants had to suffer "the precious truths of God delivered in so poor a manner" (HSP 1). The younger Edwards inherited none of the charisma of his father. "His manner was the opposite of attractive," a fellow minister remembered. "In his voice there was a nasal twang which diminished the effect of his utterance. He had little or no gesture, looked about but little upon his audience, and seemed like a man who was conscious that he was dealing with abstractions" (Sprague 1:549). Emmons made a considerable reputation, but it was as a teacher of others. "His appearance was unimposing, and his voice was weak and squeaky" (Peel 104). Gordon of Roxbury was "rude and blunt in his manner" and "not interesting as a preacher" (Winsor 1:350). Thus, if considered together, the New Divinity men were men without important family backgrounds, powerful friends or colleagues, in or outside the church, who held pastorates of small and uninfluential congregations and were mediocre public speakers at a time when this was a valued attribute of leadership. Moreover, their writing styles, any more than their speaking modes, were not likely to collect adherents. Such a cluster of defining characteristics did not bode well for the success of the New Divinity antislavery stance.

Despite such obstacles, the New Divinity men were as consistent in their antislavery efforts as in other areas of theology. Hopkins began his antislavery crusade just a year after acquiring a new post in Newport, Rhode Island, and remained committed to the cause his whole life. Jonathan Edwards Jr. and Edwards's friend and fellow Congregational pastor, Ebenezer Baldwin (whose early death at thirty-two, like the death of Otis, removed an antislavery voice) composed a series of antislavery essays, discussed later, for the Connecticut press. Levi Hart preached antislavery from his pulpit, and he and Hopkins were associates in antislavery activities for years. William Gordon was an in-defatigable writer of antislavery essays. In Newburyport, a Massachusetts cen-ter of slaving activity and an exception to the remote pastorates of his New Divinity colleagues, Nathanial Niles voiced the irony of calling for liberty while denying it to others (Niles). Emmons preached antislavery throughout his long life and at the age of ninety-one, in 1835, presided over a meeting of the New York Antislavery Society (Park 445–46).

Particularly interesting is the African-American New Divinity pastor, Lemuel Haynes of Vermont. In 1776, Haynes's first essay, "Liberty Further Extended" called for black liberty and equality along the lines of New Divinity theology, the same year as he completed his second tour as a revolutionary soldier (Sail-lant, Bogin, Cooley, MacLam). Like other congregationalists, the New Divin-ity men did not oppose independence or service to it. But, typified by David Avery, they presented an image of bastardy if a new nation emerged from colonial status sullied by slavery.

No consistent Calvinist was more important than Samuel Hopkins, who, in developing New Divinity, introduced America's first indigenous religious thought. The development of his religious philosophy led him both to anti-slavery activism and a particular view of American freedom. In the early 1770s, Hopkins came to believe that separation from Great Britain should be made only on the basis of virtue rather than self-interest. Similarly, abolition de-manded the same level of moral purity, and a corresponding belief in aboli-tion became the test for the true patriot. The moral purity required of those who would demand liberty could be illustrated by an opposition to slavery. "For Hopkins the slavery issue furnished an ethical test not only of the gen-eral moral purity of the struggle against Britain but of the virtue of individ-ual revolutionaries as well" (Conforti, *Samuel Hopkins* 128).

Nonetheless, Hopkins, more than any other of the New Divinity men, brought to the movement a political sense. Hopkins was willing to cross reli-gious boundaries in order to unite the religious community under an anti-slavery banner, a remarkable achievement given the Congregational antipathy toward certain branches of their own sect, much less other sects. Soon after arriving at Newport, Hopkins formed an alliance with Ezra Stiles, pastor of the Second Congregational Church and no friend to New Divinity (Birdsall). But as early as 1769, Hopkins had secured an invitation to lecture in Stiles's church (HSP 2). By the early 1770s, Stiles and Hopkins joined in efforts to launch two former slaves as African missionaries. This was a campaign that

crossed New England, where it appeared on the Boston desk of Phillis Wheatley, to New Jersey, New York, and to Great Britain (serving to connect even
Congregational antislavery activism to the British) (HSP 3). The proposal made
it clear that support for the two men was a way to demonstrate opposition
to the slave trade. Meantime, the two young men, Bristol Yanna and John
Quamine, whose faith in godly intervention was undoubtedly increased when
they were enabled to buy part of their freedom by winning a lottery, were
schooled in theology by Hopkins and his antislavery colleague Levi Hart, concluding their studies under John Witherspoon at the College of New Jersey.
By Hopkins and Stiles's later account, the campaign was on its way to completion but was sidelined by the onset of the war. By the time of the 1784 account, Quamine was dead and the donations had depreciated to a fraction of
their original worth (HSP 4).

The missionary campaign led to Hopkins's involvement in the efforts leading
to Connecticut's abolition of the slave trade in 1774. Buoyed by that success,
in 1776, he wrote his famous *Dialogue on Slavery* dedicated to the Continental
Congress as the next step in moving antislavery to a political and intercolonial audience. This broadening political awareness was demonstrated again
when he expanded his antislavery circle by collaborating with Rhode Island's
Moses Brown, a convert to Quakerism after a career as a merchant and legis-
lator in Providence (Thompson). By the early 1780s, Brown and Hopkins called
for colonywide meetings of clergy of all faiths to "seek their testimony" against
the trade (HSP 5). A year later Hopkins's "Essay on the African Slave Trade"
appeared in John Carter's the *Providence Gazette* (*ProvG* 10/6; 10/13/87). Altogether Hopkins's antislavery activities represent a remarkable politicization of
a cleric who had spent the first twenty-five years of his career in obscurity.

Brown must be credited for some of Hopkins's growing political awareness.
Known in Rhode Island's commercial and legislative circle and a member of
wealthy family, Brown used his secular connections in his antislavery work
and was able to enlist the local newspapers in his campaign. John Carter not
only published Brown's articles in his *Gazette* but also sold his pamphlets in
his shop, hardly an easy position either for an avowed patriot or for a local
businessman. Brown also found another newspaper outlet in Providence when
Bennett Wheeler established a new journal in 1784, the *United States Chronicle: Political, Commercial, and Historical* (Thompson 177–78) — a newspaper,
interestingly, that receives no mention in Isaiah Thomas's *History of Printing*.
Brown's ability to find outlets for unpopular thought must be considered part

of his considerable political savvy that was not a characteristic of the late colonial antislavery movement as a whole. Unlike many of his clerical colleagues, Brown used his writings to promote political activism, sought political allies across religious lines for antislavery ends, and urged the use of the pulpit as a network for political antislavery action.

Thanks to the partnership of Brown and Hopkins, the 1780s produced a stream of Rhode Island antislavery writings (*ProvG* 1/22/85; 6/21/87; 9/8/87; 10/6/87; 10/13/87; *USC* 3/7/85; 1/12/86; 1/19/86; 8/2/87). But Hopkins, as a consistent Calvinist, continued to voice antislavery in terms of retributive New Divinity in which the depreciation of paper money was as much a reflection of God's punishment as the plagues of Egypt. Meantime, even in Connecticut, there was evidence that the conservative message of Congregationalism was waning, not a good sign for a movement that was so closely connected to a religious sect. A newspaper correspondent wondered what the point of attending church was when "we have nothing to do with our salvation" and God found people so corrupt that "our very prayers are abominable" (Essig 105). For a nation that was turning away from a wrathful God, antislavery as an antidote for God's wrath came to have diminishing power.

In the end, even with Brown at his side, Hopkins was not able to divert the course of the new nation, and he finally turned his energies to colonization, concluding that God had permitted the African slave trade as a way to Christianize the African continent. By the end of the 1780s, Hopkins and Brown supported the adoption of the Constitution on the basis that, without it, the existence of slavery would lead to anarchy and further diminish the chance of abolition. As David Brion Davis observed, "Instead of being the instrument for American emancipation, the slave, it appeared, had become the greatest peril to union" (299).

Even with their growing political awareness, the New Divinity and Quaker writers were not propagandists. They sought to persuade along religious lines, not force the issue regardless of means. Despite any other drawbacks, that characteristic alone disadvantaged the antislavery activists when compared to the patriot press. Although religious leaders would involve themselves in seeking political solutions and, in Rhode Island and Connecticut, at least, have some success in utilizing local venues for the discussion, the major hindrance to the broad dissemination of the antislavery discussion was the patriots' rapid influence over the press. After 1774, newspapers increasingly aligned themselves with the patriots and a rhetoric that had no place for an antislavery discussion framed in the shame and guilt of New Divinity theology, the sentimental excesses of Quaker writing, or the lecturing of British antislavery leaders. Only in Connecticut, where newspapers were in the hands of the Congregationalist Greens, was the New Divinity slavery debate thoroughly aired in the 1770s, perhaps playing the essential role in bringing about that colony's abolition of the trade. But the system of exchange newspapers, which had proved so helpful for the dispersal of the *Boston Gazette*'s revolutionary thought, would be a rare conduit for the dispersal of antislavery essays by either the New Divinity ministers or the Quaker writers.

A broader acceptance of antislavery discussion was likely at the hands of a third group of antislavery activists less easily defined than either the Quaker activists or New Divinity ministers. This was an eclectic group that included patriots such as Thomas Paine and Benjamin Rush, Boston merchant James Swan, Baptist preacher John Allen, and even occasional satirists such as Connecticut's John Trumbull. These writers sought to place antislavery in an emerging American ideology. That was a frame that lessened the threat of New Divinity apocalypse, distanced antislavery from the British, and tempered the Quaker sentimental tradition by finding a middle ground that did not eschew practical considerations. Nonetheless, by the mid-1770s the attempts of powerful writers as Rush and Paine were not sufficient to break the antislavery arguments out of the mold of British Quakerism or a form of Congregationalism that viewed slavery as another evidence of a slothful, secular society. Thus, dominant American antislavery rhetoric came to reflect regular characteristics: the Golden Rule, the displeasure of God, natural law as expressed by John Locke, the cult of sensibility, and the portrayal of America as corrupt and guilty. The theme of American guilt became the defining one at a time of the increasing articulation by patriots that America was already pure, even given the existence of slavery, and needed only to reject the Old World as *its* corrupting influence. The continuance of the slave trade was put at British feet, and thus served to exempt colonial Americans from taking on other antislavery actions on a colonywide or national level.

At the same time, proslavery argument also had regular characteristics that tended to maintain the slavery debate in the arena as defined by the Quakers and Calvinists. On occasion, relocated West Indian planters joined the debate to charge inborn racial differences. Antislavery writers who wrote in the Calvinistic and Quaker modes generally avoided such invitations to bring to the fore this most deeply felt and least eradicable prejudice. One of the remarkable aspects about Benjamin Rush's antislavery discussion, as the next chapter explores, was that it did discuss perceptions of inborn racial difference. Although a large number of American colonists, northern as well as southern, may have held views of inborn racial difference, the argument or its response played a minor role in the slavery debate when compared to other characteristics. Jordan believes the view of black racial inferiority was changing during the revolutionary period, noting that Arthur Lee concluded his 1764 diatribe proclaiming black inferiority by indicating that lack of education might be as much to blame as inborn characteristics, although it might be noted that the pamphlet was written when Lee was in Scotland and published in London (Jordan 309). Lee's rejection of inborn inferiority did not translate into his later antislavery views. In 1767, his newspaper essay addressed to members of the Virginia House of Burgesses called on divine retribution and natural law as reasons to oppose the institution, not equality of racial characteristics (*VG*-Rind 3/19/67).

This refusal of most indigenous colonial essayists, pro or con, to confront perceived racial difference worked to maintain the public slavery debate in biblical argument and ignored the practical concerns of colonists, whose understanding of blacks in terms of racial stereotypes gave them limited imagination as to the role of slaves once freed.

Almost missing from the public debate were American southerners. Only the first part of Lee's 1767 essay was published, although even the one part played some role in Virginia's bill a month later, laying a higher tax on imported slaves. After Lee, however, an early iron curtain descended over the southern colonies. Slave advertisements served as the public rationale for southern slavery, and the advertisements provided no room for an opposing voice. Faced with the ongoing negative portrayal of blacks in newspapers and advertisements, much less the institutional support of slavery, the slavery debate was challenged to alter notions that undergirded the institution and relegated slave and free blacks to subservient positions.

CHAPTER SIX

Shame and Guilt in
the Garden of the Innocent

James Otis may be said to have ushered in the antislavery debate of the revolutionary period in his 1764 pamphlet that clearly put antislavery on the radical agenda. Otis's example was followed in 1767 when a Bostonian Son of Liberty, Nathaniel Appleton, sought to anchor the antislavery debate amid the wave of early patriot successes. "The years 1765 and 1766 will be ever memorable for the glorious stand which America has made for her liberties; how much glory will it add to use if at the same time we are establishing Liberty for ourselves and children, we show the same regard to all mankind that came among us?" (Appleton 2).

From this unctuous and flattering beginning, Nathaniel Appleton eschewed religious argument to make a place for antislavery along economic and practical lines: the slave trade only enriched its traders while preventing the white immigration that would serve to settle the continent; always expecting the slave to "throw off his burden" by revolt, the institution kept communities in constant fear; work taken over by slaves served to prevent white servants from similar work because they would not do work they associated with slavery. In an argument that offered an alternative to the religious discourse that dominated the issue, Appleton even suggested the institution promoted prostitution among lower-class girls because slaves took over the work that such girls could perform.

Appleton was a man of influence in Boston's revolutionary circles (although not to be confused with the earlier Congregational minister of the same name), a Harvard graduate (admitted as fourth in social standing of his class), son of a Congregational minister, and eventually a successful merchant and candle manufacturer (*Sibley's* 12:354–59). His position in the movement is suggested by the pamphlet publication of the essay by Edes and Gill, although it did not appear in the *Gazette*. The essay was undoubtedly prompted by Massachusetts's increasing antislavery activities. In 1765 and 1766, Worcester, then Boston, instructed their representatives to seek legislation to end slavery. In 1767, a vigorous effort was made in the Massachusetts House of Representatives to restrict the importation of slaves, and Appleton's essay, calling on the patriot fervor engendered by repudiation of the Stamp Act, was part of efforts to push the issue. As noted earlier, after much maneuvering, the antislavery bill was simply lost, disappearing suddenly and silently when legal maneuvers to kill it were exhausted (G. Moore 126–28). Appleton remained an active patriot but wrote no more antislavery essays.

Unlike Appleton's pamphlet, the 1770 election sermon by Samuel Cooke, New Divinity pastor of Cambridge's Second Church, was published as both a pamphlet and a newspaper insertion (*MS* 7/29/73). Appleton had made no excuses for American slavery, but Cooke, in the section addressing slavery, put the slave trade at British feet and was undoubtedly intended to embarrass Governor Thomas Hutchinson. Cooke's conclusion, however, served to separate the issue from the patriots by calling upon issues of conscience: "Ethiopia has long stretched out her hands to us. Let not sordid gain, acquired by the merchandize of slaves, and the souls of men harden our hearts against her piteous moans. When God ariseth, and when he visiteth, what shall we answer!" (Cooke 22).

It is unlikely that the sermon was heard by many Massachusetts legislators in any case. Following the Boston Massacre, Hutchinson ordered the colony's general court to meet in Cambridge. In response, the Sons of Liberty scheduled a separate election day sermon for Boston (continuing to give a sacred air to the revolutionary cause). Their choice for the occasion was one of Boston's revered old guard ministers, Charles Chauncy, of the Old Brick Church. In the remonstrances over the move and with blood from the Boston Massacre undoubtedly still fresh on King Street, there was no room for antislavery in Chauncy's call for retribution (Griffin 147–49).

Yet even in this period of propagandistic fervor and after the failure of the 1771 bill, Massachusetts antislavery activists managed to maintain the pressure on the colony's House of Representatives. As Adams and his circle sought to build a colonywide coalition against Great Britain that ignored the slavery issue, Massachusetts antislavery activists persistently brought the antislavery issue to the political forefront by means of a series of slave petitions from 1773 to 1777 and the pamphlets that called attention to them. Each time, the petitions failed, disappearing into the nether world of committee assignment. The petition barrage kept alive the discussion, insisting the issue was not simply the end of the slave trade, as the patriots argued, but abolition. In the third of a series of petitions, for example (Aptheker, *And Why Not* 5–10), a group of Boston slaves asked not only for an end to the slave trade, as a minimal effort, but for redress of those already in slavery.

Like Appleton's essay, this petition made its case on a base of secular concern — the role and cost of free blacks in society. Blacks who were "vicious," would be punished by law, but "there are many others of quite different characters, and who, if made free, would soon be able as well as willing to bear a part of the Public Charge." Challenging the assumptions embedded in advertisements, news stories, and common wisdom, the petition addressed perceived differences. Bondsmen and women "are discreet, sober, honest, and industrious; and may it be not said of many, that they are virtuous and religious" (Aptheker, *And Why Not* 47–48).

The petition also attempted to confront the practical concerns of European colonists, and, in retrospect, public discussion of these issues expressed by bondsmen and women themselves would have been among the most important. But the voices of Boston's black colonists were seldom heard in the realm of public discourse. Their circulation most often came by hand — presented personally to the legislators by the black petitioners. Although James Bowdoin was known to make public many documents that came to the council during his long tenure from 1757 to 1774, slave petitions were not among them. Nor did Adams choose to give them public voice in the *Boston Gazette* despite his apparent role as an intermediary between one group of black petitioners and the House, as demonstrated in a request to John Pickering to be kept abreast of the petition's development in order to "enable me to communicate to them the general outlines of your Design" (Adams, *Writings* 3:78; G. Moore 136). It is not to be unnecessarily cynical to suggest that such a piece of information would also have been helpful to the revolutionary circle who wished to avoid confrontation on the issue.

The petition did find publication in the *Massachusetts Spy,* although how it came to be published in this patriot organ that so seldom strayed from the patriot line is unclear. The petition also found publication as part of a pamphlet of four antislavery pieces that included a rare essay by a black writer, "Felix." Like the petition writers, Felix argued that freed bondsmen and women would not necessarily be a charge to the society but concluded on a dramatic note: "We have no Property! We have no Wives! No Children! We have no City! No Country! But we have a Father in Heaven and we are determined as far as Grace shall enable us" (*Appendix* 9–11; Aptheker, *And Why Not* 6). The pamphlet was published in the shop of Ezekiel Russell, who had already alienated much of patriot Boston by printing Thomas Hutchinson's political organ, the *Boston Censor,* and whose brother, Joseph Russell, was a printer of the loyalist hybrid, the *Massachusetts Gazette and Boston Post-Boy and Advertiser* (Thomas 229). Since Ezekiel Russell was a publisher of most of Boston's antislavery works, his connection to Hutchinson undoubtedly served to further attach antislavery with Toryism. Writing for posterity, his fellow Boston printer, Isaiah Thomas, dismissed him: "He published nothing of more consequence than pamphlets, most of which were small" (Thomas 153).

The petition that had encouraged so much written attention was read in the House of Representatives January 28, 1773, and recorded succinctly, probably by Adams as clerk: "A petition of a Number of Negroes, praying that they may be declared free, on certain conditions." Once read, it was "ordered to lie," a tabling act. A motion, whose author is not recorded, resuscitated it sufficiently for the formation of a committee to prepare a bill for preventing the "future Imports of Slaves into this Province," an immediate dilution of the original request (*Journal* 195). But, as in the past, the proposed bill was never presented.

Although encumbered by continuing tory associations, Boston's black campaign against slavery continued. In 1777 another slave petition was offered to the Massachusetts legislature that expressed "Astonishment" that slavery had not been ended by the revolutionary fervor (Aptheker, *And Why Not* 47–48). Signed by Prince Hall, then emerging into leadership of Boston's black community, and five others, the petition made no headway. The Massachusetts legislative chose a delaying action, moving to obtain Congress's view on abolition. As Philip S. Foner commented, "Since Congress never bothered to reply, the Massachusetts legislature could console itself with having acted in the nation's interest by refusing to enact an abolition law" (351).

It was not until eleven years later, when slavery was less of a propagandistic concern, that Massachusetts ended slavery by legislative action. In 1788, spurred by the kidnapping of three black Bostonians subsequently sold into slavery in Martinique, Hall initiated a protesting petition, this time accompanied by another petition from Boston's church leadership that argued for both an end to the slave trade and protection of Boston's black population. The resulting legislation outlawing slavery in Massachusetts concluded a colonial and state history of delay on the subject. John Adams blamed the delay on white laborers fearing the competition of black workers (P. Foner 354), although Adams was clearly part of the revolutionary cadre that had been successful in keeping even the discussion of abolition off the patriot agenda until the Revolution was well commenced.

As Boston's black colonists turned to petitions to catch the eye and sympathy of Boston leaders, one black American had already captured attention on both sides of the Atlantic. Phillis Wheatley, however, had no more success in breaking down patriot barriers than the petitioners. In 1770 her "An Elegaic Poem to George Whitefield" was put forward in the antislavery campaign to counter the argument of inborn racial differences that was so seldom discussed publicly. Indeed, the Boston broadside of the poem prominently displayed her name, "Phillis — a Negro" in type larger that the subject of the poem. The second edition (although not the first) of her 1773 book of collected poems, published in London, included the testament from the colony's governor and councilors that she was both a Negro and composer of the work (W. Robinson 15).

The Whitefield elegy, the first publication of her public career, came at the hands of Boston printers known for their Tory associations, most prominently, Ezekiel Russell, less so, John Boyle, who was nonetheless copublisher of the loyalist *The Massachusetts Gazette and Boston News Letter* (Thomas 230). Whether by accident or design, this established an ongoing association between Wheatley and the Tory press. The 1772 advertisements for a public subscription to her first proposed book of poems was made in the *Boston Censor* (*BC* 2/29; 3/14; 4/18/72) and the *Boston Post-Boy* (*BPB* 4/1/73); a subsequent proposal for the book's publication in London was made in the *News-Letter* and the *Post-Boy* (*BNL* 4/29/73; *BPB* 4/16/73); her "Farewell to America" poem was published in the *News-Letter* (4/22/73); and both newspapers published accounts of her trip to London (*BNL* 5/6/73; *BPB* 5/10/73) and the return of the "extraordinary Poetic Genius" (*BNL* 9/16/73; *BPB* 9/20/73). The *Post-Boy* published a letter lauding her abilities (*BPB* 3/21/74), and Ezekiel Russell used her famous image for his 1782 almanac (A3). Meantime, her book was published in London, her poetry in British magazines, and she became a colonial celebrity even before her collection had been published in the colonies. Benjamin Rush referenced her abilities in a footnote in his 1773 antislavery pamphlet (Rush 2n); Richard Nisbet referenced her, negatively, in his response to Rush (Nisbet 17). A Boston satirist made Wheatley the subject of attack (*IC* 1/29/78).

Through it all the *Boston Gazette* was mute, although not so the *Boston Evening-Post* or the *Massachusetts Spy*. And outside of Boston, the Whitefield poem extended her reputation. But in Philadelphia, the Tory association was furthered when her poems were published by Joseph Crukshank, the Quaker printer of most of the city's antislavery pamphlets; still, it should be noted that William Goddard, later the most ardent of patriots, also published the Whitefield poem, as did Solomon Southwick in Newport, Rhode Island (W. Robinson 17–19).

What can explain the *Gazette*'s silence on this colonial phenomenon? Like Crispus Attucks, Wheatley was destined to play no role in approved revolutionary rhetoric. Adams and Edes's refusal to acknowledge Wheatley was not out of character for the newspaper that had confused Attucks's racial identity and misinformed readers about the Somerset decision. But it also represented the difficulty posed by the American-English connections of religious reform movements that would most affect Quaker antislavery activities.

Like the Quakers, although to a less extent, George Whitefield had established an English-American binary for evangelical congregationalism, and Phillis Wheatley was one casualty. Influenced by her mistress, Susanna Wheatley, Phillis Wheatley was a pious follower of the New Divinity strain of Congregationalism represented by Samuel Hopkins. She was also part of the Anglo-American evangelical circle that swirled around Whitefield, which included the countess of Huntingdon and the earl of Dartmouth, both of whom became Wheatley supporters. Wheatley's admiring tribute to the earl of Dartmouth when he was named secretary of state for the American colonies in August of 1772 was not an act to endear her to the patriots under any circumstance perhaps but was particularly "insurrectionary," in Betsy Erkkila's analysis, because of its direct use of her own slave experience (Erkkila 234).

Perhaps more disturbing, however, was the Wheatley connection to the British humanitarian John Thorton, a philanthropist who supported Christianization efforts through the auspices of the Society of the Propagation of the Gospel in Foreign Parts. Apart from any patriot desire to repress antislavery activity, her connection by way of Thorton to the feared and despised S.P.G. was sufficient reason to ignore her work and discourage its colonial dissemination.

Wheatley's publication history in the Tory press bears some resemblance to that of her predecessor, Briton Hammon, whose work was published by Green and Russell in 1760. Although he was born a slave in Boston, Hammon's narrative of his subsequent adventures in the West Indies and London did not reference race, constructed instead along the lines of the familiar and popular tradition established by Mary Rowlandson in her story of Indian capture. Hammon's race was not a secret, and, indeed, the attachment "by a Negro" suggests race was a conscious element (Hammon). But printers Green and Russell had long-lived connections to the evangelical tradition and its antislavery stance. Not surprisingly, Hammon was connected, like Wheatley, to the countess of Huntingdon and the British antislavery circle. While it may seem ironical that the first narrative of a black American writer was in the frame of an Indian captivity tale, Hammon's choice to tell his story this way might be considered an early strategy to include black colonists under the powerful mythological umbrella of the genre as described by John Sekora and provide an alternative to the rhetorical choices of the Quaker antislavery writers. By 1760, however, Adams was already a political writer, the *Boston Gazette* already a vehicle of demonstrated political power, and Hammon's connection to the countess of Huntingdon and its perceived connections to the S.P.G. was no more attractive at that time than it would be fourteen years later.

One scholar believes it was Wheatley herself, as a "sagacious business woman," who called off the Boston publication of a volume of her poems for the chance to make more money in England (Rawley 676). Another scholar argues that the move to seek British publication came after the book was rejected for "racist reasons," although the letter he cites seems to suggest it was Wheatley's Boston friends who wanted a London publication (Robinson 13). The collection was available in Boston in 1774 and sold by the Loyalist booksellers Cox and Berry, who advertised the book in the Tory newspaper (*MG&BPB* 7/4/74). By this time, any window that may have allowed Wheatley to become a spokeswoman for indigenous antislavery had closed. The sale of the book by Cox and Berry; the publications of her poems by nonpatriot printers; the attention she received in colonial loyalist publications; the much-heralded London publication and the resulting reviews in British magazines; the connection with Wheatley's admirer, the countess of Hungtingdon; and Wheatley's connection, even tenuously, to the S.P.G all worked to confine Wheatley to the British, rather than American, antislavery movement.

For such reasons, antislavery discussion in the 1770s remained primarily in European hands in Boston and throughout the colonies. Periodically, however, Wheatley's succinct quatrains were reprinted in newspapers, as "By a Negro," in the *New-London Gazette*:

> *O mighty God! let conscience seize the mind*
> *Of inconsistent man, who wish to find*
> *A partial god to vindicate their cause*
> *And plead their freedom while they break its laws.*
>
> (NLG 5/1/72)

Boston's antislavery activity of 1773 prompted revisions of two already-published Boston antislavery pamphlets, both written by British immigrants, the first being the merchant James Swan's 1772 work. Swan called the work a "sermon," noting that he believed himself called upon to write it upon his arrival in America. The pamphlet argued on religious, economic, and moral grounds but concluded with some rather specific recommendations for the ending of the slave trade.

How a "sermon" at the hands of a newly arrived British merchant was received by the colony legislature is unknown, but clearly more of a crowd pleaser was that of another "British Bostonian," as he signed himself. John Allen published a best-selling pamphlet as a result of the popular reception given his sermon as a visiting preacher at Boston's Second Baptist Church (Bumstead and Clark). Allen arrived from Great Britain shortly after the *Gaspee* incident, when Rhode Islanders set fire to a British revenue cutter run aground as it was chasing a colonial ship suspected of carrying smuggled cargo. Patriots sought to rekindle a slumping patriot flame by turning the incident into a new propaganda thrust. Allen's sermon used the Rhode Island action as a call for the recognition of America's "blood bought... native laws." They were as much rights, he said in what was possibly a Somerset reference, as the "air they breath in or... the light in the morning when the sun rises." In 1773, for its fourth reprinting, Allen added antislavery to the polemic because, he said, the antislavery piece had been turned down when offered individually to an unnamed newspaper (Allen 1).

Once it included the antislavery addendum, the subsequent printing history of Allen's pamphlet evidences how the patriot fold and its printing-house followers distanced themselves from antislavery discussion. Kneeland and Davis were probably delighted to publish the first two editions of Allen's original *Oration Upon Liberty.* Its accessible, popular style and patriotic theme helped promote a brisk sale — not to be eschewed by the struggling firm just established by Samuel Kneeland's son, Daniel (Thomas 146). Allen, as a Baptist, represented a sect that had not previously committed itself to the revolutionary column. When the antislavery remarks were appended, the pamphlet — no matter its previous popularity, its Baptist connections, or the economic straits of Kneeland and Davis — found publication only in the shop of Ezekiel Russell. Its fifth edition fared slightly better, at the hands of Ebenezer Watson in Hartford, printer of many antislavery works and a patriot of moderate stripe. A sixth appeared in Wilmington, Delaware, from the shop of Irishman James Adams without the addendum.

In his next pamphlet, Allen attempted to meld the patriot ideology and a call for the freedom of slaves into one work. Despite its ostensible patriot theme, it concluded with a diatribe aimed at patriot leaders. "Blush ye pretended votaries for freedom! yet trifling Patriots! who are making a vain parade of being the advocates for the liberties of mankind who are thus making a mockery of your profession, by trampling on the sacred natural rights and privileges of the Africans; for while you are fasting, praying, non-importing, remonstrating, resolving, and pleading for a restoration of your charter rights, you are at the same time continuing this lawless, cruel, inhuman, and abominable practice of restraining your fellow creatures" (27).

No one clamored for this printing contract; once again, Allen's antislavery work ended up in the shop of Ezekiel Russell, now seeking a fresh start in Salem. There were no republications. Russell made several more moves but never became an official loyalist and returned to Boston after the war to print ballads that were sold by peddlers (Thomas 153).

Allen disappeared from the revolutionary scene. Present-day scholars wonder how to reconcile the "almost total lack of connection between Allen and the Revolutionary leaders with the incontrovertible fact that the *Oration Upon Liberty* was one of the most popular pamphlets of the prewar period" (Bumstead and Clark 560). Revolutionary leaders would not have appreciated Allen's murky past, but there clearly was no place for his revolutionary rhetoric when it was tied to antislavery.

Thus, antislavery received limited public hearing in Boston, the most influential of all colonial cities in establishing the revolutionary rhetoric. Once removed from Boston, antislavery discussion largely lost the voices of the slaves themselves. Also lost were writers like Appleton, Swan, and Allen, who were exploring antislavery discussion in ways that addressed secular concerns. Their place was primarily filled by religious reformers whose rhetoric failed in its efforts to make antislavery a revolutionary issue.

Philadelphia's Anthony Benezet established Quaker themes in a 1767 pamphlet, a "short representation" that combined the cult of sensibility with an appeal to natural law by quotations from dozens of learned and legal references (Benezet, *Caution*). But it was in 1771 that another Benezet "pamphlet" (a loose term to accommodate this 153-page publication) firmly established the major Quaker theme of African innocence. Quoting early explorer Francis Moore, Benezet wrote that Africa "'abounds with grains and fruits, cattle, poultry, etc. The earth yields all the year a fresh supply of food: Few clothes are requisite and little art necessary in making them.'" Marriage was sacred in this new world in which no corrupting serpent appeared until the arrival of the European. The Eden theme was clearly made. "'The whole revived in my mind the idea of our first parents, and I seemed to contemplate the world in its primitive state.'"

Africa in this state of nature was compared to the capture of the natives, the horrors of the Middle Passage, and the cruelty of the auction block. "Mothers are seen hanging over their daughters, bedewing their naked breasts with tears, and daughters clinging to their parents, not knowing what new stage of distress must follow their separation, or whether they shall ever meet again. If they will not separate as ready as their masters think proper, the Whipper is called for, and the lash is exercised" (Benezet, *Some* 16, 128).

Soon after this publication, Benezet's Quaker printer, Joseph Crukshank, printed an antislavery tract by Methodist John Wesley that reinforced the theme of African innocence. "Guinea ... far from being an horrid, dreary, barren country, is one of the most fruitfel, as well as one of the most pleasant countries in the known world." Until the Europeans debauched the "pleasant contries," there "were seldom any wars, but were in general quiet and peaceable. But the white man taught them drunkenness and avarice, and then hired them to fell one another" (Wesley 8, 17).

The theme of African innocence found further support in the argument of natural rights as espoused by John Locke. Whatever his real influence, Locke was certainly the most *acknowledged* philosophical influence of his time and, next to the Bible, may have been the most-quoted authority in colonial political writing. As antislavery writers unendingly pointed out, Locke, writing in *Two Treatises on Government,* pronounced that natural law entitled all men to life, liberty, and protection of property, including property in self as a right of birth. But proslavery writers could also turn to Locke. In the same work, in a passage intended to indicate opposition to slaveholding, Locke argued bondage could be justified on one basis — the capture of men in a "just war," that is, not slave-catching expeditions, in which perpetual slavery was the only choice over certain death.

Juxtaposing European corruption to the picture of African innocence, Quaker antislavery writers claimed that Europeans had promoted African wars merely for the capture of slaves. Since the capture of men was the intrinsic purpose of such wars, the offer of slavery as an escape from death did not satisfy Locke's ground rules. "Did Sir John Hawkins, and many others seize upon men, women, and children, who were at peace in their fields or houses, merely to save them from death?" Wesley asked. "Was it to save them from death, that they knocked out the brains of those they could not bring away?" (Wesley 37).

The New Jersey Quaker, David Cooper, another of Crukshank's clients, carried European culpability to American shores. Although arguing a religious view, Cooper was typical of all antislavery writers in his refusal to excuse Americans from responsibility, even on the basis that slavery was an accepted practice by the African. "Every one of those unfortunate men who are pretended to be slaves has a right to be declared free, for he never lost his liberty; he could not lose it; his prince had no power to dispose of him. This right he carried around with him, and is entitled every where to get it" (Cooper 8). White colonial Americans, regardless of whether they had not participated in the original purchase, could not escape the guilt by blaming the practice on its British antecedents. In fact, the culpability of Americans was emphasized by the American system of slavery. Benezet charged that bondage in the South "was more oppressive than the most of us in the northern colonies have had an opportunity of forming any idea of" (Benezet, *Some* 6). Sharp was most critical. The treatment of slaves in Virginia was as barbarous as in Jamaica and in Barbados. He was appalled that escaped slaves were pursued as a matter of public policy (Benezet, *Some* 85).

No pamphleteer addressed American guilt as dramatically as Wesley. To plantation owners, he cried: "*You* therefore are guilty, yea principally guilty, of all these frauds, robberies and murders . . . the blood of all these wretches, who died before their time . . . lies upon your head" (Wesley 52).

Thus, the philosophy of natural rights, already powerful, was coupled with the lost Eden-like innocence of the African. When Africa was pictured as the Garden, the black family as the original inhabitants, and the European as the despoiler and serpent, enormous visual and religious imagery was added to philosophical theory.

In this Quaker meld of sensibility, the Golden Rule, and natural law, the role of freed slaves in a contemporary society received little attention. But William Dillwyn, a former pupil of Benezet, addressed the practical concern of support for the freed bondsman and undoubtedly would have played a larger role in the rhetoric of antislavery had he not settled in England and adopted the British antislavery movement as his primary objective.

By virtue of Benezet's influence, however, Philadelphia produced the antislavery pamphlet of the colonial period that most approached the stature of *The Selling of Joseph*. Benjamin Rush's *An Address to the Inhabitants of the British Settlements in America upon Slave-Keeping* was published in 1773 from the shop of the patriot John Dunlap rather than Crukshank's Quaker press. At least three other publishing houses printed it, although Dunlap was the only patriot printer to do so. It was the only pamphlet of the period other than Tom Paine's *Common Sense* that was to be reprinted in a colonial newspaper (*CC* 3/30; 4/6; 5/4; 5/11/73).

It was not a pamphlet that sprang spontaneously from the pen of this peripatetic figure of revolutionary America. Although Rush was born and raised a Presbyterian, his family came from Quaker stock, and Quakers, including Benezet, were among his wide range of friends (Essig 22–24). In 1773, with a bill calling for the prohibition of the slave trade before the Pennsylvania General Assembly, Benezet asked him to write the pamphlet to gain support of the Presbyterian members of the assembly. The resulting pamphlet and a second edition that defended the original work were Rush's primary antislavery publications of the period. Indeed, Rush owned a slave himself at this time, a man he did not free until 1788, soon after he (along with Benjamin Franklin) joined the Pennsylvania Society for Promoting the Abolition of Slavery. Rush was not a member of the society when it was first formed in 1774, nor did he participate directly in efforts to obtain the passage of the Pennsylvania abolition law of 1780 (Hawke).

However, late in 1772, when asked by his friend Benezet to write the essay, Rush had been back from his medical studies in Edinburgh for less than three years. Not only was he fresh from the liberalizing Scottish Empiricist influences of that city but, according to a biographer, he carried a sense of personal guilt possibly connected to a sexual incident, which may have made the abolition movement as then defined particularly meaningful (Hawke 41). Those influences converged into a major statement that brought the many threads of the discussion into an American context.

Much of the essay had discernible roots in the Quaker rhetoric, yet Rush gave them his own flavor that showed sensitivity to an emerging American nationalism. His efficient summary of antislavery rhetoric suggested the arguments were well-known enough to need no further explication: to say that the black race descended from Canaan's curse was "absurd"; free men were much more economically productive than slave labor; if God had permitted Jews to keep slaves in the time of the Old Testament, it was for reasons that were appropriate at the time; if planters really wanted to save the souls of Africans, they would allow them to read and write; and there could be no just war when Africans had been stolen.

From this detached précis, Rush moved to sensibility. In a passage that could have been written by Benezet, he called upon his readers to imagine West Indies slavery. "Behold one covered with stripes, into which melted wax is poured—another tied down to a block or a stake—a third suspended in the air by his thumbs—a fourth obliged to set or stand upon red hot iron—a fifth I cannot relate it. See here one without a limb, whose only crime to regain his Liberty—another led to a Gallows for eating a morsel of bread . . . a third famishing on a gibbet—a fourth, in a flame of Fire!—his shrieks pierce the very heavens—O! God! Where is thy Vengeance!—O! Humanity—Justice—Liberty—Religion!—Where,—where are ye fled?"

Rush's solution for ending slavery was a call to end the slave trade by petitioning colonial assemblies. In the only reference to the Somerset case, Rush noted a *united* strategy of petition—another point that most Quaker writing failed to make—would be more successful than an effort based on "a late decision in favor of a Virginia slave, at Westminster-Hall."

Despite its Quaker referents, the Rush pamphlet sought new paths. The picture of horrors that Rush painted was of the West Indies, not of the slave block in Philadelphia or a South Carolina plantation, and, unlike the British writers such as Sharp and Wesley, Rush did not equate the West Indies with American slavery. Nor did Rush explore the stolen-from-paradise theme. His emphasis was on the African, not the birthplace. Rush did not ignore the theme of guilt, concluding, indeed, that "national crimes require national punishments." But he did not make America the carrier of debauchery. Instead, Rush called upon the American sense of mission as part of his antislavery argument: "Remember the eyes of all Europe are fixed upon you, to preserve an asylum for freedom in this country, after the last pillars of it are fallen in every other quarter of the Globe" (Rush, *Address* 3, 22–24, 28, 26).

Rush's second antislavery tract was a response to the reaction of a former West Indian slave owner residing in Philadelphia. Richard Nisbet, in his own thirty-page pamphlet, argued that Negroes were "naturally inferior to whites." Although Nisbet contended that West Indian slavery was not as heartless or as cruel as pictured by Rush and that slavery was economically necessary, his major affirmation of slavery was on the question of perceived racial differences. At a time when most proslavery argument was anchored in the Old Testament, Nisbet was unabashedly a writer who believed the white race was inherently superior to the black. "There never was a civilized nation of any other complexion than white, nor ever any individual eminent in either action or speculation." Africans, Nisbet charged, had produced no art, science, or product and had worshiped no Supreme Being. Moreover, "they seem utterly unacquainted with friendship, gratuity and every tie of the same kind," he charged, dismissing the tears of slave-block separations as "high colouring." Finally, the unstoppable tirade referred to the "stupidity of the natives" and charged that the example "of a negro girl writing a few silly poems," presumably Phillis Wheatley, was insufficient proof that "blacks are not deficient in understanding" (Nisbet 15, 25).

In his rebuttal, Rush absolutely refused to accept the Nisbet thesis of black inferiority, claiming any differences were environmentally related, another new argument for the time most commonly associated with Scottish Presbyterian thought. Rush refused to admit natural-born inferiority, as if quite aware that any equivocation on this issue would doom the antislavery cause: "You have aimed to established Principles, which justify the most extensive and cruel Depredations which have been made by Conquerors and Tyrants" (By a Pennsylvanian [Rush] 52). Less heartrending rhetoric exists in this pamphlet than in the previous one. The essay was a carefully focused reply, addressed to Nisbet rather than the guilt of a nation, and called upon readers' sense rather than sensibility.

The Rush-Nisbet exchange was important in the dialogue on slavery, because, as in the Appleton pamphlet, it illustrated that the discussion could be framed in new approaches, including one of racial difference that so seldom appeared in the colonial discussion.

That argument, however, or any others, was not to come again from the Rush pen. It was a period of financial difficulty for him, and it may be that his stand on slavery contributed to a sudden drop in his patients (Hawke 108). His financial losses turned out to be transitory when he turned his writing talents to more acceptable subjects in the patriot arsenal and to regional interests, including a decided switch to Pennsylvania conservatives Whigs. Such essays received ready publication in the Pennsylvania press that had eschewed publication of his antislavery works (*PJ* 12/22/73; 6/22/74; 5/21/76; 6/4/76; 6/11/76).

In the summer of 1774, with the Continental Congress scheduled to begin its business in the city in August, Dunlap published a lengthy pamphlet by Philadelphian Richard Wells ostensibly devoted to a discussion of nonimportation. Upon examination, the ostensible purpose of the pamphlet seems part of yet another strategy to find a national audience for antislavery. Appearing first as a series of newspaper essays in Dunlap's *Pennsylvania Packet,* the nonimportation discussion had already drawn attention, and, if we are to believe Dunlap's introduction to the pamphlet, had established a clamor for reprints of the whole series. In the final segment of the newspaper series, however, early in August as delegates were arriving and settling in, Wells added antislavery to his discussion, which became part of the pamphlet. Not unaware of the intercolonial nature of his readers, Wells noted how the "noble, spirited, and virtuous Assembly of Virginia" had sought to end the slave trade only to have the bill disallowed by the British (R. Wells 83). Wells proposed that only the strength of intercolonial cooperation would make such British actions more difficult. The usual Quaker flourishes were generally missing in favor of the espousal of immediate and practical ways to eliminate slavery—the reduction of substantial bonds Pennsylvania and New Jersey required for the manumission of slaves, for one. Here was no dependence on British authority, he might have added if he had been less cognizant of giving political offense.

Other non-Quaker writers similarly honed their arguments on points of sense, avoiding the Quaker and New Divinity arguments of moral outrage and guilt. But no pamphlet more avoided sentimentality than a Swiftean satire of Nisbet's work. The author made short work of John Woolman's writings, "the dull productions of a visionary enthusiast," recommended intractable slaves be forced to do their work with a doorpost nailed to their ears, and finally suggested that the bodies of those who died on the Middle Passage "might be cured in pickle" for future consumption. "I have never heard that their kind of meat is deemed unwholesome, but on the contrary, that the Cannibals are a hardy robust race of people" (*Personal Slavery* 3; Scherer).

Further evidence that the slavery dialogue could be conducted outside the sphere of moral outrage was illustrated in the publication of the Harvard College commencement debate of 1773 and published by the Bostonian John Boyle, partner of loyalist-leaning Joseph Russell. As published in *A Forensic Debate*, the interpretation of natural law was the point of debate between Theodore Parsons and Eliphalet Pearson, but perceived differences quickly became part of the discussion. Indeed, for the proslavery advocate, natural law was a smoke screen preventing the discussion of perceived racial difference. The African in his natural state was already in a slavery to the "tyrannizing power of lust and passion" and thus it was unnecessary to seek permission for enslavement, any more than it was necessary to seek permission from a "child, an idiot or a madman" as the character of an African was a compound of all three (Bruns 284). His opponent responded that if the principle of natural law "lies in the quality of the hair...I would advise every person, whose hair is inclined to deviate from a right line, to be upon his guard" (Bruns 284), a line of argument that may have been picked up from the Somerset discussion reprinted from English sources (*VG*-Purdie and Dixon 8/20/72).

Samuel Hopkins used the form of a debate for his pamphlet dedicated to the Continental Congress in 1776. His argument was made on familiar ground, although the wrath of God was not introduced until the final paragraphs. What was less familiar in his argument was his discussion of the role of race prejudice. Why, he asked, are we not affected by the misery of the slaves before our eyes? "The reason is obvious. It is because they are negroes, and fit for nothing but slaves, and we have been used to look at them in a mean contemptible light, and our education has filled us with strong prejudice against them, and led us to consider them, not as our breathren [sic], or in any degree on a level with us, but as quite another species of animal, made only to serve us and our children, and as happy in bondage as in other state." The answer, he concluded, was to address the underlying prejudice. "If we could only divest ourselves of these strong prejudices which have insensibly fixed on our minds...we begin to feel towards them as we should towards our children and neighbors" (Hopkins 34).

Hopkins, even as an antislavery proponent who could synthesize New Divinity and Quaker traditions, was unable to divert the stream of Quaker emotion that called for an end to slavery on the basis of empathetic feeling. As the antislavery movement continued to base itself upon feeling into the next century, proslavery advocates found they could equally support their views by the same token, the generous feelings engendered, for example, by beneficent paternalism. What Hopkins and other congregationalists shared with the Quakers, however, was the characteristic that was most damaging to the success of the antislavery position. Both sects were out of step with a revolutionary movement that refused to carry the burden of guilt. The revolutionary generation favored a birth image of innocence rising from corruption. This way of thinking was so firmly ensconced by 1775 that the Boston selectman authorized the republication of John Mein's letters to London's *Public Ledger* in which he ridiculed the hypocrisy of revolutionary ideology. Sure of the patriots' sense of innocence betrayed, the selectmen assumed Mein's arguments would be considered outrageous enough to enrage colonial readers. That Mein's attacks included the continuance of slavery as an example of colonial hypocrisy was apparently not viewed as carrying sufficient weight to need censorship ([Mein]).

Nor is it surprising that the ever-increasing numbers of newspapers aligned with the patriots were not eager to carry the pamphlet war into newspapers that were expected to promote a new nation. Nonetheless, antislavery writers persisted, utilizing the distributive system offered by the colonial newspapers in their campaign that sought expurgation for the shame and guilt of slave keeping.

CHAPTER SEVEN

The Newspaper Debate

In the prerevolutionary period, neither Joseph Crukshank nor Isaac Collins, the two Quaker publishers who had printed most of the antislavery pamphlets, published newspapers. There was no Quaker newspaper publisher in any of the colonies until Collins was pressured into publishing a New Jersey patriot paper in 1775 (Hixson). It was in the cities of Connecticut that newspaper discussion of slavery occurred most frequently. Indeed, three of the four Connecticut newspapers gave more space to the dialogue, on a more frequent basis, than the rest of the colonies put together.

How to account for the Connecticut record? Most evident was the role of New Divinity pastors in Connecticut in the stronghold of the sternest congregationalism with a tradition of public discussion of theological issues. Connecticut also had six thousand black inhabitants in this period, the largest number in the Northeast (McManis 69n). None of these factors may have made a difference in the public discourse had it not been for the role of the Green family of newspaper publishers.

The Connecticut Greens were descendants of Bartholomew Green (Morse), the Massachusetts printer who had published Samuel Sewall's famous antislavery tract *The Selling of Joseph.* By the 1770s, Connecticut's newspapers were dominated by the sons of New London's Timothy Green, the longtime printer of the city's paper and deacon of the Congregational Church. The Green family's devotion to congregationalism undoubtedly played a role in their openness to the slavery debate.

The fourth Connecticut newspaper, the *Norwich Packet,* did not have Green connections and, indeed, its founders were clearly Tory sympathizers (Morse). Norwich still had a Green influence, thanks to a Green-financed printing house, run by a Green brother-in-law, Judah P. Spooner, and publisher of antislavery tracts.

Despite the generations of Green printers, the Greens were not in the mode of the classic colonial press whose primary obligation was to provide a conduit for whatever arrived on the doorstep. When Thomas Green initiated the *Connecticut Courant,* his opening statement illustrated a view of the newspaper in a larger role: "Was it not the Press, we should be left almost intirely ignorant of all those noble Sentiments which the Antients were endow'ed with" (*CC* 10/29/64). As the patriot noose grew tighter on newspapers seeking to convey a body of information beyond the patriot sphere, Timothy Green of New London published a letter attacking the "tyranny of patriotism." Directed at the pressures put on the colonial press by the Sons of Liberty, the letter charged: "Bad as our present Ministers are universally presented by the News Papers, they still allow us some degree of freedom; they suffer us to think, to talk, and to write as we please, but the Patriots allows us no such indulgence; Unless we think, talk, and write as they would have us, we are Traitors to the State" (*NLG* 1/24/72). The paper changed its name in 1773, but the free-speech tone remained: "Some of our readers may perhaps think it amiss that we inserted a tory piece in our last," he wrote in the unusual practice of writing in his own voice, "but as this was done with a View to serve the cause of Liberty by affording a fair opportunity for exposing the Errors of these ill-natured Men and Pests of Society... Where there can be no Contradictions there can be Argument" (*CG-NL* 8/12/74).

Nonetheless, none of the Connecticut newspapers can be said to have taken an antislavery stance, for proslavery discussion was well represented in the debate. During this period, the Connecticut Greens also carried periodic news of blacks and slaves in their newspapers that were as negative as any that appeared in the colonial press.

Colonial essay writers were discursive by nature. This was nowhere more true than in the Connecticut slavery essays, in which one essay could account for half a dozen insertions, providing as much discussion as could be found in many pamphlets. One essay ran for three parts in the *Connecticut Journal* and was concluded in three more parts in the *Connecticut Courant.* A single debate appeared in half a dozen lengthy insertions that began in the fall of 1773 and did not conclude until the following September. During the same period, Timothy Green's *Connecticut Gazette* was publishing essays on both sides of the subject by writers who identified themselves by an alphabet of initials — "O.S.T." and "Q.X.Z."

The essays reflect the moral and philosophical arguments of the pamphlet press, including thousands of words combating the Old Testament biblical arguments posed by proslavery advocates. To a modern perspective, it is difficult to see how the recitation of the familiar arguments could have ignited any sparks, although the Baldwin-Edwards series is credited as having a role in the passage of Connecticut's 1774 antislavery legislation. Still, the proslavery "Philemon" admitted: "I well know how lightly people in general read newspaper controversies," he began as a way of introduction to the familiar story of God's curse on Ham (*CJ* 2/11/74).

Throughout the period, occasional pieces attempted to wrench the debate from the turgid theme of sin and guilt. In 1770 the poet and satirist Jonathan Trumbell included antislavery in his series of thirty-eight "Correspondent" essays that appeared in the *Connecticut Journal and New-Haven Post Boy,* an insertion that may have influenced later satirical work, such as *Personal Slavery Established.* Enslavement was the most charitable act in the world, Trumbell wrote. Such toil and pain, such disinterested benevolence, such trouble of conscience and fatigue of the body, all for the Christianization of the African! Indeed, why not enslave other groups, the numerous Turks and Papists for example, for similar charity? (*CJ* 7/6/70).

But, as in the pamphlet press, such attempts were swamped by the ongoing insistence that America was a guilty nation. "It is very evident, my dear countrymen," began a typical essay, "that our ways do not please the Lord, and that He has been manifesting His displeasure against us in various ways" (*CG-NL* 9/9/74). A Norwich writer began: "Among all the wicked customers that are in the nation, none appear to bring down the just vengeance of Heaven more than that of enslaving the Africans" (*CJ* 1/21/74).

The opening newspaper essay — of five lengthy parts — was written by the New Divinity ministers, Ebenezer Baldwin and Jonathan Edwards Jr. The opening paragraphs called for the consistency that New Divinity demanded. Americans were calling for liberty while "reducing a large body of people to complete the perpetual slavery" (*CJ* 10/8/73). The Baldwin-Edwards series, however, shared a number of characteristics with the Quaker essayists, insisting the Old Testament was not an appropriate defense of slavery and finally dismissing the Old Testament argument with a tone of impatience: "The truth is that the scriptures were never designed to be a system of politics" (*CJ* 10/15/73). Instead, the two New Divinity adherents substituted the New Testament's Golden Rule as part of a meld of religious and philosophical defenses that included natural rights, the hypocrisy of slave owners claiming to be saving the souls of their slaves, and the illogic of the just-war defense.

The series indicates how Congregational and Quaker thinking combined in antislavery thought, a major achievement for two sects that had a history of contention in Connecticut. The Sharp and Benezet influence is apparent in the parallel between West Indian and southern slavery, as it noted "the condition of the slaves in the southern colonies and the West-India islands, who are often most cruelly whipped and tortured . . . and sometimes killed at the pleasure of the masters" (*CJ* 12/24/73). One insertion also noted Scottish empiricist, Francis Hutcheson, whose *System of Moral Philosophy* had been quoted in Benezet's 1767 essay (*CJ* 12/31/73). In political terms, the series also shared the Quaker antipatriot stance. If it is lawful for Americans to enslave Africans, "Why is it not as right for Great Britain, France or Spain to reduce us to the same state of slavery, to which we have reduced them?" (*CJ* 10/8/73).

An antipatriot stance was a characteristic of the next extensive series. Before the essay of Baldwin and Edwards had finished its run, the Greens had already begun the publication of the writer "Antidoulious." The arguments of the essay, which stretched across two Connecticut newspapers and was referred to in a slavery essay in a third (*CG* 1/6/75), called upon emerging attitudes of sensibility. Africans were "a harmless, inoffensive people, but little disposed to engage in wars with one another" until enslaved by European greed. The tortures of the Middle Passage, "a floating dungeon," and the barbarity of the auction block were established in terms of family separation: "Little children torn from the bosoms of their indulgent parents" (*CC* 10/3/74).

Having portrayed the sinfulness of the slave trade, "Antidoulious" sought expurgation. He found it in the Sons of Liberty. As British writers shifted guilt from Great Britain to the American colonies, this colonial writer moved blame from one American to another. The patriots must bear the responsibility for the continuance of slavery, he intimated, because they refused to acknowledge the colonial guilty past and, indeed, conducted themselves with a feckless audacity: "A Son of Liberty must blush to reflect that, in one breath he has been loudly exclaiming against the Tyranny of the British Parliament in but attempting to deprive him of his natural rights; while in the next he is exercising a far worse Tyranny over his Negro Slaves" (*CJ* 10/22/73).

While "Antidoulious" chose a far-ranging landscape for his antislavery argument, the terrain sketched out by "Philemon" was a land bounded by the Old Testament and ruled by a merciless God whose instrument, Noah, destined the black race to perpetual enslavement because of the disrespect given to him by his son, Ham. As "Philemon" described the event from the ninth chapter of Genesis: "Ham the father of Canaan, saw his father's nakedness and . . . told it to his brethren without; thereby, in a public and open manner, disgracing his father." Noah condemned Ham and his posterity to be "a servant of servants," that is, a slave. Abraham subsequently prospered in the land of Egypt, presumably with God's blessing, even surrounded with Ham's slave posterity. Finally, "Philemon" asserted no servant race could still exist without defying natural law as it had been God's decree that certain men be servants to others, but not necessarily because they were less talented. Indeed, he acknowledged talent was no observer of racial lines, but even possession of talent did not necessarily lead to social or political equality. It was God's right to dispose of man any way He wanted without calling into question the moral perfectibility of His handiwork — an indication that Congregationalism could be used for either side of the slavery argument (*CJ* 1/7/74).

The antislavery "Philander" challenged the argument in excruciatingly thorough detail. Like other antislavery writers who answered the Old Testament arguments, "Philander" denied that what was permissible for Israelites was also right for all others and put his argument in a contemporary setting: "Because God had a right to set Sodom on fire and burn it to the dust; therefore I have a right to set on fire and burn down Boston or New York" (*CJ* 9/16/74).

The "Philander"/"Philemon" exchange may be the best example of the religious debate on the issue. Its length almost buried an extract from a letter written by Phillis Wheatley to the Native American Congregational minister, the Rev. Samson Occum, wondering, like others, at the absurdity of calling for freedom while denying it at home (*CJ* 4/1/74). But as the familiar Old Testament explorations came to a close in New Haven, the slavery dialogue had taken a new turn in Hartford.

Watson's *Connecticut Courant* was the only newspaper to publish the Rush pamphlet. It appeared in five parts beginning March 3, 1773. While it was usual practice to publish essays in many parts, it was not usual to republish a pamphlet in newspaper form. If a publisher thought a pamphlet of interest, he would more likely have published it separately under his own imprint for profit. To republish the Rush pamphlet in the *Courant,* Watson, by then proprietor of the paper, must have viewed its assured dissemination in the newspaper as more important than its profit, as the introduction to the first insertion suggests: "As it seems to be the prevailing Opinion of Mankind at present in the American Colonies that the Slave Trade is unreasonable in itself and directly contrary to the Principles of Liberty and the Rights of Mankind, of the Violations of which the Americans justly complain, it is hoped the Re-publication of the Whole of said Pamphlet in this Paper will be acceptable to our Readers" (*CC* 3/30/73).

Up until the publication of the Rush pamphlet, the *Courant* had published no discussion of the slavery issue outside of its coverage of the Somerset decision. And after the Rush piece was concluded, silence descended until September of 1774, when the *Courant* published the final three parts of "Antidoulious," an unusual step as already noted.

It was not until 1774 that the next extended discussion of slavery occurred. The Quaker influence was clear, but "Q.X.Z." was one of the colonial writers to confront prejudice. If all mankind was not born equally free, he asked, how are we to tell who is to be the slave? Shall it be the British? "No; they are a noble, generous people, they excel in arts and manufacturers." What about the French? "No; they are good warriors, an airy, polite people, they must not be slaves." The Indians then. "No; if we enslave any of them the remainder will be an enraged enemy, continually on our borders." The Africans? "Yes; they will do; they are black and ugly, and a wide Atlantick secures us against their resentments." He predicted that in the end even color prejudice would not be enough for some. "One will say, I am white enough to be free, and another will say you are black enough to be a slave" (*CG* 1/21/74).

But once again an examination of prejudice was sidelined by calls for the expiation of guilt. "E.M." passionately called for repentance for the "evil of our ways" (*CG* 8/4/74). A month later, another essayist insisted, "Those abominations which are the cause of God's anger, must be sought out and done away" (*CG* 9/9/74). The guilt was set on the doorstep of the revolutionary movement by the essayist "Liberty." He was moved to write because of a petition to the Sons of Liberty from a group of slaves who asked for consideration "whilst we are consulting, asserting and maintaining our natural rights. Like "Antidoulious," the writer portrayed guilt as an appropriate impediment to the revolutionary movement. "Under such a load of guilt, how can you with any face contend for your own rights? How can you condemn a North, or a Bute, or the greatest parricide that ever disgraced the British court?" (*CG* 10/28/74).

When the newspaper published the act that prohibited the importation of slaves (*CG* 11/24/74), opposition voices were again engaged. One essayist made a direct reference to the Sons of Liberty, suggesting the call to liberty was hypocrisy. If New Englanders wished to remain free, they must be ruled by "men of virtue, such as are for universal liberty" (*CG* 12/2/74).

A second insertion called for a limited emancipation but marked a new direction for discussion. Although the writer argued Africans had a right to sell their captives, he nonetheless urged the legislature to consider emancipation as long as freed slaves would not become a community burden "whenever by their folly or otherwise they are disabled from supporting themselves" (*CG* 12/23/74). Following Connecticut's prohibition on the importation of slaves, the writer was less concerned with the morality of slave keeping as with the practical concerns of emancipation, assumed to be on the horizon.

The potential charge to the public that would be caused by the emancipation of slaves was also the concern of the final essayist of 1774. Expressing sympathy for the slave, the contributor could only find three choices existing if slaves were freed—that they be returned to Africa, settled elsewhere, or given permission "to run at Large among us." None was feasible, particularly the last. "They would be greatly exposed to strong Temptations to Idleness, Debauchery, Stealing, and many other Vices very Pernicious to public Order and Safety." The writer only favored emancipation if former slaves could be removed from white society. Otherwise many of them would become "a pest to civil society, and an insupportable Charge to the public" (*CG* 12/30/74).

Early in 1775 the debate moved again into practical concerns in which the writer argued that if slaves appeared unprepared for freedom, it was because the condition of slavery promoted certain characteristics. "The native spark of ambition which inkindles and rises to a flame in the breast of a freeman, withers and expires in the breast of a slave; and leaves as a substitute, a sullen melancholy, lost to all the noble excitement which spring from a laudable ambition" (*CG* 3/17/75). That brought on a final two-part essay response that antislavery persuasion was not at the expense of the political maneuvering. "It is a fact well known, that there was an agreement entered into among a considerable number of persons in divers towns, not to vote for any man in any office whatever, who kept a negro servant." The writer called for antislavery advocates to cease their "intermeddling, not only in politics but in families, and making servants uneasy" (*CG* 3/17/75).

Besides giving us a glimpse of the machinations that went on behind the discussions of slavery, this essay brought to the surface the long-held colonial attitude that emancipation would lead to social disorder. The writer allowed he favored ending the slave trade, but that would not solve the problem of what to do with the slaves already here. Since it was impractical to return them to Africa, no alternative existed except continued enslavement. Education was not likely to change the character of bondsmen. Indeed, "there is a much great probability that the negroes, if released, would grow worse" (*CG* 2/24/75). At any rate, it was felt that the question of slavery must not be allowed to take precedence over other, pressing matters, and it was on this note that the debate ended.

The thousands of words given over to discussion of the slavery issue in the Green-dominated papers was in contrast to the *Norwich Packet.* There was not one word of debate of the slavery issue in the three years of the newspaper's existence and, outside of the Lord Dunmore coverage, bare mention of blacks or slaves at all. Connecticut's 1774 prohibition of the importation of slaves passed without notice. It appears that the slavery discussion was kept out of the *Packet* by editorial decision. At a time when the *Connecticut Gazette* was still running extensive discussions, the *Packet* published what is perhaps the clearest statement of editorial stance on the slavery issue that appeared anywhere in the colonial press: "The Printers hereof present their Compliments to the two African Advocates [possibly Moses Brown and Samuel Hopkins] who have lately honoured them with very polite epistles, and request that these HEROES would excuse their declining to enter a Contest with them whom they consider insolent, stupid, and extremely insignificant" (*NP* 2/16/75).

The inhospitable context of the newspaper indicates a previous insertion having to do with a townsman's emancipation of his slaves "from a laudable sense of freedom" was intended sarcastically (*NP* 12/15/74). There was no attempt at irony in a subsequent item that warned that a free Negro had been arrested in Massachusetts in what Boston colonists believed was his role in a plot "to destroy the White People" (*NP* 3/9/75). Whether these views on blacks and slaves were connected to a patriot stance is not clear because of the paper's muddy political history. But when one of its publishers announced the dissolution of the original partnership in 1776, he identified his paper as one that had been "friendly to Liberty" and pledged to continue the policy (*NP* 5/13/76).

Only New Jersey could challenge Connecticut for the breadth of the slavery debate. The *New Jersey Gazette* was established in 1777 by patriot pressure on the colony's public printer, Quaker Isaac Collins, in exchange for exemption from military service for himself and his workmen. Collins was an intimate of George Dillwyn, whose pamphlet he had published, and his Quaker views toward slavery likely had been intensified during his apprenticeship in Virginia (Hixson 68–70). From early in 1780 into the next year, the *Gazette* reflected New Jersey's active antislavery movement. Collins's sympathies were clear, calling the abolition of slavery in Pennsylvania "an act of humanity, wisdom and justice" (*NJG* 2/13/80) and later publishing the Pennsylvania abolition bill (*NJG* 5/17/80). The pages of the *Gazette* nonetheless presented both views. John Cooper called for immediate emancipation (*NJG* 9/20/80), answered by "A Whig" who urged caution on the basis that former slaves were not prepared for the responsibilities of free men (*NJG* 10/4/80). A Cooper supporter thence took the "Whig" to task not only for his proslavery views but for the use of the name Whig, reserved as a designation, he charged, for someone who "Abhors the very idea of slavery" (*NJG* 11/7/80).

The most extreme of the proslavery views appeared in a new newspaper, the *New Jersey Journal*, established in 1779 by patriot pressure in the north-central part of the state. Faced with competition from New York papers, there were reasons for another patriot organ. The reasons for a new paper may also have included Collins's discussion on slavery and suspicions aroused by his Quaker affiliation — although Collins had been dismissed from the Quaker meeting on the basis of his patriot newspapers, considered a tool of war (Hixson 80–84). In this new paper, the proslavery writer "Eliobo" put on the table such negative attitudes toward blacks and slaves (*NJJ* 11/29; 12/27/80) that it set off an exchange, including ridicule from the Presbyterian minister, the Reverend Jacob Green (*NJJ* 11/20; 12/27/80), in which, as described by Arthur Zilversmit, "succeeding letters becoming more vituperative" (145).

What can be concluded from New Jersey's newspaper debate was the depths of proslavery attitudes that were not so different from those of southern planters or West Indian slaveholders. What can also be concluded is that arguments based on religion, national pride, or sentiment did not appear to sway New

Jersey proslavery writers, whose major stated fear was economic loss (Zilversmit 146).

The practical concerns that were found in New Jersey and even in the Connecticut bastion of Congregationalism were not reflected in the hub of patriot activity. In Boston, the single newspaper that came closest to rivaling the Connecticut discussions of slavery in the 1770s and the New Jersey discussion in the 1780s was Thomas Fleet's *Boston Evening-Post,* a series that turned on biblical approval (*BEP* 9/7; 9/21; 10/2; 10/12; 10/19; 10/26; 11/2; 11/30; 12/28/72). Thomas's *Massachusetts Spy* published a similar series based on biblical approval appearing in the same year as the Somerset decision, although without mentioning it (*MS* 2/27; 10/1; 10/27/72). Outside of Boston, however, in another newspaper connected to Thomas, the slavery debate was framed in a startling new way,

Thomas founded the *Essex Journal* in Newburyport, Massachusetts, with Henry Walter Tinges, a former apprentice, who had also worked for the accused Tory sympathizer John Fleming (Thomas 179–89). The first edition, December 4, 1773, was distributed free in this bustling port town that had a fifty-year history of antislavery activity (Thomas 369; Coffin 241, 372). It was Newbury's most famous son, Judge Samuel Sewall, who had written the early antislavery tract *The Selling of Joseph.* But what put Newbury in the center of antislavery activity just a month before the first edition of the new paper was the successful suit of a Newbury slave, Caesar, for his freedom. The jury not only granted the suit but awarded the plaintiff eighteen pounds in damages (Coffin 373).

The appearance of the paper also coincided with the colony's activity to prohibit the slave trade. By January 1774, a bill had passed both houses. Hutchinson's refusal to sign it only renewed antislavery activity. In Newbury, Nathanial Niles took the antislavery message to the town's North Church pulpit — "Let us either cease to enslave our fellow-men, else let us cease to complain of those who would enslave us" (Niles). Meantime, the fiery Benjamin Colman (not to be confused with the Boston minister), deacon of the Byfield Parish Church, found the new paper a hospitable place to continue his antislavery crusade. Colman called on readers to refrain from criticism of the British ministry until Americans had removed the yoke of bondage from "our brethren, the negroes" (*EJ* 6/20/74). Colman, indeed, took his own advice to look to one's own house. In the 1780s the church was split when Colman charged his own pastor as a "thief" and slave keeper (Coffin 341–44; *Sibley's* 10:56–58).

The Thomas-Tinges partnership failed, perhaps because Colman reflected an antislavery position that was out of step with patriot ideology. In the first appearance of the newspaper under the new partnership of Tinges and Ezra Lunt, a major antislavery essay was found front page. Since Lunt was not a printer but an investor—owner of a stagecoach line between Newburyport and Boston (*BG* 9/20/73)—the decision to print the essay seems to have belonged to Tinges. The essay that launched the partnership also broke new ground, having been written by a former slave, Caesar Sarter, perhaps, but not indisputably, the same individual whose freedom had been granted in 1773 (Coffin 339).

The essay has obvious Quaker influences, touching on the themes of African natural rights, African innocence, the irony of the patriot cause, and scripture. What made the Sarter essay memorable, however, was an egalitarian style that refused subservience. Traditionally, Quaker essays called upon white readers to think of themselves as slaves in order to understand the brutality of the system. Ignored in the rhetoric was a call to imagine the reverse—to picture the African in mainstream society in which the African is at home. One problem in the Quaker's argument of the Golden Rule was that it never addressed the issue beyond emancipation, leaving that discussion open to essayists who could not imagine former bondsmen and women operating in any way other than as members of the lowest rung of society, even as free. When petitions appeared, their supplicating nature tended to reinforce the role of blacks, even free, as subservient.

In contrast, the assurance of Sarter's style raised the concept of equality of black and white, even in the Quaker rhetorical frame. Sarter asked readers to put themselves in the place of stolen Africans, a usual Quaker device. "Suppose that you were trepanned away," he asked, "the husband from the dear wife of his bosom—the wife from her affectionate husband—children from their fond parents—or parents from their tender and beloved offspring who, not an hour before, perhaps they were fondling in their arms and in whom they were promising themselves much future happiness?" (*EJ* 8/17/74).

What Sarter rejects is the Quaker language of horror, choosing instead the language of civilized society that assumes an equality of expectations and experience. In the same way as the Somerset coverage had noted two years before blacks "and their ladies" enjoying an evening out after the Somerset success, the way any English group might celebrate the success of a court battle, Sarter described Africans experiencing the slave block not in dramatic terms of rivulets of blood that Quaker writers often favored but in the genteel language of family separation that reflected common white perceptions about themselves. For white colonists concerned with emancipation as disorder, here was evidence that belied the newspapers' emphasis on black crime.

The Sarter approach was seldom seen in the antislavery discussion of the time. But there was at least one other example of a former slave rejecting Quaker sensibility in favor of a political argument. In January of 1780, a Trenton doctor, David Cowell, inserted an advertisement in the *New Jersey Gazette* offering to sell or exchange an able-bodied Negro man. The man in question, Adam, replied in an essay to the *Gazette* charging that Cowell had signed a contract for his freedom, and calling for freedom, justice, and protection, "which I am entitled to by the laws of the state, although I am a Negro." Cowell replied, although he had to take out an advertisement to do it, denying he had promised such freedom and blamed two white men for instigating trouble. Adam replied, again in the columns of the *Gazette,* in an onslaught charging an array of specific wrongs including an attack of Cowell's ability as a surgeon. Cowell rallied to respond, again in terms of specificity. The argument went to the Supreme Court of New Jersey, which declared Adam to be Cowell's property, but in 1783, a notice informed *Gazette* readers of Cowell's death, and it is to be surmised that Adam found a way to maintain his freedom (White 117–19).

Shane White interprets the episode as a remarkable example of black challenge to white "monopoly of the printed word" (119). That view is supported when it is considered that Adam made his case without any reference to the antislavery arguments of the period. Instead, Adams's argument, as Cowell's response, was in the specificity of promises made and promises broken, a rare alternative to the religious rhetoric.

The voices of the enslaved were seldom heard in the colonial press, and that lack left the antislavery argument to till dusty soil. The tone of some essays suggested the writers themselves were tiring of restating arguments already well known. "We all know that they are purchased from their princes, who pretend to have a right to dispose of them," according to a Salem writer, as if too obvious to repeat (*EG* 8/25/72).

Through it all, the dull and not-so-dull, the *Boston Gazette* chose to ignore the debate. Despite the considerable agitation for the abolition of the slave trade that came before Massachusetts's legislators in 1767, 1771, 1773, 1774, and 1776, the patriot's flag carrier remained silent. Other Boston newspapers, forced or otherwise, generally followed suit. One exception was Edward E. Powars and Nathaniel Willis's *Independent Chronicle,* a latecomer to the Boston press community, which published a contribution from Roxbury's New Divinity minister, William Gordon. Gordon, like Paine and Rush, made an effort to confront the question of physical difference: "Would it not be ridiculous, inconsistent and unjust, to exclude freemen from voting for representatives and senators, though otherwise qualified, because their skins are black, tawny or reddish? Why not disqualify for being long-nosed, short-faced, or higher or lower than five feet nine?" (*IC* 1/8/78).

The *Chronicle* also provided a glimpse of the debate in the state's legislative convention of 1777–78 in which blacks, Indians, and mulattos were excluded from citizenship. In opposing the exclusion, Gordon pointed to political motivation: to grant citizenship to blacks would be to offend "the sister States," a rare instance when that issue was discussed openly. The proposed constitution was defeated, perhaps in some small part because of Gordon's attacks on the exclusionary clause, which, when coupled with a perceived insult to that most easily offended colonial gentlemen, Governor John Hancock, led to his dismissal as chaplain to both houses of the Massachusetts legislative (G. Moore 194). Later, Gordon was fired from his Roxbury pastorate, whereupon he returned to Great Britain in 1786 to write the *History of the American Revolution* and survive as best he could. Described by a nineteenth-century historian as possessing a "warmth of temper and lack of prudence" (Winsor 350), Gordon came to the American colonies in 1770 with an unfettered and uncompromising outlook on slavery that he was unable to integrate into the American cause. And even with his clear patriot sympathies, Gordon's British birth, like that of Swan and Allen, likely did not serve to advance his theories on abolition.

On safer ground, the *Chronicle* limited other slavery debate to a pro-and-con versification war in early 1778 (*IC* 1/29; 2/19/78). It would not be surprising if these insertions had been prompted by the *Chronicle's* secret partner, John Green, a member of the peripatetic printing family whose members carried the antislavery debate in Connecticut (Thomas 139).

The outbreak of war ended the partnership of Edes and Gill. Gill was imprisoned in 1775 while Edes moved the *Gazette* to Watertown and then back to Boston at the end of 1776. In 1776, Gill was also back in the newspaper business as the founder and proprietor of the *Continental Journal,* which published Gordon's second essay on the proposed constitution (*ConJ* 4/9/79). Gill has always been regarded as the silent partner in the Edes and Gill relationship, apparently doing most of the day-to-day business, freeing Edes for his Loyall

Nine activities. However, both in the fisticuffs incident with John Mein and in his imprisonment, Gill took on the lion's share of the punishment. The publication of the unpopular Gordon in his new paper leads to speculation that Gill may have been finally challenging the patriot hegemony that had ruled the *Boston Gazette* for so many years.

Meantime, quite apart from the publication record of Boston newspapers, the question of the role of slaves in the Revolution was causing civil disorder in the city. A proposal to raise a detachment of blacks for military service resulted in a Congress Street riot led by the patriot incendiary, Isaac Sears. Sears's connection to the riot suggests it was hardly spontaneous but likely a propaganda assurance to the "sister States" of Massachusetts's political commitment to the continuance of black subservience.

One of the last antislavery essays — before the Declaration of Independence — was written by another British immigrant, Thomas Paine, and, as the last piece of editorial matter before the advertising, was tucked onto page three of the *Pennsylvania Journal.* The newspaper was an odd venue considering the *Journal* did not print even an extract from the pamphlet written by Rush, who was a family friend of the publisher, and accepted the piece after it was rejected by Robert Aiken for the *Pennsylvania Magazine* (Woodward 61). The *Journal* was no hospitable context for antislavery discussion. Its publisher William Bradford was long an opponent of Quakers and Quaker positions; indeed, it was Bradford who commanded the military contingent that arrested Philadelphia's Quaker leaders for exile to Virginia (Gilprin).

The *Journal* had published just one letter objecting to slavery prior to the Paine piece (*PJ* 9/24/74) and published a series of letters by a spokesman defending slavery during the debate on the proposed modification of Pennsylvania's 1780 abolition bill (*PJ* 1/31; 2/5; 2/21/81). The response to these letters came not in the *Pennsylvania Journal* but in a new, politically active newspaper, Frances Bailey's *Freeman's Journal,* which also published a "postscript" from a black correspondent who argued for the retention of the original bill (*FJ* 6/13; 9/21/81).

Paine had not been long in the colonies when he wrote the essay, and his familiarity with the arguments indicated their British sources. Paine was master, however, in his grasp of colonial thought. After the traditional arguments, Paine moved the discussion into the realm of practical concerns, as if recognizing that it was not John Locke or biblical command that prevented most white colonists from moving vigorously on antislavery issues but the lack of solutions to perceived problems, such as the role of freed bondsmen in a new society. Paine's proposal strikes no egalitarian chord, suggesting initial segregation until the former slaves believed they had a stake in the new nation. "Perhaps they might sometime form useful barrier settlements on the frontiers. Thus they become interested in the public welfare, and assist in promoting it" (*PJ* 3/8/75). However, Paine's acknowledgment of the practical concerns of the colonists and his attempt to address those fears in ways that would be beneficial to the patriot cause suggest an awareness that continued ruminations would likely serve to maintain, not alter, positions. His attempt to connect the freedom of black Americans with the revolutionary movement came too late for impact on the Revolution's ideology, however. The antislavery rhetoric was well established along tracks that carried into the antebellum era.

The newspaper essays calling for an end to slavery were dominated by issues from the pens of the British-influenced Quaker pamphlet writers. For Great Britain, the Somerset decision provided redemption. The guilt of the British nation for its role in establishing slavery in the world was shifted to American shoulders. The Quaker writers carried this British agenda to the Puritan soil of the colonies, where shame and guilt were not unknown. However, the descendants of the Puritans were now part of the revolutionary generation, a generation that emphasized American purity and European corruption. Colonial Americans refused to take on this British burden, put on them as if the British expected to extract a tithe from colonists to pay for British sinfulness, as surely as they taxed colonists to pay for British interests in European wars. Colonists refused to pay such debts and rejected them wholly, even their own legitimate part in them.

Although the religious arguments carried weight in certain colonies, the antislavery rhetoric of the New Divinity and other congregational ministers was best appreciated by a regional audience, and its regional nature must account for its failure to be reprinted in other areas of the colonies. When antislavery addressed secular concerns, as in the Rush pamphlet, dissemination increased. Further, the antislavery cause had no proponent who was as skilled in the manipulation of attitudes as Samuel Adams, nor did it boast any printer who could carry out the propagandistic mission as well as Benjamin Edes. Even the most sympathetic of printers, the Greens in Connecticut and Collins in New Jersey, were compelled to offer their columns to the opposite views. Meantime, antislavery patriot supporters who remained in good standing — Rush, Paine, and Appleton — were taken up by other aspects of the Revolution.

The antislavery agitation that remained within the patriot fold was confined to calls for slave trade prohibitions. Quaker antislavery activists found themselves cornered into Toryism, an alienation that carried into the new nation. And all antislavery essayists, whether Tory or not, did their cause little good by taunting patriots for their lack of antislavery sentiment.

Thus, mired in arguments that often lacked intercolonial appeal, the antislavery essayists failed to make a place for the cause beyond the end of the slave trade. At the same time, the Somerset decision had indicated that it served the patriot cause to promote the fear that the British regarded colonists on the same level as slaves. It became an even more compelling fear when embodied by the decision of Virginia's governor to set free the colony's slaves on the proviso they would make war on their former owners.

CHAPTER EIGHT

Insurrection

In the early fall of 1774, Abigail Adams informed John that a Boston "conspiracy of the Negroes" had failed. This was not the usual conspiracy of revolt. Adams was referring to the presentation of two petitions by Boston's black leaders to General Thomas Gage, the British commander-in-chief in America, "telling him that they would fight for him provided he would arm them and engage to liberate them if he conquered" (*Adams Family* 1:161).

This was not news that a reader could find in the Boston newspapers. Although the colonial press had not been adverse to printing stories that engaged colonial fear of slave uprising, such stories and others related to slave agency became less common as the Revolution approached. James Madison, writing to his best friend, William Bradford Jr. of Philadelphia, about a 1774 incident in which a group of Virginia slaves had met to select a leader in readiness for British liberation, cautioned, "It is prudent such things should be concealed as well as suppressed" (Madison 1:130) — clearly not a casual warning to Bradford as son of the *Pennsylvania Journal's* publisher. John Dunlap of the *Pennsylvania Packet,* introducing a letter from Williamsburg, noted: "The letter goes on farther, and relates a great deal about the Negroes in South Carolina; but we think it prudent to suppress the account. It may be necessary, however, to mention to our readers, that we have entirely overcome that body, in the aforesaid quarter, and reduced them to their former submission" (*PP* 12/25/75).

Both by formal action in colonial legislatures and by informal self-censorship in the colonial press, patriots sought to mute the news of slave insurrection lest the contagion of liberty be misinterpreted by bondsmen and women as having something to do with them. The *Georgia Gazette* did provide an account of the St. Andrew Parish Revolt, but likely only because it could relate that its leader and a compatriot had been captured and executed, both burned alive (*GG* 12/7/74).

But by 1775, even the ongoing use of the metaphor of slavery did not seem able to quell the dangers of its reality. If there was an official silence on the subject, it only could have been an effort to avoid attention to the nightmare of the American Revolution — that American slaves would take up arms against white colonists. A Georgia delegate to the Continental Congress had no rosy view that the slaves would stand by their owners if the British made an offer of freedom. He predicted to John Adams that it would take just two weeks for the British to take Georgia and South Carolina once slaves began to flock to the British standard (*Works* 2:458). Madison shared the view: "It is imagined our Governor has been tampering with the Slaves & that he has it in contemplation to make great Use of them in case of a civil war in this province. To say the truth, that is the only part in which this Colony is vulnerable; & if we should be subdued, we shall fall like Achilles by the hand of one that knows that secret" (Madison 1:153).

In 1775, in the House of Commons, Edmund Burke proposed a general emancipation of American slaves. The proposal failed, but it only forwarded the long-held colonial attitude, as represented by Captain Wilson's comment the previous decade in Boston, that the British would unleash American slaves on their masters in case of rebellion. It was clearly an innuendo that the British found useful and periodically invoked. General Gage panicked South Carolina into virtual military rule when South Carolinians interpreted a casual remark (at least, an ostensibly casual remark) as a veiled threat that the British intended to enlist black slaves (J. R. Alden).

In the face of patriot preference for suppressed accounts of slave revolts, rumor flourished. In April of 1775, word swept into the Connecticut town of Killingly that former slaves were actually on the march, leading residents to post sentinels and boil kettles of water in preparation for battle (*Sibley's* 11:438). More typical were the responses of Edenton and New Bern, North Carolina, where new committees were authorized to "patrol and search the Negroes Houses" for arms and ammunition (Frey, *Water* 59). South Carolina could call on its already established Patrol Act, in existence since 1737, stiffened in 1740 in the wake of the Stono uprising, with further calls for stronger enforcement in 1766 and 1773 (G. Wood 276–77). Meantime, the discovery of slave plots challenged white hegemony as never before. An insurrectionary plot in the heavily slave-populated Wilmington, North Carolina, was crushed by patrols whose members arrested, shot, whipped, and cut suspected conspirators. In Charleston, after the discovery of a plot thought to be connected to the arrival of the British, South Carolinian Henry Laurens, president of the First Provincial Congress, ordered patrols of the city and established a special committee to investigate slave insurrections. Under the authority of the Provincial Congress, the alleged Charleston leader, a free black man, Thomas Jeremiah, was convicted of "intended sedition," hanged and burned to death in Charleston. The execution did not deter a later group of South Carolina slaves, including several black preachers who included two women, to mount a countywide plan of death to whites. George, one of its leaders, was hunted down and hanged. In Wilmington, North Carolina, a slave uprising was discovered hours before it was to go into effect over three counties (Frey, *Water* 56–62). Compared to earlier years when the *Boston Evening-Post* and other newspapers had published accounts of such events, the patriot newspapers were more silent than not.

By 1775, the question of slavery was becoming less a metaphor for the treatment of American colonists at British hands than a military problem with the American Revolution in the balance. The British, who for years had been cautious about openly calling on the support of the slaves without offending the considerable number of their own supporters who were slave owners, were pressing their campaign of innuendo. Increasingly, southerners saw the British "tampering" in slave unrest. Local political differences were shunted aside in a cooperative white response to the "instigated Insurrections," the code phrase for British involvement.

The final turn on the wheel came when the British governor of Virginia, Lord Dunmore, ignoring British hesitancy, issued a proclamation that promised freedom to all slaves who would fight for the British cause. Long awaiting such a call, hundreds of Virginia slaves threaded their way through the Virginia patrols to join Dunmore's fleet (Frey, "Between" 378). The British caution turned out to be well founded; perhaps no other single event could have driven Virginians so quickly and so absolutely into patriot arms. Edward Rutledge reported to the Continental Congress that the Dunmore proclamation had done more "to work an eternal separation between Great Britain and the colonies than any other expedient which could possibly have been thought of" (D. Robinson 103).

Although silence had been the press code of the day for many of the previous slave insurrections, the scope of the Dunmore Proclamation not only made it impossible to ignore but presented to the radicals a grand opportunity to promote united opposition to Great Britain by giving example to the metaphor of slavery. News of the event, coming from the mouths of the aggrieved Virginians, conveyed Virginians' views of betrayal. In the resulting call to race solidarity, colonial newspapers played a pivotal role by extending the Virginian view of the episode across the colonies. The Dunmore chapter, climaxing the suspicions set in place by the Somerset decision and the antislavery discourse, seemed proof of the various warnings implicit in the patriot metaphor of slavery. Here was evidence that the British would break any compact — including, in the Virginians' view, the sacred one between master and slave. Could any further evidence be needed, for any colony, that Great Britain was not to be trusted?

From the beginning, Virginia Whigs should have viewed the last royal governor of Virginia with some suspicion. John Murray, Earl of Dunmore, was a Scottish peer at a time when Scots in America were perceived as pro-Tory. Dunmore was not only Scottish but a descendant of the House of Stuart. His father, William Murray, participated in the 1745 rebellion that led to the ignominious defeat at the Battle of Culloden and retained his title only after an official pardon. Dunmore was raised in Scotland in the years after the defeat and, suffused in this atmosphere of a cause permanently lost, became one of the sixteen representative peers of Scotland to sit in the British Parliament as part of efforts to unify the nation.

In his role as a Scottish representative, Dunmore spent the nine years before his appointment to the American colonies in London, mixing with the eminent men of the day. His life in London, any more than his Scottish background, gave him little in common with the New Yorkers, then Virginians, whom he was appointed to govern. His own history was a minority history, a history of a lost cause. He was a man who saw that position was not necessarily ordained, and it is not surprising that he did not take as sacred the Virginian view that their society was immutable and unchanging (Caley; Selby 15).

The event that challenged the Virginian view of the world occurred in November of 1775 when Dunmore issued a proclamation offering freedom to slaves who would leave their patriot masters and join the British forces. The cries of anguish, disbelief, and anger spilled immediately onto the pages of the three Virginia newspapers (all called the *Virginia Gazette,* making identification by publisher important). In the thousands of words that sprang from the pages of the Virginia press, Dunmore was accused of hypocrisy, political machinations, indeed, the abandonment of all principles. Slaves were ominously warned to return to their "homes" — that is, the plantations — or suffer assured death upon capture.

The common wellspring for this flood of emotion was the challenge posed to Virginians' sense of themselves as not only kind, but, most important, *necessary* masters of their slaves. The Dunmore Proclamation forced Virginians to face the possibility that the only necessity that called them to be masters was not the needs of the slave but their own need of definition. Unlike the Georgia delegate's assessment to John Adams, the Virginians seemed genuinely surprised at the flight of their slaves, giving some indication of the depths of the society's paternalism. The slaves who escaped to join Dunmore were, as in the advertisements, "runaways," still ungrateful for the kind care of their masters, who told them to return "home" if they knew what was best for them. The Virginians viewed the slaves as having been "carried off," men and women unable to act on their own behalf. The real anger, however, was reserved for Dunmore, the man who had broken faith with the loyalty of white to white. Dunmore, the representative of the British crown, was the traitor, the "Lord Kidnapper" of John Leacock's propaganda play.

The sense of betrayal that marked so much of the Virginian attack on Dunmore may be in part explained by Dunmore's original popularity and the trust Virginians placed in him. Dunmore arrived in the American colonies in 1770 as governor of New York. In an episode redolent of the events that led to the Peter Zenger decision, Dunmore, like William Cosby, alienated colonial leadership by demanding full salary for the period before he had actually taken up his colonial gubernatorial duties. But the New York unpleasantness was behind him when, vigorous and under forty, Dunmore took on the governorship of the southern colony. His popularity was increased when he named his fifth child Virginia; his own name was given to the new counties of Dunmore and Fincastle; and his physical bravery was demonstrated in his personal leadership of the campaign against the Shawnee Indians in 1774 — Lord Dunmore's War (Caley).

It has been suggested that Dunmore's attack on the Indians was not so much to please the Virginian thirst for new lands as to satisfy his own land hunger, already demonstrated when he purchased fifty thousand acres in New York. The campaign against the Shawnees promised additional holdings for land speculation and was conducted despite a British policy that discouraged further internal developments. By the time of his proclamation, Dunmore had shown himself to be a man who had little sense of allegiance either to the American colonies or to the policies of the British government. Dunmore's popularity at the time of Lord Dunmore's War had come about more by accident than design. He was not the man to nurture the considerable Virginia loyalism that continued even in face of British policies that kept Virginians in debt to British merchants and held back Virginian hopes of expansion. Indeed, some of Dunmore's actions seem aimed at the destruction of British loyalism. After receiving months of support from Norfolk merchants, for example, he decided to fire on Norfolk's patriot-controlled warehouses that had been used to ambush British ships. In retaliation, patriots had an excuse to set fire to the town that had served as Dunmore's loyalist stronghold. Norfolk's resulting decimation was blamed entirely on Dunmore, despite the patriot torch, and became another rallying cry for separation from Great Britain (Harrell 13–15; Selby 81–84).

The Virginians' honeymoon with their new governor was intense but relatively short. In 1773 Dunmore dissolved the House of Burgesses for proposing a committee of correspondence on colonial grievances. The following year he dissolved the House again when the burgesses set aside a day for fasting and mourning in connection with the Boston Port Bill. But Virginian resentment came to the boiling point when the governor, noting the extent of the enlargement of the Virginia militia, ordered the removal of the gunpowder from the public magazine in Williamsburg and had it transported to a ship on the James River. Dunmore agreed to pay for the powder after an armed party under the leadership of Patrick Henry demanded restitution. However, the removal of the gunpowder produced months of controversy and gave Dunmore time to return his family to England and take up residence himself on a British man-of-war on the York River. Joined by other ships, some of them carrying Virginians who defined themselves as loyalists, Dunmore's fleet provisioned itself by conducting a guerrilla war on the plantations that lined the Virginia shores.

Virginians complained, and perhaps with some justice, that Dunmore had taken to the man-of-war precipitously. Yet his action is consistent in terms of his family's nationalism. By choosing to live outside Virginian society, Dunmore was replaying his Scottish history. He became the rebel again, leading a marine force and choosing confrontation at his will. The Virginian Whigs were stripped of the romantic lead and were instead forced into the role of the lumbering defenders of the status quo. If the Virginia response to Lord Dunmore has never taken hold of the American popular imagination in the same way as the Battle of Bunker Hill or the Boston Tea Party, it is because Dunmore reserved for himself the role of challenger of authority, as if he were once again playing out the rebellion of 1745 on the inlet coastal ways of Virginia instead of on the heather and hills of the Scottish highlands.

On November 17, 1775, Dunmore, still on shipboard, climaxed the months of controversy by declaring martial law in a proclamation that offered freedom to the slaves and indentured servants "appertaining to rebels" who would "repair to his Majesty's standard" (Force 4:1103–4). The announcement was not a surprise. Eight months before he had threatened such a proclamation when Virginians opposed the confiscation of the gunpowder. He had been building his army of black conscripts as part of his raids on the Virginia plantations.

By the time of the announcement, Virginians had established a precautionary network of slave patrols. Slaves were allowed to move about the countryside only when vitally necessary and then only with passes. Despite such surveillance, perhaps as many as a thousand slaves escaped the dragnet to join Dunmore (Frey, "Between" 378). Virginians insisted the slaves had been "seduced" or kidnapped (Force 4:1385). Impressment was certainly a British tradition, but given the insurrectionary climate of the period, it seems probable that the majority of Dunmore's black regiment was composed of men who voluntarily joined him. Dunmore certainly reported the ex-slaves were "flocking to him" and Virginians expressed fear that indeed they were (*VG*-Purdie 1/26/76).

Dunmore assembled a regiment of former slaves on the basis of the rumored announcement. Dunmore issued the proclamation shortly after his force had been prevented from burning Hampton by the sharpshooting skills of Virginia riflemen, who simply picked off the British sailors as the ships tried to get close to shore. He chose to publish the proclamation a week later following a small military success when his force had routed a detachment of colonial militia at Kemp's Landing near the Elizabeth River (Selby 64).

It was a particularly humiliating defeat for the Virginians, all of whom fled before the first shot even though it was Dunmore's regiment that was taken by surprise (Harrell 39). One of the militia commanders, Colonel Joseph Hutchings, was among those fleeing into the surrounding woods. He was followed by a member of the regiment who, in, what must have been a dramatic moment, took his former master into British custody (Force 4:292; Caley 647).

The Virginians avenged their honor a month later at a fort at Great Bridge, near Norfolk, which the Virginians occupied and surrounded in wait for Dunmore and his troops to appear. For several days the Virginians remained concealed around the causeway that led to the fort. Finally, the British, apparently misinformed about strength of the militia, chose to attack. In the dawn of December 9, a detachment of British soldiers, including members of the black regiment, crossed the causeway with bayonets fixed. But exposed to the unerring Virginia fire and trapped by the narrow causeway, the British lost sixty-one men, including their captain. One Virginian was slightly wounded. Dunmore hurriedly retreated to Norfolk and thence to his ships and never faced the Virginians on land again (Selby 70–73).

In the end, however, it was the ravages of smallpox that most defeated Dunmore and his ambitions for the black regiment. The close quarters of the ships and the lack of inoculation among his black troops encouraged the spread of the disease. In June 1776, the flotilla landed and occupied Gwynn's Island in the Chesapeake in an effort to restore health to the troops by quarantining the ill. But soon attacked by Virginia fire and left with only a handful of black and white troops, Dunmore finally abandoned his dead on the island, burned ships he could no longer man, and dispersed in various directions the much-dwindled "pestilential fleet."

Dunmore rejoined his wife and children in England but returned to the colonies in 1781 when he expected to resume his governorship in the wake of Cornwallis's victories. After the surrender at Yorktown, Dunmore turned his attention to arming loyalist blacks for the purpose of seizing New Orleans and West Florida as a haven for all British loyalists — Dunmore again putting himself in the role of the rebel leader. The plan never materialized, but it has been speculated that Dunmore accepted the post of the governor of the Bahamas in 1787 as a power base to continue his plan to establish a loyalist colony on the North American continent, again utilizing black troops. He was, however, abruptly recalled from his Bahamian post in 1796, a result of both his turbulent stewardship and the secret marriage of his daughter to the king's son, which the king quickly had annulled (Wright 379).

Dunmore died at age seventy-seven, in sedate retirement at the English seaside resort of Ramsgate. Patriot predictions of ministerial punishments because of his actions in Virginia never came about. But neither was Dunmore ever to fulfill his ambitions for glorious leadership by sparking in the British a coordinated plan that would have provided American slaves a stake in maintaining British America.

Modern historians conclude that the British government's attitudes toward slavery were not any different from those held by the American colonists (Quarles, *Negro* 156–57; D. Davis 278; Selby 67). Dunmore's actions are explained in terms of a rash and impulsive personality, because the proclamation excluded slaves owned by loyalists and Dunmore himself was a slave owner. While Dunmore and the British command considered emancipation of the rebel slaves in military rather than in humanitarian terms, the emphasis of historians has been on the failure of the British to live up to the liberal promise of the proclamation, rather than taking into account that Dunmore armed the escaped slaves, provided them with uniforms, and allowed them the prestige and history of a regiment with the opportunity to face their Virginia oppressors as equals.

The Virginians' response to Dunmore's actions was the first time the Virginian view of slavery had been expressed in the public prints. Despite the private dilemmas experienced by many Virginia leaders (Morgan, *American*), only Arthur Lee had publicly denounced slavery, seven years before in Rind's *Virginia Gazette*, although in ways that hardly promoted abolition: "They [slaves] depend on their tyrants for what they are pleased to grant them, property, or life, or honors, to which they aspire not by virtue, but by cunning, servility and wickedness, from which they soon become habitually vicious, weak and insensitive" (*VG*-Rind 3/3/68). The young Lee, like Benjamin Rush, fresh from his studies in Edinburgh, was not permitted the opportunity of completing the essay, and his considerable writing skills were spent as the representative of the American cause in Great Britain without further reference to slavery (Riggs).

In this, then, the first widespread, public representation of the Virginian view, the theme that spread from the Virginia hub across the colonies thanks to the system of exchange newspapers was betrayal, specifically the betrayal of Dunmore as a representative of Great Britain to white colonists. The theme dovetailed easily with what the patriot propagandists had been promulgating as Great Britain's view toward the colonies. As Lord Dunmore had betrayed the men and women under his charge, the British were betraying the colonies as a whole.

Virginian newspapers were unsurprisingly similar in their response to the crisis. In examining seventy-three separate items taken from the three *Virginia Gazettes* in connection with the episode, several themes emerge. However, almost half of the items deal with betrayal. Dunmore and other whites sympathetic with his cause were categorized as evil, traitorous, hypocritical, and themselves deserving the status of slaves. A second group of responses (25 percent) described blacks and slaves in relatively neutral terms but a third group (15 percent) characterized blacks and slaves as a threat to whites and portrayed them as thieves, potters, and murderers. A small but intense group of items (10 percent) gives some indication of the conflicted nature of the Virginian attitudes. Here slaves and blacks were characterized as being threats to themselves, easily taken advantage of, misguided, gullible, and fearful. Slaves were viewed as basically loyal to Virginian masters if outsiders would simply leave them alone. Just two percent of the items described blacks and slaves in positive terms.

Betrayal was clearly sounded with the response to the Proclamation, as prefaced by Purdue's *Virginia Gazette*: "Here you have a proclamation that will at once show the baseness of lord Dunmore's heart, his malice and treachery against the people, who were once under this government and his officious violation of all law, justice and humanity; not to mention his arrogating to himself a power which neither he can assume, nor any power upon earth intend, etc. Not in the legions of horrid hell, can a devil more damned that D......E" (*VG*-Purdie 12/24/75).

The final three lines are Macduff's lines in Act IV, Scene III of *Macbeth,* in which Dunmore's initials replace the name of Macbeth—an interesting literary comparison.

The criticism of Dunmore often took the form of angry sarcasm, as in the report of the seizure of three slaves captured on their way to join the Dunmore fleet. The anger appears directed not so much at the escaping slaves as at Dunmore for accepting such "shoe blacks" into his service. "It is to be hoped, however, that General Lee, so soon as he finds it convenient, will take care to provide our governor with a more suitable household, agreeable to his *highbirth,* and distinguished merit" (*VG*-Purdie 2/17/75). Dunmore was not sole representative of British betrayal. The depredations along the Virginia coast by a Captain Squires of the British sloop *Otter* in late summer produced the sarcastic outburst: "A very pretty occupation for the captain of one of his majesty's ships of war!" (*VG*-Purdie 9/15/75). Squires came in for a more underlined sarcasm a few days later. The movement of the sloop suggested Squires was up to "*old trade*" — "negro-catching, pillaging farms and plantations of their sock, and other *illustrious actions* highly becoming a *squire* in the king's navy" (*VG*-Purdie 9/22/75).

Concomitant with these expressions of outrage was the idea that such betrayal was tantamount to the surrender of white class standing to the status of the blacks. Dunmore was quickly characterized as "king of the blacks, alias *pirates*" (*VG*-Pickney 11//9/75). In one account British prisoners were grouped as "Jack Dunmore's *hopeful gang*, consisting of soldiers, sailors and negroes" (*VG*-Pickney 1/6/75). Members of a British raiding party were reported to have had their faces "blacked like Negroes, whose *dear* companions they are" (*VG*-Pickney 11/30/75). This concern with loss of status was most clearly represented in accounts of the battle of Great Neck, published as "extracts of letters" in the three newspapers. "We have taken up some of the worst of the tories and coupled them to a negro with handcuffs," according to one letter (*VG*-Pickney 12/16/75). Readers of the Virginia press were not left in doubt that this coupling of black and white prisoners was a symbolic gesture meant to insult the British. In a letter published in Purdie's newspaper, Colonel William Woodford, the commander of the Virginia troops, informed Edmund Pendleton, president of the General Convention, "I ordered him coupled to one of his black brother soldiers, with a pair of handcuffs, which is the resolution I have taken shall be the fate of all those cattle, till I am farther instructed by your Honorable House" (*VG*-Purdie 12/15/75). In another letter sounding the same theme, Woodford referred to the British troops as the "black and white slaves" (*VG*-Purdie 12/15/75).

While the Virginians condemned Lord Dunmore and the British ministry for jeopardizing the status of whites by permitting blacks to serve the king, the published reports of the battle at Great Neck indicated that not all the British were tarred with the same brush. Woodford ordered the leader of the British forces, killed early in the battle, to be buried "with all the honors due him" (*VG*-Dixon and Hunter 12/6/75). Generous in victory, Virginians treated white prisoners, especially officers, with humanity, as if Virginians were showing by example the benefits of the white brotherhood.

Next to this theme of betrayal was the use of items in which slaves are described in relatively neutral terms, although, obviously, such a classification does not mean that the accounts were intended as neutral or read as neutral. The Virginian practice of breaking down all black and white encounters into numerical accounting by race suggests the overriding concern of race in the culture. The Virginia press, therefore, included many items that used race as an organizing principle. "Our people took a small tender with five men, a woman, and two slaves, six swivels, seven muskets, some small arms, a sword, pistols, and other things" (*VG*-Purdie 10/17/75). When the Virginians regained Gwynn's Island, they found "a large number of cannon, swivels, thirty black prisoners, and three tenders" (*VG*-Dixon and Hunter 7/13/76). One item, ostensibly neutral, undoubtedly raised different feelings in many Virginia breasts. In a captured letter from Dunmore to the British command, Virginia readers learned, in Dunmore's own words, of his plans for the black regiment. "You may observe by my proclamation that I offer freedom to the slaves of all rebels that join me, in consequence of which there are between 2 and 300 already come in; and those I form into a corps as fast as they come in, giving them white officers, and non-commissioned officers in proportion" (*VG*-Purdie 1/26/76).

Making "examples of" escaped slaves played a prominent role in the Virginia response. Several of the items are concerned with the consequences to blacks who were seized on their way to join the British as in an account of nine blacks, including two women, who were fired upon as they put ashore near Norfolk. "Two of the fellows are wounded, and it is expected the rest will soon be made example of" (*VG*-Dixon and Hunter 12/2/75). To be made an "example of" probably meant execution, as was made clear in another item in which slaves on their way to join Dunmore had been captured: "Two of the Negroes who mistook one of our armed vessels at Jamestown for a tender, and expressed their inclination to serve Lord Dunmore, are under sentence of death, and will be executed in a few days, as an example to others" (*VG*-Dixon and Hunter 4/13/76). Items in this category also include those that almost routinely reflect on slaves as thieves and "banditti." One item that originated in Philadelphia (and reprinted only in Purdie) suggested that all blacks, slave and free, were only waiting for the opportunity to join the British: "Late last night, a gentlewoman, going along second Street, was insulted by a negro, near Christ Church; and upon her reprimanding him for his rude behavior, the fellow replied, 'Stay your d-----d white bitch till lord Dunmore and his black regiment come, and then we will see who is to take the wall' " (*VG*-Purdie 12/29/75).

A sarcastic item in which blacks aboard the fleet were predicted to perform military exercises to the "martial tune of 'Hungry Niger, parch'd Corn!' and which from henceforward is to be styled by way of eminence, the BLACKBIRD MARCH" (*VG*-Purdie 3/22/76) indicated an uglier tone, coming at a time between the success of the battle of Great Neck and Dunmore's continued depredations along the coast.

The fourth category in order of use identified slaves as gullible and needing Virginia masters to survive. Although few items appeared in this category, they included two essays written at the time of the proclamation. The first called upon slaves "not to be seduced from their duty to their masters by the treacherous and cruel tools of administration." Dunmore and the British were not sincere in their offer, readers were told, for the British had insisted on a continuance of the slave trade in order to reap profits from the sale of tobacco. Moreover, if the British were to win they would immediately sell the blacks to the West Indies for profit; if blacks did enlist, they would be hanged if seized, and ran the risk of having their wives and children murdered, "cut off by our riflemen from the back country, who never wish to see a negro, and who will pour out their vengeance upon them whenever it is desired." If masters had told their slaves these things "they would be contented with their situation, and expect a better condition in the next world" (*VG*-Purdie 11/17/75).

In a second essay the author similarly doubted Dunmore's motives, suggesting Dunmore would either return the slaves to their owners, or, repeating a familiar theme, sell them in the West Indies. "Can it then be supposed that the Negroes will be better used by the English, who have always encouraged, and upheld this slavery, than by their present masters, who pity their condition, who, in general, to make it as easy and comfortable as possible, and would willingly, were it in their power, or were they permitted not only prevent any more Negroes from losing their freedom, but restore it to such as have already lost it" (*VG*-Dixon and Hunter 11/25/75). Five days later, the view that the slaves had been taken advantage of by false promises was expressed in Pickney's *Virginia Gazette*. "Lord Dunmore's cruel policy begins at length to be discovered by the blacks," the piece began, contending that Dunmore was holding the former slaves in a new bondage. "But such is the barbarous policy of this cruel man, he keeps these unhappy creatures not only against their will, but intends to place them in the front of battle, to prevent them flying in case of engagement, which, from their utter ignorance of firearms, he knows they will do" (*VG*-Pickney 11/30/75).

Blacks as fearful was a characterization that appeared in an account of Great Bridge. "Captain Leslie, being unable to rally the Negroes, who could not stand the severe fire from hundreds of marksmen, retreated into the fort, and that night abandoned it" (*VG*-Pickney 12/30/75). Blacks as unsuspecting victims at the hands of Lord Dunmore was a theme sounded at the conclusion of the episode when the Virginia troops took over Gwynn's Island, at which time "many poor Negroes were found on the island dying of the putrid fever. Dunmore's neglect of those poor creatures, suffering numbers of them to perish for want to common necessaries and the least assistance, one would think enough to discourage others from joining him" (*VG*-Dixon and Hunter 7/20/76).

The final grouping, in which blacks were defined in only positive ways, contains just two items: one in which a black pilot, simply defined as "a valuable Negro man" without any qualifications, was reported shot in an engagement with a British vessel (*VG*-Purdie 5/3/76). The second item was the characterization of Joseph Harris, a slave who had escaped from his Virginia owner to serve the British as a pilot. This appeared in a letter by a British sea captain who said that Harris was "too valuable" in his knowledge of the rivers not to be used by the British and, additionally, was "a very useful person." As in the captured Dunmore letter, it should be noted that the publication of this was not to present the former slave in a generous light as much as it was to indicate that the British would stoop to the enlistment of a slave. The paragraph introducing the letter pointed out, with ironic emphasis, that the British considered Harris as "a proper person" to be employed in the king's service (*VG*-Purdie 9/15/75).

Certainly, many of the themes that have come to be associated with paternalism were represented in the Lord Dunmore coverage, including the belief that the Virginia masters knew what was best for their bondspeople as well as the notion that slaves were basically loyal if their perceived gullibility was not taken advantage of. This view of essential attachment could seem to support the concept of black and white Virginians as composing a single family of shared traditions, work patterns, and family ties (Sobel), if family is defined to include many subordinate members. The Virginian response is in terms of family, if we consider family in a traditional patriarchal structure characterized by ownership and domination of family members. Virginians clearly expressed the view that masters had to be willing to use force to support the system.

Most of the published accounts of the Dunmore period fall into the first grouping that cluster around the theme of white male self-definition and the threat posed to that definition in the face of desertion by others of similar or upper classes. The large number of these stories compared to the other groups suggests that what Virginians feared most was the breaking of ranks among whites. Paternalism could not succeed as a mode of domination, the items indicate, if the dominant whites did not agree upon its principles.

The concern in maintaining the system already in place was so overriding that the Virginians allowed themselves no flexibility to bargain. Only one item suggested anything like a promise of freedom to the slave, an item in which the writer indicated that while the British had opposed the ending of the slave trade, the Virginians had worked to bring it to a close "and would restore freedom to those that had lost it" (*VG*-Dixon and Hunter 11/25/75). Otherwise, slaves were told to "return to their duty" and to "return home" or risk death. With the single exception of the item cited, Virginians refused to make any concessions, at least in the public prints. There was only the prediction that the escaped slave could expect worse treatment at the hands of the British than their former Virginia masters, not the promise of eventual emancipation; indeed, not even earned emancipation by serving the patriot side was promised. Even in the face of Dunmore's offer, Virginians refused to consider any change in slave status. Trapped in a closed society, Virginians seemed unable to allow a change in status for the slave without challenging their own view of themselves.

It was a view that was to be promulgated throughout the American colonies by a press that relied almost exclusively on the Virginia newspapers for its news of the event. The propaganda press only had to use what was at hand to promote its agenda. The less ardent patriots had little choice but to use what was at hand. Inevitably, the Virginia reaction became the historical account of the event.

With twenty-eight uses each, the *Pennsylvania Evening Post* and the *Pennsylvania Gazette* had the highest utilization of the Virginia press items. The *South-Carolina Gazette,* whose curtain of silence had been long lowered on issues to do with slavery, used just one item. The *Boston Gazette* used twelve items, about the middle of the rankings. (Other newspaper use as follows: *CJ* 21; *NYJ* 21; *PJ* 20; *CJ* 13; *PP* 10; *CC* 9; *PG* 9; *MG* 9; *EJ* 8; *PL* 7; *NM* 7; *CG* 4; *EG* 4; *NYG* 3; *GG* 2.)

The range in the usage must be qualified by external factors. The first has to do with the unreliability of the colonial mail, particularly to and from the southern colonies. The *Georgia Gazette,* for example, did not receive the Virginia newspapers as promised: "A Gentleman immediately from Virginia, who brought the publick papers with him but left them in the country." The gentleman from Virginia had a good memory for he supplied the Georgia paper with an accurate summary of the proclamation but without the invective that accompanied the Virginia publication (*GG* 1/3/76). The relative high percentage of use represented by the Philadelphia press has some obvious explanations, the most important one being that Philadelphia was the seat of the provisional government and the papers represented the wide sphere of interests of the convention. Nor can competition be ignored. Benjamin Towne's attractive and well-printed *Pennsylvania Evening Post* was published three times a week, carried relatively light advertising, and thus had more space available than many other newspapers. In fact, the *Post* may have established a rather rigorous news standard for its competitors, as many of the Dunmore items that appeared in the Philadelphia papers had been published the day before in the *Post*. Moreover Towne's paper carried a wider spectrum of news than its competitors, including the related news of Burke's address to the House of Commons and the execution of Thomas Jeremiah in Charleston (*PEP* 7/27; 8/20/75).

The use of the Virginia press items by the Philadelphia papers does not appear related to a particular political pattern. In classic rendering, Towne is always drawn as a Tory sympathizer—"a clever printer without any apparent principles" (Mott 88), hardly the appropriate carrier for Virginia Whiggism. Nor was Franklin's old paper, the *Pennsylvania Gazette*, now under the unhindered stewardship of David Hall, a propaganda organ. But William Bradford, proprietor of the *Pennsylvania Journal* (twenty items) was a Son of Liberty and a Presbyterian who, as mentioned, had little patience with antislavery. Holt's *New-York Journal* (twenty-one items) was clearly part of the core patriot press. Holt was undoubtedly a Virginia sympathizer as a former Virginian, mayor of Williamsburg from 1750 to 1753. He was also a slave owner, and in a later period blamed his slave for the theft of a batch of lottery tickets that he likely stole himself (Walker 48). In Norfolk, a radical newspaper run by his adopted son, John Hunter Holt, was closed down by Dunmore, who called the closure a "public service" (Palsits 490).

The most frequently reprinted item, with twelve uses, was Dixon and Hunter's December 2, 1775, item that had to do with the enlistment of blacks who were to wear "this inscription on their breasts—'liberty to slaves'" and concludes, "As the rivers will henceforth be strictly watched, and every possible precaution taken, it is hoped others will be effectually prevented from joining those his Lordship has already collected." The mention of slaves was incidental in an item used eleven times that was an account of the taking of a British tender (VG-Purdie 10/17/75). Also reprinted eleven times was the account of the battle of Great Bridge in which Edmund Pendleton is assured that "none of the blacks, etc., in the rear with Capt. Leslie, advanced farther than the bridge" (*VG*-Purdie 12/15/75).

The *Boston Gazette* supplemented its coverage of the Great Bridge attack outside of the Virginia press by publishing part of a letter from a Virginia correspondent, one that relayed the common perception of black ineptitude on the field of battle: "Blacks were found rather an encumbrance than a service to his lordship, destroying one another more than the enemy" (*BG* 1/15/76).

One item that had nine uses was the account, already mentioned, of a British captain's depredations along the Virginia coast — "a very pretty occupation for the captain of one of his Majesty's ships of war." Another item that received a similar number of uses was an account of the widely held view, even to modern times, that Dunmore and the British sold all blacks who came to them. "Lord Dunmore intends shortly for the West Indies with his cargo of slaves, to make the most of them before his departure for England" (*VG*-Purdie 12/15/75).

All of the above items contain racial messages, as do all the accounts in some degree, even the numerical cordoning of black from white, that had to do with the Dunmore episode. But the use of a Virginia press item that first appeared on November 30, 1775, and reprinted eight times, gave readers outside Virginia a full-fledged example of Virginia paternalism. In this account, the writer asserted blacks were realizing that Lord Dunmore did not have their best interests in mind. The blacks were kept "digging entrenchments in wet ground," and they could expect to be placed "in the front of battle, to prevent their flying in case of engagement, which, from their utter ignorance of firearms, he knows they will do." The blacks are characterized as "unhappy creatures," who are "kept against their will" (implicating, perhaps that they remained with their Virginia masters out of preference), frightened by guns and deluded by false promises (*VG*-Pickney 11/30/75), almost all the earmarks of the slave "Sambo" personality that was to appear so frequently in the antebellum period.

But the tone of this item is calm and reasonable. What the press outside Virginia did not represent to the same degree as the newspapers inside Virginia was the tone of fury that appeared in some of the Virginia items. For example, the text of the proclamation and the accompanying furious introductory paragraph that condemned Dunmore to the legions of hell were republished in just five newspapers outside Virginia: the *Boston Gazette,* the *New-York Journal,* the *Pennsylvania Journal,* the *Providence Gazette,* and the *Pennsylvania Evening Post* (*BG* 12/25; *NYJ* 12/7; *PJ* 12/6; *PG* 12/23; *PEP* 12/5/75). The account of the landing of British troops on Gwynn's Island that was celebrated by "a promiscuous ball which was opened we hear, by a certain spruce little gentleman with one of the black ladies" (*VG-*Purdie 5/31/76) was not used outside Virginia.

Nonetheless, the press outside Virginia generally tended to use the Virginia items in the same proportions as in the Virginia colony, as in the use of items in which the British are seen as betrayers. The exception is in the use of items where slaves and blacks were portrayed as a threat to whites as thieves, plotters, barbarians, and murderers. In the press outside Virginia, these items composed a significantly larger share, almost double, of the Dunmore coverage than they did in the Virginia papers (my count).

Taken together, the published reports suggest that the main concern of the Virginians was the abandonment by the British leadership of the Virginia value system. It is significant that none of the coverage was concerned with the economic loss the slaves represented, obviously less important to the planters, even as debt-ridden as they were, than the threat of a change of status between black and white. Instead, Lord Dunmore's abandonment left Virginians without British support to carry the standard for their philosophy of enslavement, and much of the coverage was the articulation of values that had been part of Virginian life for more than 150 years.

The sense of the betrayal that Virginians experienced was double-sided. The loss of slaves could be explained on grounds of "gullibility," but the Virginian sense of betrayal at the British could only be translated into anger at Great Britain, a view that was carried into the rest of the colonial press that had been primed for years by the Boston radicals. Outside Virginia, Dunmore's action was likely to represent another example of a Mother Country rejecting established responsibilities in favor of privileging a subservient class. An essay first appearing in the *Pennsylvania Journal* and then in the *Boston Gazette* expressed the culmination of the Dunmore episode to the colonial sensibility: First, the writer charged, the British had instigated "the Indian savages to ravage our frontiers, and murder, after their inhuman manner, our defenceless wives and children." Now, the writer asked, "Have not yet Negro slaves been incited to rebel against their masters and arms put into their hands to murder them?" (*BG* 3/25/76; *PJ* 2/26/76). Colonial readers, however, no strangers to finding large meaning in homely detail, would have noted the metaphor in another story that appeared during the period. A British soldier's wife, employed to care for a sick woman, was found dead "with a little tender infant; with all the horrors of death in its face, sucking the dead mother's breasts" (*NYJ* 3/2/75).

Even before the Dunmore episode was concluded, its reverberations had become part of the patriot call to arms. Certainly the event was reflected in the Declaration of Independence in the claim that the king "has excited domestic insurrections against us." Its purpose as propaganda was extended from the colonial press into revolutionary theater and provides an example of how the Virginian view came to dominate revolutionary politics.

The Philadelphia artisan and Son of Liberty, John Leacock, devoted the fourth act in *The Fall of British Tyranny; or, American Liberty Triumphant the First Campaign* to Dunmore and is used here as an example of the spread of ideas articulated in Virginia press into the revolutionary culture, as well as the incorporation of racist ideas into patriot propaganda.

Published in Philadelphia in 1776, *The Fall of British Tyranny* is a chronicle play, presenting the early events of the Revolution with sweep and grandeur in what has been recognized as one of the most ambitious of the period (Silverman 310–13). In well-paced scenes, the play moves from the English Parliament to Boston; Lexington, Virginia; and Cambridge. Leacock gave his Tory players names considered telling for their roles. Lord Dunmore is thus "Lord Kidnapper," Thomas Hutchinson is "Judas," and the Earl of Bute appears under the title "Lord Paramount," who opens the play by plotting the return of the Stuart dynasty — that favorite theme of the British Whigs.

Lord Dunmore appears in Act IV in action that is confined to his ship. The act opens with the arrival of a boatload of escaped slaves. They are greeted without enthusiasm by the ship's boatswain and a sailor.

> *Sailor:* Damn my eyes, Mr. Boatswain, but here's a black flag of truce coming aboard.
> *Boatswain:* Sure enough . . . where are they from?
> *Sailor:* From hell, I suppose . . . for they're as black as so many devils.
> *Boatswain:* Very well — no matter — they're recruits for the Kidnapper.
> *Sailor:* We shall be all of a color by and by — damn me —

The boatswain disappears below deck to inform Dunmore of the volunteers, but he is stopped at Dunmore's door by a servant because Dunmore is in bed with two women. The boatswain demands entrance, calling the servant a "pimping son of a bitch," and muttering to himself that the "pimp guard" would be of better use as a ship lookout. Dunmore finally appears, in an amiable mood, laughing pleasantly as he tells the boatswain to bring the recruits on board. In a falsely humble manner, the boatswain suggests, "I think we have gallows-looking dogs enough on board already — the scrapings of Newgate, and the refuse of Tyburn, and when the wind blow aft, damn 'em, they stink like Polecats." Dunmore laughs again, but the boatswain persists, indicating, in the same humble manner, that Dunmore will sell the slaves to the West Indies when he has used them to cut the throats of their old masters. "And that will be something in your honour's pocket, d'ye see — sell, ev'ry man to his trade."

Awaiting Dunmore on deck, the sailors grumble he will appear only when he is finished with his sexual encounters and complain the blacks will consume space and food. By contrast, Dunmore, finally arriving, greets the recruits cordially: "Well, by brave blacks, are you come to 'list." The spokesman for the group speaks in dialect, both as comic relief and to suggest that Dunmore cannot mean his detailed promises of rank and privilege: "You shall be called major Cudjo Thompson," Dunmore informs him, "and if you behave well, I'll soon make you a greater man than your master, and if I find the rest of you behave well, I'll make you all officers, and after you have served Lord Paramount for a while, you shall have money in your pockets, good cloaths on your backs and be as free as them white men over there."

Back in the cabin, Dunmore makes it clear to his second-in-command he cares nothing for freedom of the slaves. "I look upon this to be a grand maneuver in politics; this is making dog eat dog — thief catch thief — the servants against his master — rebel against rebel." The scene and act close as Dunmore's compatriots josh him about his "brace of whores" to which he responds with yet another pleasant laugh and excuses himself to take a nap. Clearly, manners did not make the man (Philbrick 106–12).

The Dunmore of the play is removed from the realities of either his ship's stores or the havoc produced by his proclamation. He is infuriatingly indifferent to the troubles he has caused, indulging in his own pleasures while his troops starve. The British boatswain is the hero of the act, righteously angry at Dunmore's dalliance, which seems to represent his utter lack of interest in anything but his own ends. Leacock, in this brief scene, encapsulated the Virginia sense of outrage at Dunmore's abandonment.

The Virginia coverage also fit nicely into black stereotype that had already been seen on the colonial stage. Cudjo, the only speaking black, is shown as a man easily swayed by promises and eager to please. While he expresses no anger at his former master, he promises, as if to please, that he would shoot him if necessary. The blacks are represented in terms of speech and facial stereotypes (the sailors ridicule the size of Cudjo's mouth), a comic tradition to which Leacock gave new virulence. There is no sense among the sailors that the blacks are "brave"; and it is clearly indicated that Dunmore patronizes them for his own ends. As in the Virginia coverage of military engagements, the British common soldier or sailor is not the target of attack—indeed, the British sailors express American attitudes—but it is Dunmore, as representative of the British administration, who is the focus.

The episode quickly slipped into popular song (F. Moore 67), and Philip Freneau included Lord Dunmore in one of his first political poems. Dunmore and his "crew of banditti"—a phrase often used in the newspapers—are recognized in a series of couplets listing all the reasons for disunion from Great Britain (Freneau 149). From popular accounts, the Dunmore of the Virginia press was set into stone by early historians. In his history published in 1789, the account of the battle of Great Bridge, even by the New Divinity antislavery activist, William Gordon, appears drawn totally from the Virginia press accounts (Gordon 1:110). In 1818, thirty years after Gordon's book, David Ramsay was also influenced by the Virginia press. The slave participation at the battle of Great Bridge was dismissed. "The slaves in this engagement were more prejudicial to their British employers than to the provincials," he wrote in a sentence that is little changed from what appeared in the Virginia press (Ramsay 2:89). Such early historical accounts promulgated the eighteenth-century Virginian view of the incident into the twentieth century.

Among modern historians, only Benjamin Quarles has examined the newspaper accounts of the episode with any eye to their source, noting the "psychological warfare" of the Virginia newspaper essay that called upon blacks to return to their duty or suffer the consequences (Quarles, "Lord Dunmore" 24). Additionally, if only in a footnote, Quarles refers to another Dunmore item published in the *New-York Journal* that, in an angry quatrain, noted a black mother had named her child after Dunmore.

> *Hail! doughty Ethiopian Chief*
> *Though ignominious Negro Thief!*
> *This Black shall prop they stinking name*
> *And damn thee to perpetual fame.*
> (Quarles, "Lord Dunmore" 24n)

Those lines indicate the undertow of fury that characterized much of the Dunmore coverage. By the use of such items, the patriot press brought into high relief the racial themes that had been building during the revolutionary period. Like another Boston Massacre, the British fired into the colonial world of black and white relationships with little concern for the damage or the disarray that was left behind. That was a theme that had meaning for colonists outside colonial Virginia, a message that was brought to them in all its reverberations thanks to a patriot press that sought to unite by whatever bonds that were at hand with little thought to future consequences.

Propaganda and Patriotism

Early in his national career, Abraham Lincoln argued that the founding fathers, understanding slavery was wrong but finding its eradication a practical impossibility at the establishment of the national government, "hedged and hemmed it in to the narrowest limits of necessity." The word "slavery" was not even allowed in the Constitution, Lincoln told his audience of Nebraska-Kansas Act opponents, in order to indicate that "the cutting may begin at the end of a given time" (Donald 176).

The antislavery legislation that began to occur even before independence was won upholds the traditional view that the Revolution included the tacit promise that a new nation could be expected to move vigorously to eliminate the institution. Even Massachusetts, so resistant to antislavery legislation in the revolutionary decade, adopted a constitution in 1780 that was viewed as inimical to slavery; certainly court cases substantially, if not conclusively, halted the institution; and by the decade's end, unequivocal legislation was in place.

Lincoln did not credit propaganda as the lever that made such a promise, but it nevertheless could be argued that the Revolution's propaganda, by substantially remaining silent on the issue of slavery, did not alienate southern support and made a national independence movement possible. At the same time, the silence neither quelled nor censored local antislavery discussion. And, most important, silence further helped cement the promise by eschewing the temptation of making *proslavery* a unifying theme — certainly a strategy that would have gone a long way to break the southern tie to Great Britain.

Although antislavery was not a national standard at independence, neither was the perpetuation of the institution. Silence, it might be argued, was the only amenable choice that gave antislavery a chance. Any other position contained the seeds of dooming a national movement, and perhaps putting in the place of the present United States a North America composed of two or more nations based on attitudes toward race. In short, if this argument were framed as one of the debate questions that the colonial Harvard graduates so favored, it might be: Resolved: by avoiding the issue of slavery, the propagandists of the American Revolution made a unified revolution possible, and allowed for the development of a movement that sought full rights for all.

Another alternative is to consider that the American Revolution may have failed to materialize at all if the slavery issue was fully debated. In that case, American slavery would have been abolished by British imperial action, possibly avoiding the Civil War. But only Great Britain's own caution on the subject can be blamed for not winning the war by this means. Up until Burke's 1775 parliamentary call for the emancipation of American slaves — although a predictable failure — only Lord Dunmore chose to address the issue of American slavery directly. Instead, the British relied on innuendo, which in the end served to weaken the antislavery cause in the American colonies without strengthening the British hand.

Such speculations aside, what may be concluded is that the role of the antislavery movement in the American Revolution encouraged the continuance of antislavery voices along familiar lines. New Divinity as a religious movement did not last into the new century, but the style and passion of its antislavery arguments were carried forward by the nineteenth-century abolitionists. The reverberations of Jonathan Edwards and Samuel Hopkins were clearly to be heard in the sound and fury of the William Lloyd Garrison wing of the abolitionist movement and in the Radical Republicanism of Charles Sumner. By the same token, the American Revolution strengthened the resolve of the Quaker campaign against slavery, and the Quaker argument of sensibility would be carried forward by Theodore Parker, Lydia Marie Child, and Harriet Beecher Stowe.

But it might be considered that the rhetoric that continued to accompany the abolition movement into the new century was not any more suited to the nation than it had been to a revolutionary generation. The promise of Paine, Rush, Appleton, and Swan, who had begun to address slavery outside of moral outrage, was never fulfilled in the construction of an antebellum rhetoric that still sought to persuade by empathetic feeling and godly retribution. Antislavery would continue to be couched in terms that were not so relevant to white Americans concerned with competition from black labor or who feared social disorder, the loss of racial identity, status, or other perceived advantages. Abolition, in fact, became so removed from the general American agenda that even the word "abolitionist" came to represent an abjured, radical fringe.

The adoption of the colonization schemes, that is, the consensual removal of black Americans to the African continent, by men such as Lincoln speaks to the vacuum that occurred when antislavery adherents, before and after the Revolution, failed to put the issue on the mainstream agenda in ways that directly addressed the role of the freed slave in ordinary society. Such argument needed time for development. Because of the patriot silence on the issue, Rush, Paine, and Sarter never had the opportunity to develop the cohesive discussion that might have given the tacit promise a national springboard after the Revolution. Patriot silence on the issue stilled the development of a public discourse that explored alternative arguments so that, lacking other discussion, colonization, embedded in failure, came to fill the gap.

Among the alternative arguments stilled by the early patriot curtain of silence were those expressed by the voices of the oppressed, both slave and free. Widespread distribution of the Massachusetts petitions for freedom, the essay by Caesar Sarter, the argument offered by Adam, the actions of Prince Hall, and the poetry of Phillis Wheatley would have offered counters to the role of myth, symbol, and difference and may have influenced the essays employed by the white antislavery adherents. But into the antebellum period, the black voices most heard were, like Frederick Douglass and Sojourner Truth, those that found expression in narrative forms that had been long set in place by Quaker and Congregational antislavery adherents. Despite their considerable commitment and public voice, less destined for stardom on the antebellum trail were the members of the black middle class, whose contributions included the representation of African Americans in a world that was not only outside of slavery but also outside myth and symbol and the Quaker and Calvinist framings of white conscience. The voices of Philadelphia's James Forten family, for example, were the minority voices in the antislavery campaign of traditional Quaker and Calvinist arguments made on public platforms, in antislavery newspapers, and in the millions of pamphlets that came from abolitionist presses in the 1830s and 1840s. The antislavery arguments of the antebellum period largely worked the familiar fields of sentiment, sensibility, and white conscience, all of doubtful significance in permanently shifting white attitudes toward black Americans.

Indeed, at the turn of millennium, more than two hundred years after the American Revolution, what is striking is that the white attitudes toward black Americans do not seem so far removed from the attitudes promulgated by the metaphor of slavery in the American Revolution. Inner cities have been given over to black inhabitants thought to have no possibility of change. Politicians hesitate at strengthening, and more likely seek to weaken, the national social services network lest it be considered as assisting the black poor, who are widely seen by many white Americans as responsible for, and thus deserving of, the poverty in which they exist. Political campaigns have only to press a code word or two for familiar racial attitudes to flood into white consciousness.

As a country that always has some level of dislocation somewhere, shared emotion about race provides the comfort of solidarity as much today as it did in revolutionary times, and perhaps on the same basis — the perceived lack of solutions to old problems. Encouraged by the American media industry and its love of broad representation over factual differentiation, the use of shared emotion as a substitute for democratic participation, and the easy understanding that comes by thinking in opposites, particular ways of thinking are now embedded American characteristics for all groups and impinge upon the perceptions of race in America from many sides. Still missing is a constructive public discourse that explores and builds on the basis of exchange; instead, we are encouraged to leave in place a mode of expression that is the most characterized by its opposition to another position.

Oppositional thinking is useful for propagandistic purposes, but the danger, of course, is that its flames will continue to burn after the cause is done. Beliefs promulgated as propagandistic messages may later be difficult to dislodge, associated as they are with the satisfying emotions of rightness, solidarity, and purpose. It is no wonder that jingoism is the easiest theme to revive. Moreover, the propaganda associated with national purpose can become fixed by the firmament of success as much as by the simmering resentments that accompany an unsuccessful coup.

John Adams noted approvingly that Otis and Adams were "politick" in their use of public festival. But the propagandists of the American Revolution set in place a system of codes that utilized complicated white fears about black colonial Americans. We may appreciate that the propagandists never completely shut down antislavery discussion; nonetheless, the failure of the revolutionaries to address the issue of black Americans in a new nation served to leave intact an underworld of beliefs that could only shape the course of the republic.

Works Cited

PRIMARY SOURCES

Adams, John. *Diary and Autobiography of John Adams.* 8 vols. Edited by L. H. Butterfield. Cambridge: Harvard University Press, 1962.

———. *The Life and Works of John Adams.* 10 vols. Boston: Little Brown, 1850–56.

Adams, Samuel. *The Writings of Sam Adams.* 4 vols. Edited by Henry Alonzo Cushing. New York: Putnam's, 1907.

Adams Family Correspondence. Edited by L. H. Butterfield. Cambridge: Harvard University Press, 1963.

Alexander, James. *A Brief Narrative of the Case and Trial of John Peter Zenger.* Edited by Stanley Nider Katz. Cambridge: Harvard University Press, 1963.

Allen, John. *An Oration on the Beauties of Liberty, or the Essential Rights of Americans, Delivered at the Second Baptist Church in Boston Upon last Thanksgiving Dec. 3d, 1772.* 4th ed. Boston: E. Russell, 1773. Reprinted in *Am I Not a Man and a Brother: The Antislavery Crusade of Revolutionary America.* Edited by Roger Bruns, 257–62. New York: Confucian Press, 1980 [hereafter Bruns].

Ames, Ellis, and Abner C. Goodell, eds. *Acts and Resolves, Public and Private, Massachusetts of the Province of Massachusetts Bay, 1692–1714.* 4 vols. Boston: 1869–1922.

The Appendix: or, some Observations on the Expediency of the Petitions of the Africans, living in Boston, etc. lately presented to the General Assembly of this Province to which is annexed, the Petitions referred to. Boston: Russell, 1773.

Appleton, Nathaniel. *Considerations of Slavery in a Letter to a Friend.* Boston: Edes and Gill, 1767. Reprinted Bruns, 128–37.

Arthur. *Arthur, a Negro: The Life and Dying Speech of Arthur, a Negro Man.* Boston: n.p., 1768.

Avery, David. *The Lord is to be praised for the Triumph of his Power, Sermon December 18, 1777 Greenwich, Conn. General Thanksgiving.* Norwich, Conn.: Green and Spooner, 1778.

Benezet, Anthony. *A Caution and Warning to Great Britain and Her Colonies in a Short Representation of the Calamitous State of the Enslaved Negroes in the British Dominions: Collected from various Authors and submitted to the Serious Consideration of All, more especially of Those in Power.* Philadelphia: Hall and Sellers, 1767. Reprinted Bruns, 111–27.

———. *A Short Account of that Part of Africa Inhabited by Negroes. With Respect to the Fertility of the Country; and good Disposition of many of the Natives, and the Manner in which the Slave Trade is carried on. Extracted from divers Authors, in order to shew the Iniquity of what Trade and the falsity of the Arguments, usually; advanced in its Vindication.* Philadelphia: Dunlap, 1762. Reprinted Bruns, 145–84.

———. *Some Historical Account of Guinea, its Situation, Produce and the General Disposition of its Inhabitants. An Inquiry into the Rise and Progress of the Slave Trade, Its Nature, and lamentable Effects.* Philadelphia: Crukshank, 1771. Reprinted Bruns, 145–84.

Bristol. *The Dying Speech of Bristol.* Boston: Edes and Gill, 1763.

By a Pennsylvanian [Benjamin Rush]. *An Address to the Inhabitants of the British Settlements on the Slavery of Negroes in America, The Second Edition.* Philadelphia: John Dunlap, 1773. Reprinted Bruns, 224–31.

Byles, Mather. *Before the Execution of a Young Negro Servant for Poisoning an Infant.* Boston: Kneeland, 1754.

Chauncy, Charles. *Enthusiasm Described and caution'd against. A Sermon Preach'd . . . the Lord's Day after the Commencement.* Boston: Draper for Eliot and Blanchard, 1743.

———. *Trust in* GOD, *the Duty of a People in a Day of Trouble: A Sermon preached, May 30th, 1770.* Boston: Kneeland for Thomas Leverett, 1770.

Coleman, Ellihu. "A Testimony against the Anti-Christian Practice of making Slaves of Men, wherein it is shewed to be contrary to the Dispensation of the Law and Time of the Gospel, and very opposite both to Grace and Nature," *Friends' Review* 5 (1851): 84–85, 102–4.

Cooke, Samuel. *A Sermon Preached at Cambridge in the Audience of his Honor Thomas Hutchinson, Esq . . . , May 20, 1770.* Boston: Edes and Gill, 1770. Reprinted, *The Wall and the Garden: Selected Massachusetts Elections Sermons, 1670–1775.* Edited by A. W. Plumstead, 326–46. Minneapolis: University of Minnesota Press, 1968.

Cooper, David. *A Mite Cast in the Treasury; or Observations on Slave-Keeping.* Philadelphia: Crukshank, 1772. Reprinted Bruns, 184–91.

Dillwyn, William. *Brief Considerations on Slavery and the Expediency of the Abolition with some Hints on the means whereby it may be gradually effected. Recommended to the serious Attention of All, and especially of those entrussted with the Power of Legislation.* Burlington, N.J.: Isaac Collins, 1774. Reprinted Bruns, 270–76.

Du Simitiere, Pierre. Cartoon depicting Pope Day. Pen and ink and wash drawing [Boston, 1767]. Library Company, Philadelphia.

Edes, Peter, to Benjamin C. Edes, February 16, 1836. *Proceedings of the Massachusetts Historical Society,* Ser. 1, 12 (1878): 174–76.

Edwards, Jonathan. "Images of Divine Things," In *A Jonathan Edwards Reader,* edited by John E. Smith, Harry R. Stout, and Kenneth P. Kinkema, 16–21. New Haven: Yale University Press, 1995.

A Few Lines on the Occasion of the Untimely End of Mark and Phyliss, who were executed at Cambridge Sept. 18 for Poisoning Their Master, Captain John Codman of Charlestown. Boston: n.p., 1751.

Force, Peter, ed. *Tracts and Other Papers Relating Principally to the Origin, Settlement, and Progress of the Colonies in North America, from the Discovery of the Country to the Year 1776.* 5 vols. Washington, D.C.: n.p., 1836–46.

A Forensic Dispute on the Legality of enslaving the Africans. Held at the Public commencement in Cambridge, New-England, July 21st, 1773. By Two Candidates for the Bachelor Degree. Boston: Boyle, 1773. Reprinted Bruns, 278–90.

Fowle, Daniel. *A Total Eclipse of Liberty.* Boston: Fowle, 1755.

Franklin, Benjamin. *The Autobiography and Other Writings.* Edited by Kenneth Silverman. New York: Penguin, 1986.

———. *Papers of Benjamin Franklin.* 32 vols. Edited by Leonard Larabee. New Haven: Yale University Press, 1967.

[Franklin, Benjamin]. *Magna Britannia: her Colonies Reduc'd.* London: 1765/66.

Freneau, Philip. *The Poems of Philip Freneau.* 2 vols. Edited by Fred Lewis Pattes. Princeton: University Library, 1902.

Frugal Housewife, or Complete Woman Cook. Boston: Edes and Gill, 1772.

Gilprin, Thomas. *Exiles in Virginia; with observations on the conduct of the Society of Friends During the Revolutionary War, 1777–1778.* Philadelphia: Published for the Subscribers, 1848.

Hammon, Briton. *A Narrative of the Uncommon Suffering and Surprising Deliverance of Briton Hammon.* Boston: Green and Russell, 1760.

Hargrave, Francis. *An Argument in the Case of James Somerset.* Boston: J. Russell, 1774.

An Historical Catalogue of the Old South Church of Boston. Boston: Old South Church, 1883.

Hopkins, Samuel. *A Dialogue Concerning the Slavery of the Africans.* Norwich, Conn.: Spooner, 1776.

Hopkins, Samuel, and Ezra Stiles. "To the Public," August 31, 1773, Redwood Library, Newport, R.I. Reprinted Bruns, 293.

The Horrid Nature, and enormous Guilt of Murder — a sermon Nov. 19, 1754, the Day of the Execution of William Wier for the Murder of William Chisen. Boston; Thomas Fleet, 1754.

Hutchins, John Nathan. "The Mental and Personal *Qualifications of a Wife," Hutchin's Improved: Being an Almanack For the Year of our Lord, 1771.* New York: Hugh Gaine, n.d.

Journal of the Honourable House of Representatives. Boston: Edes and Gill, 1773.

Laurens, Henry. *The Papers of Henry Laurens.* 13 vols. Edited by George C. Rogers and David R. Chesnutt. Columbia: University of South Carolina Press, 1980.

Madison, James. *Papers of James Madison.* 16 vols. Edited by William T. Hutchinson. Chicago: University of Chicago Press, 1962–77.

Mather, Cotton. *Diary of Cotton Mather.* 2 vols. *Collections of the Massachusetts Historical Society.* 7th Ser. 7–8. Boston: n.p., 1911–12.

——. *The Negro Christianized.* Boston: Bartholomew Green, 1706.

Mayhew, Jonathan. *Discourse Concerning Unlimited Submission and Non-Resistance to the Higher Powers.* Boston: Fowle and Gookin, 1750.

——. *Observations of the Charter and Conduct of the Society of the Propagation of the Gospel in Foreign Parts.* Boston: Draper, Edes and Bill, Fleet, 1763.

[Mein, John]. *Sagittarius's Letter and Political. Speculations extracted from the Public Ledger. Boston: By Order of the Select Men and sold at Faneuil Hall for the Benefit of the Distressed Patriots.* Boston: n.p., 1775.

Niles, Nathaniel. *Two Discourses on Liberty Delivered at the North Church, in Newburyport. June 5, 1774.* Newburyport, Mass.: Isaiah Thomas and H. W. Tinges, 1774. Reprinted Bruns, 317–24.

Nisbet, Richard. *Slavery Not Forbidden by Scripture or a Defence of the West-India Planter.* Philadelphia: Sparhawk, 1773.

Oliver, Peter. *Peter's Oliver's Origins and Progress of the American Rebellion: A Tory View.* San Marino, Calif.: Huntington Library, 1961.

Otis, James. *The Rights of the British Colonies Asserted and Proved.* Boston: Edes and Gill, 1764. Reprinted Bruns, 103–5.

Parkman, Ebenezer. *The Diary of Ebenezer Parkman, 1703–1782.* Edited by Frances G. Walett. Worcester, Mass.: American Antiquarian Society, 1974.

Personal Slavery Established by the Suffrage of Custom and Right Reason: Being a Full Answer to the Gloomy and Visionary Reveries of All the Fanatical and Enthusiastical Writers on that Subject. Philadelphia: Dunlap, 1773. Reprinted Bruns, 245–57.

Probate Records, Suffolk County, Massachusetts, 84, 102 (1785, 1804).

Pruitt, Bettye Hobbs, ed. *Massachusetts Tax Valuation List of 1771.* Boston: Hall, 1978.

Record of the First Church of Charlestown, Mass., 1652–1789. Boston: Clapp, 1880.

"Records of the West Church, Boston, Mass. Admitted to Full Communion 1739–1853." *The New England Historical and Genealogical Register* 93 (1938): 261.

[Reed, Esther DeBerdt]. *The Sentiments of an American Woman.* Philadelphia: Dunlap, 1780

Report of the Record Commissioners of the City of Boston Concerning the Boston Town Records, 1756 to 1768. Boston: Rockwell and Church, 1888.

A Report of the Records Commission of the City of Boston Containing the Selectmen's Minutes from 1754 to 1763. Boston: Rockwell and Churchill, 1887.

Rush, Benjamin. *An Address on the Slavery of the Negroes in America.* 1773. Reprint, New York: Arno Press and New York Times, 1969.

Saffin, John. *A Brief and Candid Answer to a Late Printed Sheet, Entituled the Selling of Joseph Whereunto Is Vindication of the Author's Dealing with and Prosecution of His Negro Man Servant for His Vile and Exhorbitant Behavior towards His Master and His Tenant, Thomas Shepard; which Hath Been Wrongfully Represented to Their Prejudice and Defamation.* Boston: n.p., 1701.

Sewall, Samuel. *Diary of Samuel Sewall.* Edited by Harvey Wish. New York: Putnam's Sons, 1976.

———. *The Selling of Joseph a Memorial.* Boston: Bartholomew Green and John Allen, 1700. Reprinted in Sewall, *Diary,* 88–92.

Sharp, Granville. *An Essay on Slavery.* Burlington, N.J.: Isaac Collins, 1773.

A Short Narrative of the Horrid Massacre in Boston perpetrated in the Evening of Fifth Day of March 1770, by Soldiers of the XXIXth Regiment. Boston: Edes and Gill, T. and J. Fleet, 1770.

Swan, James. *A Disuasion to Great-Britain and the Colonies from the Slave Trade to Africa. Shewing the Contradictions this Trade Bears, both to Laws divine and provincial; the Disadvantages arising from it, and Advantages from abolishing it, both to Europe and Africa, particularly to Britain and the Plantations.* Boston: n.p., 1772. Reprinted Bruns, 200–215.

Thomas, Isaiah. *The History of Printing in America.* Edited by Marcus A. McCorison. 1868. Reprint, New York: Weathervane Books, 1970.

Thorton, John, ed. *The Pulpit of the American Revolution.* Boston: Gould and Lincoln, 1860.

Warren-Adams Letters Being chiefly a correspondence among John Adams, Samuel Adams, and James Warren. 2 vols. Boston: Massachusetts Historical Society, 1917.

The Watchman's Alarm to Lord North or the British Parliamentary Boston Port-Bill unwrapped being an Oration on the Meredian of Liberty; with some observations on the Liberty of the African. Salem, Mass.: Russell, 1774.

Wells, Richard. *A Few Political Reflections Submitted to the Consideration of the British Colonies.* Philadelphia: Dunlap, 1774.

Wesley, John. *"Thoughts on Slavery," The Potent Enemies of America.* Philadelphia: Crukshank, 1774.

Almanacs (A)

A1 *Bickerstaff's Boston Almanack, For... 1769.* Boston: Mills and Hicks, 1768.

A2 *The New England Town and Country Almanack... For... 1769.* Providence, R.I.: Carter, 1768.

A3 *Bickerstaff's Boston Almanack for the Year of our Redemption 1782.* Boston: E. Russel, 1781.

Historical Society of Pennsylvania (HSP)

HSP 1 Samuel Hopkins to Susa [sic] Anthony, Newport, November 14, 1769, Gratz Collection, American Colonial Clergy, Case 8, Box 23.

HSP 2 Samuel Hopkins to Susa [sic] Anthony, Newport, November 3, 1769, Gratz Collection, American Colonial Clergy, Case 8, Box 23.

HSP 3 Phillis Wheatley to Samuel Hopkins, September 11, 1773, Gratz Collection, American Poets Collection, Case 7, Box 10.

HSP 4 Samuel Hopkins and Ezra Stiles, "A Narrative of the Rise and Progress of a Proposal and attempt to send the gospel to New Guinea by educating and sending two negroes there to attempt to christianize their brethren," March 27, 1784, Gratz Collection, American Colonial Clergy, Case 8, Box 23.

HSP 5 Samuel Hopkins to Levi Hart, February 10, 1786, Gratz Collection, American Colonial Clergy, Case 8, Box 23.

Secondary Sources

Akers, Charles. *Called unto Liberty: A Life of Jonathan Mayhew, 1720–1766.* Cambridge: Harvard University Press, 1964.

———. "Religion and the American Revolution: Samuel Cooper and the Brattle Street Church." *William and Mary Quarterly* [hereafter *WMQ*] 35 (July 1977): 477–98.

Alden, John E. "John Mein: Scourge of Patriots." *Transactions of the Colonial Society of Massachusetts* 38 (February 1942): 585–87.

Alden, John R. "NOTES AND DOCUMENTS: John Stuart Accuses John Bull." *WMQ* 2 (July 1945): 315–20.

Aptheker, Herbert, ed. *And Why Not Every Man? Documentary Story of the Fight Against Slavery in the U.S.* 1961. Reprint, New York: International Publishers, 1970.

———, ed. *A Documentary History of the Negro People in the United States from Colonial Times through the Civil War.* 1951. Reprint, Secaucus, N.J.: Citadel, 1975.

Bailyn, Bernard, *The Ideological Origins of the American Revolution.* Cambridge: Harvard University Press, 1967.

———. *The Ordeal of Thomas Hutchinson.* Cambridge: Harvard University Press, 1974.

Bailyn, Bernard, and John. B. Hench, eds. *The Press and the American Revolution.* Worcester, Mass.: American Antiquarian Society, 1980.

Baldwin, Alice H. *The New England Clergy and the American Revolution.* 1928. Reprint, New York: Ungar, 1958.

Barrow, Robert. "Newspaper Advertising in Colonial America 1704–1775." Ph.D. diss., University of Virginia, 1967.

Bauer, Carol Phillips. "Law, Slavery and Somerset's Case in Eighteenth-Century England: A Study of the Legal Status of Freedom." Ph.D. diss., New York University, 1973.

Berlin, Ira, and Ronald Hoffman, eds. *Slavery and Freedom in the Age of the American Revolution.* Charlottesville: University Press of Virginia for the U.S. Capitol Historical Society, 1983.

Birdsall, Richard D. "Ezra Stiles Versus the New Divinity Men." *American Quarterly* 17 (1965): 248–58.

Black, Jeremy. *The English Press in the Eighteenth Century.* London: Croom Helm, 1987.

Bogin, Ruth. "NOTES AND DOCUMENTS: 'Liberty Further Extended': A 1776 Antislavery Manuscript by Lemuel Haynes." *WMQ* 40 (January 1983): 85–105.

Bonomi, Patricia. *Under the Cope of Heaven: Religion, Society, and Politics in Colonial America.* New York: Oxford University Press, 1986.

Botein, Stephen. "'Meer Mechanics' and an Open Press: The Business and Political Strategies of Colonial American Printers." *Perspectives in American History* 9 (1975): 127–225.

Boyce, George, James Curran, and Pauline Wingate, eds. *Newspaper History from the Seventeenth Century to the Present Day.* Beverly Hills: Sage, 1978.

Boyer, Paul S. "Borrowed Rhetoric: The Massachusetts Excise Controversy of 1754." *WMQ* 21 (July 1964): 328–51.

Bradley, Patricia. "Slavery in Colonial Newspapers: The Somerset Case." *Journalism History* 12 (Spring 1985): 1–7.

Breitenbach, William. "The Consistent Calvinism of the New Divinity Movement." *WMQ* 41 (May 1984): 241–64.

Brewer, John. *Party Ideology and Popular Politics at the Accession of George III.* London: Cambridge University Press, 1976.

Bridenbaugh, Carl. *Cities in Revolt Urban Life in America, 1743–1746.* New York: Knopf, 1955.

———. *Rebels and Gentlemen: Philadelphia in the Age of Franklin.* New York: Reynal and Hitchcock, 1942.

Brigham, Clarence S. *History and Bibliography of American Newspapers, 1690–1820.* 2 vols. 1947. Reprint, Westport, Conn.: Greenwood, 1975.

———. *Journals and Journeymen.* Philadelphia: University of Pennsylvania Press, 1950.

———. *Paul Revere's Engravings.* New York: Atheneum 1969.

Brown, Richard D. *Revolutionary Politics in Massachusetts: The Boston Committee of Correspondence and the Towns, 1772–1774.* Cambridge: Harvard University Press, 1970.

Bruns, Roger, ed. *Am I Not a Man and a Brother: The Antislavery Crusade of Revolutionary America, 1688–1788.* 1977. Reprint, New York: Confucian, 1980.

Budington, William I. *The History of the First Church, Charlestown, in Nine Lectures, With Notes.* Boston: Halres, Tappan, 1845.

Bumstead, John M., and Charles E. Clark. "New England's Tom Paine: John Allen and the Spirit of Liberty." *WMQ* 21 (October 1964): 561–70.

Caley, Percy B. "Dunmore: Colonial Governor of New York and Virginia, 1770–1782." Ph.D. diss., University of Pittsburgh, 1939.

Calhoun, Robert M. *The Loyalists in Revolutionary America.* New York: Little Brown, 1950.

Clark, Joseph S. *Historical Sketch of the Congregational Churches in Massachusetts.* Boston: Congregational Board of Publication, 1858.

Clinton, Catherine, and Michele Gillespie. *The Devil's Lane Sex and Race in the Early South.* New York: Oxford University Press, 1997.

Coffin, Joshua. *A Sketch of the History of Newbury, Newburyport and West Newbury.* 1845. Reprint, Hampton, N.H.: Privately published by Peter E. Randall, 1977.

Cohen, Bernard. "Prejudice Against the Introduction of Lightning Rods." *Journal of the Franklin Institute* 253 (1952): 422–39.

Conforti, Joseph. *Jonathan Edwards, Religious Tradition, and American Culture.* Chapel Hill: University of North Carolina Press, 1995.

———. *Samuel Hopkins and the New Divinity Movement: Calvinism, the Congregational Ministry, and Reform in New England between the Great Awakenings.* Grand Rapids, Mich.: Christian University Press and William B. Erdmans, 1981.

Cooley, Timothy Mather. *Sketches of the Life and Character of the Rev. Lemuel Haynes, A.M., For Many years Pastor of a Church in Rutland, Vt., and Late in Granville, New York.* 1837. Reprint, New York: Negro Universities Press, 1969.

Copeland, David. *Colonial American Newspapers Character and Content.* Newark: University of Delaware Press, 1997.

Cott, Nancy F. *The Bonds of Womanhood: "Women's Sphere" in New England, 1780–1835.* New Haven: Yale University Press, 1977.

Coughtry, Jay. *The Notorious Triangle, Rhode Island and the African Slave Trade.* Philadelphia: Temple University Press, 1981.

Cullen, M. R., Jr. "Scourge of the Tories." *Journalism Quarterly* 51 (Summer 1974): 213–18.

Davidson, Philip. *Propaganda and the American Revolution, 1763–1783.* Chapel Hill: University of North Carolina Press, 1941.

Davis, David Brion. *The Problem of Slavery in the Age of Revolution, 1770–1823.* Ithaca: Cornell University Press, 1975.

Davis, Thomas J. *A Rumor of Revolt: The Great "Negro Plot" in Colonial New York.* New York: Free Press, 1985.

De Armond, Anna Janney. *Andrew Bradford: Colonial Journalist.* Newark: University of Delaware Press, 1949.

Dexter, Franklin B. *Biographical Sketches of the Graduates of Yale College.* 6 vols. New York: Holt, 1885–1912.

Dickerson, Oliver Morton, comp. *Boston under Military Rule [1768–1770] as revealed in A Journal of the Times.* 1936. Reprint, Boston: Da Capo, 1970.

Dolmetsch, Joan D. *Rebellion and Reconciliation Satirical Prints on the Revolution at Williamsburg.* Williamsburg, Va.: Colonial Williamsburg Foundation, 1976.

Donald, David Herbert. *Lincoln.* New York: Simon and Schuster, 1995.

Duncan, Hugh. *Symbols in Society.* New York: Oxford University Press, 1968.

Dyer, Alan. *A Biography of James Parker, Colonial Printer.* Troy, N.Y.: Whitson, 1982.

Eaton, Arthur Wentword Hamilton. *The Famous Mather Byles: The Noted Boston Tory Preacher, Poet, and Wit, 1707–1788.* Boston: Butterfield, 1914.

Erkkila, Betsy. "Phillis Wheatley and the Black American Revolution." In *A Mixed Race Ethnicity in Early America,* edited by Frank Shuffelton, 224–40. New York: Oxford University Press, 1993.

Essig, James D. *The Bonds of Wickedness: American Evangelicals Against Slavery, 1770–1808.* Philadelphia: Temple University Press, 1982.

Finkelman, Paul, *An Imperfect Union, Slavery, Federalism, and Comity.* Chapel Hill: University of North Carolina Press, 1981.

Foner, Eric. *Tom Paine and Revolutionary America.* New York: Oxford University Press, 1976.

Foner, Philip S. *History of Black Americans from Africa to the Emergence of the Cotton Kingdom.* Westport, Conn.: Greenwood, 1975.

Forbes, Esther. *Paul Revere and the World He Lived In.* Boston: Houghton Mifflin, 1942.

Franklin, John Hope. *From Slavery to Freedom: A History of African Americans.* 7th ed. 1948. Reprint, New York: Knopf, 1994.

Frey, Sylvia. "Between Slavery and Freedom: Virginia Blacks in the American Revolution." *Journal of Southern History* 49 (August 1983): 374–98.

———. *Water from the Rock: Black Resistance in a Revolutionary Age.* Princeton: Princeton University Press, 1991.

Frost, J. William, ed. *The Quaker Origins of Antislavery.* Norwood, Mass.: Norwood, 1980.

Frothingham, Richard, Jr. *History of Charlestown, Massachusetts.* Boston: Little and Brown, 1845.

———. *The Rise of the Republic of the United States.* 5th ed. Boston: Little, Brown, 1890.

Genovese, Eugene. *From Rebellion to Revolution: Afro-American Slave Revolts and the Making of the Modern World.* Baton Rouge: Louisiana State University Press, 1979.

Gleason, J. Phillip. "A Scurrilous Colonial Election and Franklin's Reputation," *WMQ* 18 (January 1961): 68–84.

Goodell, Abner Cheney, Jr. "The Trial; and Execution, for Petit Treason, of Mark and Phillis, Slaves of Capt. John Codman, Who Murdered Their Master in Charlestown, Mass., in 1755; for which the Man was Hanged and Gibbeted, and the Woman was Burned to Death, Including Some Account of other Punishments in Massachusetts." 1883. In *Slavery, Race and the American Legal System, 1700–1872.* 107. New York: Garland, 1988.

Gordon, William. *The History of the Rise, Progress, and Establishment of the Independence of the United States of America.* 2 vols. 1789. Reprint, Freeport, N.Y.: Books for Libraries Press, 1969.

Greene, Lorenzo. *The Negro in Colonial New England.* 1942. Reprint, New York; Atheneum, 1974.

———. "The New England Negro as Seen in Advertisements for Runaway Slaves." *Journal of Negro History* 29 (April 1944): 125–40.

———. "Slave-holding in New England and Its Awakening." *Journal of Negro History* 13 (October 1928): 492–533.

Griffin, Edward M. *"Old Brick" Charles Chauncy of Boston, 1705–1787.* Minneapolis: University of Minnesota Press, 1980.

Handlin, Oscar, and Mary F. Handlin. "Origins of the Southern Labor System." *WMQ* 7 (April 1950): 199–222.

Hargrove, Richard J. "Portrait of a Southern Patriot: The Life an Death of John Laurens." In *The Revolutionary War in the South: Power, Conflict and Leadership,* edited by W. Robert Higgins. Durham: Duke University Press, 1979.

Harlow, Ralph V. *Samuel Adams: Promoter of the American Revolution.* New York: Holt, 1923.

Harrell, Isaac S. *Loyalism in Virginia: Chapters in the Economic History of the Revolution.* Durham: Duke University Press, 1926.

Hart, Albert B., ed. *Commonwealth History of Massachusetts.* 5 vols. New York: States History Company, 1927–30.

Hawke, David F. *Benjamin Rush, Revolutionary Gadfly.* New York: Bobbs-Merrill, 1971.

Heimert, Alan. *Religion and the American Mind: From the Great Awakening to the Revolution.* Cambridge: Harvard University Press, 1966.

Heimert, Alan, and Perry Miller, eds. *The Great Awakening: Documents Illustrating the Crisis and Its Consequences.* New York: Bobbs-Merrill, 1967.

Hemphill, C. Dallet. "Middle Class Rising in Revolutionary America: The Evidence from Manners." *Journal of Social History* 30 (Winter 1996): 321–44.

Hester, Al. "Foreign News in Colonial North American Newspapers, 1764–1775." *Journalism Quarterly* 57 (Spring 1980): 118–22, 44.

Hildeburn, Charles, *Sketches of Printers and Printing in Colonial New York.* 1895. Reprint, Detroit: Gale Research Company, 1969.

Hill, Hamilton A. *History of the Old South Church (3rd Church) Boston, 1669–1884.* 2 vols. Cambridge: n.p., 1890.

Hixson, Richard F. *Isaac Collins: A Quaker Printer in 18th Century America.* New Brunswick, N.J.: Rutgers University Press, 1968.

Hodges, Graham Russell, and Alan Edward Brown, eds. *"Pretends to be Free": Runaway Slave Advertisements from Colonial and Revolutionary New York and New Jersey.* New York: Garland, 1994.

Hoerder, Dirk. *Crowd Action in Revolutionary Massachusetts, 1765–1780.* New York: Academic Press, 1977.

Holmberg, Georgia McKee. "British-American Whig Political Rhetoric, 1765–1775: A Content Analysis of the 'London Gazette,' 'London Chronicle' and 'Boston Gazette.'" Ph.D. diss., University of Pittsburgh, 1979.

Horton, James Oliver, and Lois E. Horton. *Family Life and Community Struggle in the Antebellum North.* New York: Holmes and Meier, 1979.

———. *In Hope of Liberty: Culture, Community, and Protest Among Northern Free Blacks, 1700–1860.* New York: Oxford University Press, 1997.

Hosmer, James K. *Samuel Adams.* New York: Houghton, Mifflin, 1885.

Hunnewell, James F. *A Century of Town Life A History of Charlestown, Mass., 1775–1887.* Boston: Little, Brown, 1888.

James, Sydney V. *Colonial Rhode Island A History.* New York: Scribner, 1975.

Jennings, Judith. "Mid-Eighteenth Century British Quakerism and the Response to the Problem of Slavery." *Quaker History* 66 (Spring 1977): 23–39.

Jordan, Winthrop. *White Over Black: Attitudes Toward the Negro, 1550–1812.* Chapel Hill: University of North Carolina Press, 1968.

Kerber, Linda. *Women of the Republic: Intellect and Ideology in Revolutionary America.* Chapel Hill: University of North Carolina Press, 1980.

Ketchum, Ralph, ed. *The Political Thought of Benjamin Franklin.* New York: Bobbs-Merrill, 1955.

Kidder, Frederick. *The History of the Boston Massacre, March 5, 1770; consisting of the narrative of the town, the trial of the soldiers: and a historical introduction containing unpublished documents of John Adams.* Albany: Munsell, 1870.

Kiessel, William C. "The Green Family A Dynasty of Printers." *New England Historical and Genealogical Register* 104 (April 1950): 81–93.

Klingberg, Frank J. *The Anti-Slavery Movement in England.* New Haven: Yale University Press, 1926.

Knight, Janice. "Learning the Language of God: Jonathan Edwards and the Typology of Nature," *WMQ* 48 (October 1991): 531–51.

Labaree, Benjamin W. *Patriots and Partisans: The Merchants of Newburyport, 1764–1815.* Cambridge: Harvard University Press, 1962.

Lacey, Barbara E. "Visual Images of Blacks in Early American Imprints." *WMQ* 53 (January 1996): 137–80.

Lambert, Frank. "'Peddler in Divinity': George Whitefield and the Great Awakening, 1737–1745," *Journal of American History* 77 (December 1990): 814–35.

Lathem, Edward Connery. *Chronological Tables of American Newspapers.* Barre, Mass.: American Antiquarian Society and Barre Publishers, 1972.

Lemisch, Jesse. "Jack Tar in the Streets: Merchant Seaman in the Politics of Revolutionary America." *WMQ* 25 (July 1968): 371–407.

Levesque, George A. *Black Boston: African American Life and Culture in Urban America, 1750–1860.* New York: Garland, 1994.

Lewis, Paul. *The Grand Incendiary: A Biography of Samuel Adams.* New York: Dial, 1973.

Lorenz, Alfred L. *Hugh Gaine: A Colonial Printer-Editor's Odyssey to Loyalism.* Carbondale: Southern Illinois University Press, 1972.

Lovejoy, David S. "Samuel Hopkins: Religion, Slavery, and the Revolution." *New England Quarterly* 40 (June 1967): 227–43.

Lowance, Mason I., and Georgia B. Bumgardner. *Massachusetts Broadsides of the American Revolution.* Amherst: University of Massachusetts Press, 1976.

Mackay, John, and William Brown. *The Rhetorical Dialogue: Contemporary Concepts and Cases.* Dubuque, Iowa: Brown, 1972.

MacLam, Helen M. "Black Puritan on the Northern Frontier: The Vermont Ministry of Lemuel Haynes." In *Black Apostles at Home and Abroad: Afro-Americans and the Christian Mission from the Revolution to Reconstruction,* edited by David W. Wills and Rich Newman. Boston: Hall, 1982.

MacLeod, Duncan J. *Slavery, Race and the American Revolution.* Cambridge: Cambridge University Press, 1974.

Maier, Pauline. *From Resistance to Revolution: Colonial Radicals and the Development of American Opposition to Britain.* New York: Knopf, 1972.

———. "John Wilkes and the American Disillusionment with Britain." *WMQ* 20 (July 1963): 373–95.

———. "Popular Uprisings and Civil Authority in Eighteenth-Century America." *WMQ* 27 (January 1970): 3–35.

Marble, Annie R. *From 'Prentice to Patron: The Life Story of Isaiah Thomas.* New York: Appleton-Century-Crofts, 1935.

May, Herbert F. *The Enlightenment in America.* New York: Oxford University Press, 1976.

McKeel, Arthur J. *The Quakers and the American Revolution.* York, England: Sessions Book Trust, 1996.

McManis, Douglas R. *Colonial New England: A Historical Geography.* New York: Oxford University Press, 1975.

McManus, Edgar J. *Black Bondage in the North.* Syracuse: Syracuse University Press, 1973.

Merritt, Richard L. "The Colonists Discover America: Attention Patterns in the Colonial Press, 1735–1775." *WMQ* 21 (April 1964): 270–87.

Miller, John C. *Sam Adams, Pioneer in Propaganda.* Palo Alto, Calif.: Stanford University Press, 1936.

Miller, Perry, and Thomas H. Johnson, eds. *The Puritans: A Sourcebook of Their Writings.* 2 vols. 1938. New York: Harper and Row, 1963.

Miner, Ward L. *William Goddard, Newspaperman.* Durham: Duke University Press, 1962.

Moore, Frank, ed. *Songs and Ballads of the American Revolution.* Port Washington, N.Y.: Kennicutt Press, 1964.

Moore, George H. *Notes on the History of Slavery in Massachusetts.* New York: Appleton, 1866.

Morgan, Edmund S. *American Slavery, American Freedom: The Ordeal of Colonial Virginia.* New York: Norton, 1975.

———. "The Puritan Ethic and the American Revolution." *WMQ* 24 (January 1967): 3–43.

Morse, Jarvis Means. *Connecticut Newspapers in the Eighteenth Century.* New Haven: Yale University Press, 1935.

Mott, Frank Luther. *American Journalism: A History: 1690–1960.* 3d ed. New York: Macmillan, 1962.

Mullin, Gerald W. *Flight and Rebellion: Slave Resistance in Eighteenth-Century Virginia.* New York: Oxford University Press, 1972.

Nash, Gary B. *Class and Society in Early America.* Englewood Cliffs, N.J.: Prentice-Hall, 1970.

———. *Race and Revolution.* Madison, Wisc.: Madison House, 1990.

———. *Urban Crucible: Social Change, Political Consciousness and the Origins of the American Revolution.* Cambridge: Harvard University Press, 1979.

Nadelhaft, Jerome. "The Somerset Case and Slavery: Myth, Reality, and Repercussions." *Journal of Negro History* 51 (Spring 1966): 193–208.

Nell, William C. *The Colored Patriots of the American Revolution.* 1855. Reprint, New York: Arno Press and New York Times, 1968.

Nobbe, George. *The North Briton: A Study in Political Propaganda.* New York: Columbia University Press, 1939.

Norton, Anne. *Reflections on Political Identity.* Baltimore: Johns Hopkins University Press, 1988.

Norton, Mary Beth. *Liberty's Daughters: The Revolutionary Experience of American Women, 1750–1800.* Boston: Little, Brown, 1980.

Okoye, F. Nwabueze. "Chattel Slavery as the Nightmare of the Revolution." *WMQ* 37 (January 1980): 3–28.

Olton, Charles S. *Artisans for Independence: Philadelphia Mechanics and the American Revolution.* Syracuse: Syracuse University Press, 1975.

Palsits, Victor H., "John Holt — Printer and Postmaster," *Bulletin of the New York Public Library* 24 (September 1920): 483–99.

Park, Edward A. *Memoir of Nathanael Emmons.* Boston: Congregational Board of Publication, 1861.

Parker, Barbara Neville, and Ann Bolling Wheeler. *John Singleton Copley: American Portraits in Oil, Pastel, and Miniature with Biographical Sketches.* Boston: Museum of Fine Arts, 1938.

Parker, Freddie L. *Running for Freedom Slave Runaways in North Carolina, 1775–1840.* New York: Garland, 1993.

Pearce, Roy H. *The Savages of America: A Study of the Indian and the Idea of Civilization.* Baltimore: Johns Hopkins University Press, 1953.

Peel, Albert. *The Congregational Two Hundred, 1530–1848.* London: Independent Press, 1948.

Philbrick, Norman, ed. *Trumpets Sounding: Propaganda Plays of the American Revolution.* New York: Arno, 1976.

Piersen, William D. *Black Yankees: The Development of an Afro — American Subculture in Eighteenth-Century New England.* Amherst: University of Massachusetts Press, 1988.

———. *From Africa to America: African American History from the Colonial Era to the Early Republic, 1526–1790.* New York: Twayne, 1997.

Powers, Edwin. *Crime and Punishment in Early Massachusetts, 1620–1692.* Boston: Beacon, 1966.

Quarles, Benjamin. "Lord Dunmore as Liberator," *WMQ* 15 (October 1958): 494–507.

———. *The Negro in the American Revolution.* Chapel Hill: University of North Carolina Press for the Institute of Early American History and Culture, Williamsburg, Va., 1961.

Ramsay, David, *History of the United States.* 2 vols. Philadelphia: Carey and Son, 1818.

Ransom, Stanley A., Jr., ed. *America's First Negro Poet: The Complete Works of Jupiter Hammon of Long Island.* Port Washington, N.Y.: Kennikat Press, 1970.

Rawley, James A. "The World of Phillis Wheatley." *New England Quarterly* 50 (December 1977): 666–77.

Rea, Robert. *The English Press in Politics, 1760–1774.* Lincoln: University of Nebraska Press, 1963.

Rhodes, Leara. "Haitian Contributions to American History: A Journalistic Record." Unpublished paper, University of Georgia, 1997.

Riggs, Alvin Richard. "Arthur Lee and the Radical Whigs 1768–1776." Ph.D. diss., Yale University, 1967.

Ritter, Kurt William. "Rhetoric and Ritual in the American Revolution: The Boston Massacre Commemorations, 1771–1783." Ph.D. diss., Indiana University, 1974.

Robert, Oliver Ayer. *History of the Military Company of Massachusetts now called the Ancient and Honorable Artillery Company of Massachusetts, 1637–1888*, 3 vols. Boston: Mudge, 1897.

Robinson, Donald L. *Slavery in the Structure of American Politics, 1765–1820*. New York: Harcourt Brace Jovanovich, 1970.

Robinson, William H. *Phillis Wheatley: A Bio-Bibliography*. Boston: Hall, 1981.

Rodgers, Daniel T. "'Republicanism' the Career of a Concept." *Journal of American History* 79 (June 1992): 11–38.

Rossiter, Clinton. *The Political Thought of the American Revolution*. New York: Harcourt, Brace and World, 1963.

Rosswurm, Steven. *Arms, Country, and Class: The Philadelphia Militia and the "Lower Sort" during the American Revolution*. New Brunswick, N.J.: Rutgers University Press, 1987.

Ruchames, Louis. "The Sources of Racial Thought in Colonial America." *Journal of Negro History* 52 (October 1967): 252–72.

Ryerson, Richard Alan. *The Revolution Is Now Begun: The Radical Committees of Philadelphia, 1765–1776*. Philadelphia: University of Pennsylvania Press, 1978.

Saillant, John. "Lemuel Haynes and the Revolutionary Origins of Black Theology, 1776–1801," *Religion and American Culture* 32 (1992): 89–102.

Scherer, Lester B. "A New Look at 'Personal Slavery Established.'" *WMQ* (October 1973): 645–52.

Schlesinger, Arthur M. *Prelude to Independence: The Newspaper War With Britain, 1764–1776*. New York: Knopf, 1957.

———. "Propaganda and the Boston Press." *Transactions of the Colonial Society of Massachusetts* 32 (April 1936): 397–416.

Selby, John E. *The Revolution in Virginia, 1775–1783*. Williamsburg, Va.: Colonial Williamsburg Foundation, 1988.

Shaw, Peter. *American Patriots and the Rituals of Revolution*. Cambridge: Harvard University Press, 1991.

Shipton, Clifford K. *Isaiah Thomas, Printer and Philanthropist, 1741–1831*. Rochester, N.Y.: Hart, 1941.

Shyllon, F. O. *Black People in Britain, 1553–1833*. London: Institute of Race Relations by Oxford University Press, 1977.

Sibley's Harvard Graduates. 17 vols. Clifford K. Shipton, ed. Boston: Massachusetts Historical Society, 1975.

Siebert, Frederick. *Freedom of the Press in England, 1476–1775*. Urbana: University of Illinois Press, 1952.

Silverman, Kenneth. *A Cultural History of the American Revolution*. New York: Crowell, 1976.

Slotkin, Richard. "Narratives of Negro Crime in New England, 1675–1800." *American Quarterly* 25 (March 1973): 3–29.

Smith, Billy G., and Richard Wojtowicz, eds. *Blacks Who Stole Themselves: Advertisements for Runaways in the Pennsylvania Gazette, 1728–1790.* Philadelphia: University of Pennsylvania Press, 1989.

Smith, Robert W. "What Came After? News Diffusion and Significance of the Boston Massacre, 1770–1775." *Journalism History* 3 (August 1976): 71–75, 85.

Sobel, Mechal. *The World They Made Together: Black and White Values in Eighteenth-Century Virginia.* Princeton: Princeton University Press, 1987.

Soderland, Jean R. *Quakers and Slavery: A Divided Spirit.* Princeton: Princeton University Press, 1985.

Sprague, William B. *Annals of the American Pulpit.* 8 vols. 1866–77. Reprint, Worcester, Mass.: American Antiquarian Society, 1994.

Steiner, Bernard C. *History of Slavery in Connecticut. Johns Hopkins University Studies in Historical and Political Science,* edited by Herbert B. Adams. Baltimore: Johns Hopkins Press, 1893.

Stewart, Charles J., Craig Allen Smith, and Robert F. Denton Jr. "The Persuasive Functions of Slogans." In *Propaganda,* edited by Robert Jackall, 400–22. New York: New York University Press, 1995.

Stout, Harry S. "Religion, Communications, and the Ideological Origins of the American Revolution." *WMQ* 34 (October 1977): 519–41.

Sutherland, James. *The Restoration Newspaper and Its Development.* Cambridge: Cambridge University Press, 1986.

Teeter, Dwight L. "John Dunlap: The Political Economy of a Printer's Success." *Journalism Quarterly* 52 (Spring 1975): 3–8; 55.

———. "'King Sears,' the Mob, and Freedom of the Press in New York, 1765–76," *Journalism Quarterly* 41 (Autumn 1964): 539–44.

Thompson, Mack. *Moses Brown, Reluctant Reformer.* Chapel Hill: University of North Carolina Press, for the Institute of Early American History and Culture, Williamsburg, Va., 1962.

Tise, Larry E. *Proslavery: A History of the Defense of Slavery in America, 1701–1840.* Athens: University of Georgia Press, 1987.

Towner, Lawrence W. "The Sewall-Saffin Dialogue on Slavery." *WMQ* 21 (January 1964): 40–52.

Tucker, Bruce. "The Reinvention of New England, 1691–1771." *New England Quarterly* 59 (September 1986): 315–40.

Twombly, Robert C., and Robert H. Moore. "Black Puritan: The Negro in Seventeenth-Century Massachusetts," *WMQ* 26 (April 1968): 224–42.

Tyler, Moses Coit. *The Literary History of the American Revolution, 1776–1783.* 1897. Reprint, New York: Frederick Ungar, 1957.

Walett, Francis B. "James Bowdoin, Patriot Propagandist." *New England Quarterly* 23 (September 1950): 320–38.

Walker, Leola O. "Officials in the City Government of Colonial Williamsburg." *Virginia Magazine of Biography and History* 75 (1967): 35–51.

Wallace, David Duncan. *The Life of Henry Laurens.* New York: Putnam, 1915.

Walsh, Evelyn Marie. "Effects of the Revolution upon the Town of Boston: Social, Economic, and Cultural." Ph. diss., Brown University, 1964.

Wells, William V. *The Life and Public Service of Samuel Adams.* 3 vols. Boston: Little, Brown, 1865.

White, Shane. *Somewhat More Independent: The End of Slavery in New York City, 1770–1810.* Athens: University of Georgia Press, 1991.

Wiecek, William M. *The Sources of Antislavery Constitutionalism in America, 1766–1848.* Ithaca: Cornell University Press, 1971.

Williams, Daniel. "The Gratification of That Corrupt and Lawless Passion: Character, Types, and Themes in Early New England Rape Narratives." In *A Mixed Race Ethnicity in Early America,* edited by Frank Shuffelton, 194–221. New York: Oxford University Press, 1993.

Wilson, Joan Hoff. "The Illusion of Change: Women and the American Revolution." In *The American Revolution: Explorations in the History of American Radicalism,* edited by Alfred F. Young. DeKalb: Northern Illinois University Press, 1976.

Windley, Lathan Algerna, comp. *Runaway Slave Advertisements: A Document History from the 1730s to 1790.* 3 vols. Westport, Conn.: Greenwood, 1983.

Winsor, Justin, ed. *The Memorial History of Boston, 1630–1880.* 4 vols. Boston: Osgood, 1881.

Wood, Betty. *Slavery in Colonial Georgia, 1730–1775.* Athens: University of Georgia Press, 1984.

Wood, Gordon S. "Conspiracy and the Paranoid Style: Causality and Deceit in the Eighteenth Century." *WMQ* 39 (July 1982): 401–41.

———. *The Radicalism of the American Revolution.* New York: Knopf, 1992.

Wood, Peter H. *Black Majority Negroes in Colonial South Carolina: From 1670 through the Stono Rebellion.* New York: Knopf, 1975.

Woodward, William E. *Tom Paine: America's Godfather, 1737–1809.* New York: Dutton, 1945.

Wright, J. Leitch, Jr. "Lord Dunmore's Loyalist Asylum in the Floridas." *Florida Historical Quarterly* 49 (Winter 1971): 370–79.

Wroth, Lawrence C. *The Colonial Printer.* Portland, Maine: Southworth-Anthoensen Press, 1938.

Wyman, Thomas Bellow. *The Genealogies and Estate of Charlestown in the County of Middlesex and Commonwealth of Massachusetts, 1629–1818.* 2 vols. Boston: Clap and Son, 1879.

Yodelis, Mary Ann. "Boston's First Major Newspaper War: A 'Great Awakening' of Freedom." *Journalism Quarterly* 51 (Summer 1974): 207–12.

———. "Who Paid the Piper? Publishing Economics in Boston, 1763–1775." *Journalism Monographs* 38 (February 1975).

Zilversmit, Arthur. *The First Emancipation: The Abolition of Slavery in the North.* Chicago: University of Chicago Press, 1967.

Zuckerman, Michael. "The Fabrication of Identity in Early America." *WMQ* 34 (April 1977): 183–214.

Index

Jamaica, 8

James River, 137

Jamestown, 143

Jeremiah, Thomas, 134, 147

Johnson, Michael. *See* Attucks, Crispus

Journal of Occurrences (Journal of the Times), 51–53, 56, 58, 60, 62

Kemp's Landing, 138

Killingly (Conn.), 133

Kneeland, Daniel, 107

Kneeland, Samuel, 49, 54, 88, 107

Laurens, Henry, 17, 66–67, 134

Leacock, John, 136, 150–52

Lee, Arthur, 98, 140

Leslie, Captain, 145, 148

"Letters from a Farmer in Pennsylvania," 51–52

"Liberty," 121

"Liberty Song," 4

Liberty Tree, 56–57, 58

Lincoln, Abraham, 154, 156

Locke, John, 26, 97, 108–09, 129

London, 66, 67, 135

London Chronicle, 5

London Gazette, 5

Loring, Joshua, 63

Loyall Nine, 57, 129

Lunt, Ezra, 126

Madison, James, 132, 133

Magawley, Elizabeth, 15

Mansfield, Lord, 67, 68, 70, 71, 72, 74, 76–78

Marrant, John, 23

Maryland, 26, 32, 34, 36, 38, 39

Maryland Gazette, 37–38

Massachusetts, 10, 17, 18, 19, 29, 36, 45, 53–54, 71, 81–82, 90, 91, 100–03, 128, 154

Massachusetts Gazette and Boston News-Letter, 2, 28–29, 69, 79–80, 103

Massachusetts Gazette and Boston Post-Boy and Advertiser, 79–80, 102

Massachusetts General Court, 4

Massachusetts Spy, 47, 62, 69, 71, 75–76, 102, 104, 125

Massachusetts Stamp Tax, 49

Massacre of St. George's Field, The, 58

Mather, Cotton, 8, 10, 22, 86–87

Mayhew, Jonathan, 3, 49, 87, 88, 90, 93

Mecom, Benjamin, 47

Mein, John, 1, 55, 115, 129

Merriam, Caesar, 63

Methodists, 83, 84, 86, 108

Middle Passage, 108, 114, 119

Middlesex Journal, 72

Miscegenation, 18–20, 36, 70

Moore, Francis, 108

Mountains, Joseph, 19

Murray, John, Earl of Dunmore, 42, 123, 134–45, 146, 147, 148, 149, 150–53, 155

Murray, William, 135

Nantucket, 84

Natural law, 108–10, 114, 126

Nell, William C., 61

New Bern (N.C.), 133

New Divinity, 83, 84, 86, 87, 89–94, 95, 97, 104, 113, 115, 116, 118, 119, 128, 130, 155

New England Courant, 22

New Hampshire Gazette, 71

New Haven, 10, 120

New Jersey, 9, 10, 95, 109, 113, 116, 124–25

New Jersey, College of, 95

New Jersey Gazette, 124, 127

New Jersey Journal, 124

New Light ministry, 48, 49, 88–90, 93

New London, 18, 116, 117

New-London Gazette, 106